Come Back
to Afghanistan

Come Back to Afghanistan

Trying to Rebuild a Country with My Father,
My Brother, My One-Eyed Uncle,
Bearded Tribesmen, and President Karzai

SAID HYDER AKBAR
and Susan Burton

BLOOMSBURY

For my parents, Nadera Akbar and Said Fazel Akbar,
to whom I will be forever indebted.

And for Abdul Haq, Said Bahauddin Majrooh, and the countless
heroes who gave their lives for Afghanistan.

"Love Rescue Me" by Paul Hewson, Dave Evans, Adam Clayton, Larry Mullen.
© 1988 by PolyGram International Music Publishing, B.V.
All rights in the United States administered by Universal-PolyGram
International Publishing/ASCAP. Used by permission. All rights reserved.

"Stand," by John M. Stipe, Michael E. Mills, Peter L. Buck, and William T. Berry.
© 1988 Night Garden Music. All rights on behalf of Night Garden Music, administered by
Alfred Publishing Co., Inc. All rights reserved. Used by permission.

Published by Bloomsbury USA, New York
Distributed to the trade by Holtzbrinck Publishers

All papers used by Bloomsbury USA are natural, recyclable products made from
wood grown in well-managed forests. The manufacturing processes conform to the
environmental regulations of the country of origin.

The Library of Congress has cataloged the hardcover edition of this book as follows:

Akbar, Said Hyder.
Come back to Afghanistan : a California teenager's story / by Said Hyder Akbar
and Susan Burton.—1st U.S. ed.
p. cm.
ISBN-13: 978-1-58234-520-8 (hardcover)
ISBN-10: 1-58234-520-1 (hardcover)
1. Afghanistan—Description and travel.   2. Afghanistan—Politics and government—2001–
3. Afghanistan—History.   4. Akbar, Said Hyder—Travel—Afghanistan.
I. Burton, Susan, 1973– II. Title.

DS352.A39 2005
958.104'7—dc22
2005009249

First published in the United States by Bloomsbury in 2005
This paperback edition published in 2006

Paperback ISBN-10: 1-59691-068-2
ISBN-13: 978-1-59691-068-3

3 5 7 9 10 8 6 4 2

Typeset by Westchester Book Group
Printed in the United States of America
by Quebecor World Fairfield

Sta de ishq de weeno daq sho zegaronah
Sta puh meena ke byley zalmey saronah
Ta tuh rashema zergai ze mah farigh shey
Bey ley ta mai andekhney de zlar maronah
De Delhi takht hayrawooma chey rayad kum
Ze mah de khweley Pashtunkhwa de ghru saronah
Ke tamamah dunya yohkhwa tu belkhwa ay
Ze mah khwakh dey sta khali tush dagaronah

By blood, we are immersed in love of you.
The youth lose their heads for your sake.
I come to you and my heart finds rest.
Away from you, grief clings to my heart like a snake.
I forget the throne of Delhi
When I remember the mountaintops of my Pashtun land.
If I must choose between the world and you,
I shall not hesitate to claim your barren deserts as my own.

—Ahmed Shah Durrani (1722–72),
the founding father of modern Afghanistan

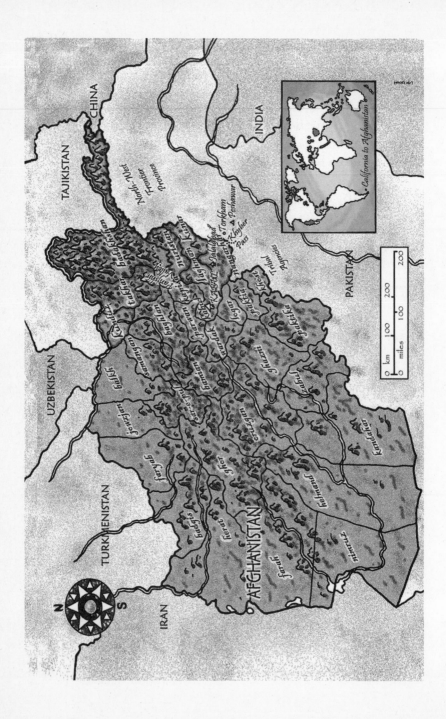

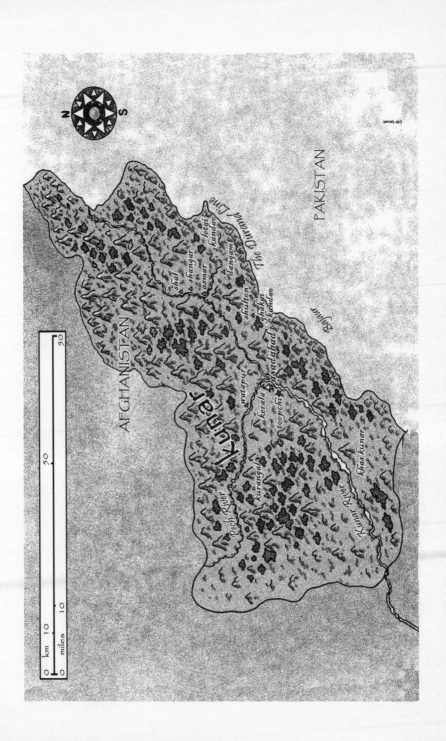

Characters

NADERA AKBAR: my mother

SAID ALI AKBAR (ALI): my nephew (Omar and Sofia's son)

SAID FAZEL AKBAR: my father; President Hamid Karzai's spokesman and, later, governor of Kunar

SAID OMAR AKBAR (OMAR): my brother

SOFIA AKBAR: my sister-in-law

ZULIKHA AKBAR: my sister

ABDULLAH ALI: my uncle; succeeded Haji Qadir as Minister of Public Works

HAZRAT ALI: warlord bolstered by the Americans; security chief of Jalalabad

JAHAN DAD: warlord; former governor of Kunar

"MARBLE" JAHAN DAD: detained by the Americans for unknown reasons

RASHID DOSTUM: warlord from the north; said to have crushed prisoners with tanks

MUHAMMAD FAHIM: defense minister; Panjshiri

ABDUL HAQ: mujahedeen commander executed by the Taliban after 9/11; family friend

Characters

JALLALUDDIN HAQQANI: mujahedeen commander now wanted by the Americans; my father and brother traveled with him during the resistance

GULBIDDIN HEKMATYAR: supported by the ISI during the Soviet war; extremist troublemaker whose efforts have continued since 9/11

MR. HUNTER: State Department representative stationed at the Asadabad base

ALI AHMED JALALI: interior minister

HAMID KARZAI: president of Afghanistan

ZALMAY KHALILZAD: U.S. special envoy to Afghanistan

DAOUD KHAN: brother of King Zahir Shah; killed by Communists in 1978 coup

ISMAIL KHAN: warlord and governor of Herat

NARAY LALA: my cousin and companion in Tora Bora

SAID BAHAUDDIN MAJROOH: Said Shamsuddin Majrooh's son; poet, scholar; assassinated in 1988

SAID SHAMSUDDIN MAJROOH (BABA): my father's great-uncle; architect of 1964 constitution; justice minister

WALID MAJROOH: Said Shamsuddin Majrooh's grandson

GHOUSOUDIN MAMA: Rauf Mama's brother

RAUF MAMA: my uncle who lost an eye in the Soviet war; former front-line commander of Kunar's Wahhabi party

AHMED SHAH MASSOUD: Northern Alliance leader assassinated on September 9, 2001

HAJI DIN MUHAMMAD: brother of Abdul Haq and Haji Qadir; succeeded Haji Qadir as governor of Nangarhar

SAID AHMED PACHA: my mother's father

SHAL PACHA: my father's grandfather

DAVE PASSARO: CIA contractor accused of assaulting Abdul Wali

HAJI QADIR: brother of Abdul Haq and Haji Din Muhammad; vice president of Afghanistan; assassinated in July 2002

YUNUS QANOONI: education minister; Panjshiri

BURHANUDDIN RABBANI: former president of Afghanistan; lives in the northern province of Badakhshan

Characters

RUHULLAH: adversary of my father's; imprisoned at Guantánamo for alleged connections to Al Qaeda

SALAAM: Rauf Mama's son

SARTOR: our driver and close family friend

ZAHIR SHAH: former king of Afghanistan

GUL AGHA SHIRZAI: warlord and governor of Kandahar

SHOHAB: Rauf Mama's nephew

COLONEL THOMAS: head of Kunar's Provincial Reconstruction Team (PRT)

ABDUL WALI: prisoner who died in U.S. custody in June 2003

SHAH WALI: accused of extortion by Kurangal villagers

YOSSEF: my father's aide

AHMED ZAHIR: famous Afghan singer from the 1970s

MALIK ZARIN: Kunar warlord and commander of the Ninth Division

Prologue

Kabul International Airport,
August 2003

THE LETTERS LOOK LIKE they are going to fall off the airport. That's
what you notice as you approach the terminal by car. By air the approach inspires even less confidence: you fly over rugged mountains only to
arrive at a field littered with airplane parts. You descend right into this
dump. Taxiing toward the terminal along a U-shaped runway, you take in
the wreckage strewn across the grass: planes with pieces snapped off, a
huge wing all by itself, a crashed helicopter.

You know, rationally, that these were shot down or bombed. But the
scene is so surreal that you wonder, *Who put these things here?* It doesn't
look like something humans could have done. Instead you picture a giant
monster stomping down the runway, scooping up everything in its path,
crumpling the aircrafts and hurling them to the ground like garbage.

You realize immediately that this is a different kind of airport.

Today I'm driving to Kabul International in a white Ford Ranger pickup
with my dad. Afghanistan is scruffy in the summer; the place just keeps
kicking up dust. But you can't always tell from pictures: in a video I show
to the rest of my family back in California, the air looks brisk and clean. I
don't understand where the dust goes, how it disappears. When you're here,

it's impossible to ignore: from the powdery ground up, the country is constantly on the verge of falling apart.

But it may be years before the dust settles in Afghanistan, and in the meantime the country's roads will be characterized by its presence—and by checkpoints like this one up ahead. We pass five or six guys standing around with guns. It's a couple hundred yards from here to the airport; usually you see a few people making their way on foot. Most people who can afford to get out of Kabul can afford a taxi to the front of the terminal, so anyone walking probably isn't really leaving the city—just here to meet someone, or on their way to work.

Near the end of the road there's a big circle in which you might expect to see a burbling fountain. Instead there's a Soviet fighter jet mounted on top of a pole, looking like it's about to fly off. It seems out of place, this monument left over from an agonizing era. I have no idea why it's still here. There's so little left standing in Kabul that it seems like it must have required a lot of effort to preserve this. You can see someone thinking about knocking it down, but deciding not to, because at least it still exists. When so much has been obliterated, it's hard to know what to save.

I've been in Afghanistan since June—mostly in Kunar province, where my father, Said Fazel Akbar, is the governor. Like almost everyone gainfully employed in Afghanistan, he's new to his job. This time two years ago he was standing behind the counter of the hip-hop clothes store he owned in Oakland. Then September 11th happened, and the Taliban fell, and everything changed. My father sold the store and left for Afghanistan; at the end of my senior year of high school, in May 2002, I joined him. That was the first time I'd ever been to Afghanistan—by the time I was born, in December 1984, the Soviet war was well under way, and my parents had already left the country. Last summer my father—who was then working as President Hamid Karzai's spokesman—and I lived together in a room in the blasted-out Kabul Hotel. Now we sleep on rope beds on the balcony of the governor's house in Kunar. So this is my second summer vacation in Afghanistan. That's what I like to tell people: that I'm here in Afghanistan on vacation.

My father's in Kabul this week for some meetings with Karzai and others, and after spending so much time in Kunar—a remote tribal area with scant electricity and ample rocket fire—my perspective is all askew. I actually catch myself thinking, *Kabul's tight, man.* For example, here we drive on paved roads. The roads outside the capital are so bad—in places, nonexistent—that the 150-mile trip from the governor's house to Kabul takes eight hours.

The trip from California takes two to three days—a long time, too, but one that at least bears a more reasonable correspondence to the map. I don't know for sure, but I think that Rahman, a friend of mine from high school, may be arriving with his family this afternoon. Now we approach the terminal, and I get out of the pickup and start looking around, hoping Rahman will pop up. As usual, there's a crowd out front—as many as a couple hundred people have gathered to meet the arriving flight—because the guards won't let anyone go inside.

The guards in Afghanistan never seem to have uniforms that fit them. Mostly they are really, really baggy. Just about all of the guards are carrying AK-47s. They seem stressed, hollering contradictory commands at cars—*Park here!—No, don't park here!*—and at people—*Stay here!—No, don't stay here!—No, you can't come in!* They're jittery, heightening an already emotional situation. It's not like the vibe you get at an airport in America: a girlfriend waiting for her boyfriend to show up, casually shaking her car keys; a wife flipping through a magazine, glancing up every now and then for her husband. Here the whole family comes, and the people they're coming to meet are probably other family members whom they haven't seen in years, maybe decades. Women in burkas sit on the ground, looking raggedy and hot. In a little while you know that someone—an aunt or a cousin or a sister—is going to walk out of the door of the terminal, wearing nice clothes, looking fresh and very clean. I keep picturing how it will be when they greet each other, the one who managed to get out and the one who stayed back.

The guards harass the anxious families, literally pushing them from one area to another, and as the tension escalates, I realize that they have no idea what they're doing. Afghanistan's new police force is in desperate need of training of all kinds. Some of these men are probably barely used to being in a big city. My father tells a story of riding in a taxi through Kabul. The traffic was bad, as always, and a policeman was trying to get control of the situation; but he was saying, *Usha, usha,* which is what you yell to an ox when you're trying to slow it down. It's not a command you give to a car or a human; it's a farming term. (Imagine an old-time cowboy trying to make the merging cars on the Los Angeles freeway do his bidding with whoops and hollers.) Many of those charged with restoring order in Kabul are completely unprepared for their responsibilities. But after twenty-three years of war, there are few qualified people left in Afghanistan.

I get worried that I won't see Rahman when he comes outside, so I ask my dad if he can do anything to help me get into the terminal. We look around a little bit and see an official we recognize from last summer. Back then he had a mustache, but now he's shaved it off. The official tells me that he can get me in, and I follow him behind the building. We're right by the runway, but it's not like other airports, where you'd hear the rumble of planes pushing back from the terminal, or feel them exploding into the air at regularly timed intervals. Here it's practically silent.

I notice an unusually luxurious array of cars, a few Land Cruisers, maybe three Mercedes sedans. A small pack of men is crossing the tarmac toward a plane.

"Who's the VIP?" I ask the official.

He looks over. "Oh, him? That's the national murderer," he says casually.

I can tell he's joking—making a play on the phrase "the national hero." The national hero is Ahmed Shah Massoud, the Northern Alliance commander who was assassinated just days before 9/11, presumably as a preemptive maneuver by Al Qaeda. Osama bin Laden and his deputies wanted to weaken the Northern Alliance, Afghanistan's only functioning anti-Taliban military force, before the retaliatory strike that might follow their suicide hijackings in the United States.

"The national murderer," the official says again, "you know—Ismail Khan."

Ismail Khan is one of Afghanistan's best-known warlords. Some Western journalists might write that sentence differently: describe Khan as "notorious" and cite his recent, abominable human rights record. (Khan's men have reportedly administered electric shocks to political dissidents and virginity tests to women.) But among warlords he's not particularly known for his brutality. For a time after the Soviet withdrawal, he was even considered a hero: he stayed out of the civil war that consumed many of his peers, and he maintained relatively peaceful conditions in his province, Herat. Later he escaped from a Taliban prison and sought sanctuary in Iran. Now he is seen as Iran's man in Afghanistan. These days he stubbornly resists sharing the revenue he collects with the central government in Kabul, making him in this, and other ways, a major obstacle to reconstruction. (Many government employees—including those of the Interior Ministry, which is responsible for the policemen out front—haven't been paid in recent months.) So I could be wrong, but I interpret the "national murderer" remark not as an assessment of Khan's savagery but as a measure of the threat he, and other warlords, pose to national unity. After a quarter-century of turmoil, people are desperate for stability, and the prospect that someone like Ismail Khan might wreck the chances for everyone else inspires powerful anger.

The official and I continue along until we reach the back side of the luggage belt. I'm surprised to see that it works—the last time I was here, they just dumped all the bags in a pile. Some men are unloading a dolly of suitcases. It's the same kind of luggage you might see anywhere, except there are almost no small bags. It's funny: when Americans talk about an upcoming trip, they never mention the weight limit, but that's always the first thing Afghans bring up. (On international flights it's usually seventy pounds per bag.) Wherever you go, there are lots of relatives, and lots of stuff to take them, and I've never gone on a trip, even domestically, where the weight limit hasn't been an issue: squatting down and moving two pounds from one suitcase to the other at check-in, stuffing the overflow into a carry-on bag. And you don't get a break coming back, either: by the end of the trip you have your own load of presents for everyone on the other side, plus you've accommodated various requests—for my mother, dried fruit, certain spices.

The official looks at me, looks around, looks at the belt, and looks around again. "Sit on this belt, and it will take you inside," he says.

"No way," I refuse. "What if they say something? I don't want to get you in trouble."

"No, no, no," he says. "It's fine, it's fine. I'll stand here until you get across. I'll watch you get off."

"Okay, then," I say. The belt is the regular black rubbery kind that loops around. It enters and exits the terminal through holes cut into the wall before us. The holes look to be about three feet high. As I lower myself onto the belt, all I can think is, *I'm going to hit my head; I'm going to be really embarrassed.* I squat, tuck my head, drive a knee down, and I'm off.

It's a short ride—a matter of seconds—and before I'm even all the way inside the lobby, I see faces, people peering right into the hole I'm coming out of. Everyone's leaning in, anxious to get their bags, but as soon as I emerge, the passengers jump out of the way. I straighten, and one goofy small guy, maybe eighteen, spazzes out and starts pointing. "Oh my God!" he says. "Look at that!"

I'm wearing my regular Afghan clothes—a kameez partoog, which is a long nightshirt top and baggy pants. On my head I have a pakol, a hat with a flat top and a rolled brim, like the puffy edge of a pizza crust. I haven't had a haircut in a while—my sideburns are sticking out a little bit—and it's been a day or two since I shaved, which means I have a strong shadow growing. It's strange to realize that people are scared of me. You carry with you a certain image of yourself, and it's never occurred to me that I might inspire fear. But to a new arrival, I guess I do seem frightening. They've gazed out at the wreckage on the airfield, are already on edge, and then here I come, ready to leap forward and launch whatever they're primed for—a hand grenade, an uprising, a terror attack.

If I screamed "Allah-u-Akbar" right now, there would literally be a stampede toward the door, I consider. Instead I hop off the belt and start weaving through the lobby. Soon nobody's even giving me a second glance. That's the other side of it—for every terrified person, there's another who couldn't care less. In the United States the entire airport would shut down, and you'd tune in to breaking news about a security breach, but here nobody even bothers to report the incident. After so many years of chaos, they employ the shoulder-shrug approach: *This is Afghanistan, what do you expect?*

The lobby is hot, hotter than it was outside, and loud, with everyone crammed into an area the size of a single gate at JFK. Most of the travelers seem to be Afghans returning from abroad, the rest are foreigners, and almost everyone from both groups is wearing Western clothes. I position my-self so that I have a view of the arriving passengers. Hopefully I'll see Rah-man as soon as he gets off the plane.

A few days ago I called my friend Matin in California. It was the first time I'd talked to him all summer. Matin was at someone's house playing video games, and he told me that Rahman had just left for Afghanistan. Rah-man's sister was getting engaged, and our friends had teased that his par-ents were actually secretly lining up some crazy arranged marriage for him.

I told Matin I was coming back to California soon, in just a little more than a week. Matin said that they were planning a hiking trip to Tahoe for right around then and that I should come along. I thought back over my summer, of trekking with my uncle across the border to Pakistan up terrain so steep I thought I would fall backward, and I joked, "I don't think that's what I want to do when I get back from Afghanistan, hike some more mountains." But I hoped I'd get back in time to go with them anyway.

I watch the passengers lining up, the guards flipping open passports, check-ing visas. Beside me two American guys are talking. They seem like foreign correspondents—khaki pants, button-down shirts with rolled-up sleeves. I notice that whenever Western-looking people walk by, these two guys lower their voices and quiet down their conversation. But I'm standing right on top of them, and still they keep going in their loud voices, clearly never thinking that I might understand. It's almost voyeuristic: these people have no idea that I'm hearing every single word they're saying. Then suddenly, they notice me.

"Like look at this guy," one of the guys says. "Now, this is a light-skinned Pashtun from the eastern region. You can tell because he's wearing that hat, a pakol."

I turn to face them. They're the same height as I am, five eleven, and we're at eye level. "Actually," I say, "I'm from northern California."

They become completely silent. They literally just look at me in shock. I wait for them to say something, and when they don't, I turn around. They just stay quiet. Now I feel awkward—do they think I'm mad at them? Or maybe I didn't speak clearly, and they think I've just told them off in

Pashto. But I'm pretty sure they've understood me. Except for a mellow note of California teenager, my English is accent-free.

Do you feel more Afghan or more American? I get asked this a lot. It's a fair question, and the simplest answer is, more Afghan. My first summer here, I worked this over in my mind a good deal—identity is a powerful thing—but at this point it's more of a low-level backdrop. When I arrived in Kabul in June, I took off my Ralph Lauren polo shirt and khakis and slipped on my kameez partoog. I spent the summer in the middle of nowhere, sitting around a fire with a bunch of people with pakols and long beards, and the only weird thing about it was that I didn't feel weird, and when I think of changing back into my khakis a week from now and spending the fall in Concord, California, sitting around a big TV with a bunch of friends, I don't feel weird, either.

So I'd rather answer that question by saying this: My identity itself isn't intrinsically interesting; it's the perspective it gives me that's compelling. I probably don't totally understand either world, but I understand more of both than most.

Rahman and his family are literally the last five people off the plane. I'm waiting and waiting, and then I see him, fifteen feet away, in line for his paperwork. I stand there, and stand there, and Rahman's eyes come across me about twenty times, and he doesn't notice anything. Then he looks at me really hard. I nod my head—*Yeah, it's me*—and his face shows surprised recognition—*Oh my God.* He points me out to his family—*Look, there's my friend Hyder*—and then finally he's finished, and I'm helping him and his family get outside.

As soon as they see each other, the women in the family start crying, and I feel like I should get out of there. Rahman and I exchange local phone numbers, though things are so hectic that we probably won't meet again until we're back in America.

Then I say goodbye and I head off through the crowd, a light-skinned Pashtun from the eastern region wearing a pakol. The American guy nailed it: he was right about everything.

Part One

"This Must Be Your First Time in Afghanistan."

Summer 2002

I've conquered my past
The future is here at last
I stand at the entrance to a new world I can see
The ruins to the right of me
Will soon have lost sight of me

—U2, "Love Rescue Me"

I

THE GUARD PEERS INTO the open car window. "Where are you from?" he says.

I've been in Afghanistan for five hours. Five hours total, ever. Until I crossed the border this morning, I had never been inside the country in my entire seventeen years of life. In my pocket is a blue passport stamped United States of America, issued just months ago by the agency in San Francisco, a forty-five-minute commuter-train ride from my home. I know what I should tell the guard. But instead I say the name of the Afghan province my family's from—where I feel like I'm from, where I want to be from. "Kunar," I reply.

"Pull over," the guard says.

The taxi I'm riding in—a '99 Toyota Corolla decorated with fuzzy dice and pictures of Indian actresses—pulls to the side of this checkpoint on the outskirts of Kabul. The guard strides over and says—in Dari, the Afghan language we've been speaking—that he has to do a search. I unlock my bags for him, and he sifts through my clothes. When he checks my passport, he says derisively, "Oh, you must be one of those Afghan-Americans, huh?"

"Yeah," I say, trying not to get ruffled. "I'm coming back to see my country."

Then the guard opens a small bag in which I've packed some U2 CDs. Okay, *a lot* of U2 CDs—more than eighty. I'm going to be in Afghanistan for the whole summer, and I want at least one form of entertainment. I'm carrying all ten of their studio albums, their singles and B-sides, bootlegs of concerts.

"What's all this?" the guard says. "What if this is bad stuff? We should test this," he announces. Now he's really just posturing; there's no stereo equipment in sight.

When at last we're allowed to pass, our driver starts cussing the guard out. "They don't do this every time," he says angrily. "It's just because you said you're from Kunar." Being from Kunar means I'm an ethnic Pashtun; the guard was an ethnic Tajik. As we approach Kabul—where I'll meet up with my father—the driver continues his screed. Little does he know I could give him a lecture of my own. For months I've been reading at the pace of a Ph.D. student about Afghanistan. But this is the first time I've been directly affected by ethnic tension, and foreknowledge or not, the actual experience feels weird.

The whole day has felt weird. I didn't expect to be transformed the moment I touched Afghan soil (or did I? . . .); but I thought I could reasonably expect to feel some connection to the place. Instead I'm carsick, dust-choked, and shocked by the barren landscape; I feel no affinity with the bearded men and shrouded women in our path. The only thing that's clear to me is that I'm a total outsider. It wasn't supposed to be like this.

What was it supposed to be like? I don't know. During all the months I've spent dreaming of Afghanistan, I've never been able to put into words what I wanted to feel when I finally went inside. A rush of excitement was the best I could do. It was easier to picture actual things that might happen later, scenes here and there: walking along a street in Kabul with my father, meeting Karzai in the presidential palace, driving through mountains in an SUV actually necessitated by the terrain. A lot of kids my age dream of playing football with the pros, or making the last shot to win the basketball game. I dream of going to Kunar and helping my dad land a big UN reconstruction project. That's the kind of stuff I've been thinking about all spring; it's what goes through my mind when I'm lifting weights or running on the treadmill in my garage.

For years Afghanistan has existed only in my imagination. My dad would tell me about it, and I would learn about it and read about it, but it was a story; it wasn't real. Not long after 9/11 I bid on eBay for a *National Geographic* that featured an article called "Afghanistan: Crossroad of Conquerors." The issue was from September 1968—a time in Afghanistan that now seems like paradise. Radical political movements had yet to gain significant momentum. There were universities in Kabul, moderate social mores, and European college students traipsing through as they wound their way to Kathmandu along the "Hippie Trail." There were archaeologists digging for Paleolithic tools instead of dogs sniffing for landmines; farmers tending wheat instead of poppies in the agricultural countryside. These were the days in which my parents met in Kabul and married. My mom can go on for hours.

I won the auction for the *National Geographic,* and when it came, I paged through it. A photograph of the Kabul stadium later notorious as a site of the Taliban's public executions offered no hint of the field's grim future; it was cheerily festooned as if for the Rose Bowl. Another picture showed a woman with makeup and a stylish haircut. But my favorite photograph in the issue showed a countryside landscape that seemed not to have changed for four hundred years. A man herded cattle along a path. In the background there were desertlike hills, but also green grass, and a rushing blue river. In the middle of the river was a rock with a house set on it. I'd stare at the picture, wondering how the person who lived in the house on the rock got home across the water.

My house in California is on a cul-de-sac, and I get there the regular way teenagers in California do, whipping around the corner, playing music loud in the car. I usually park on the street, because our garage is filled with gym equipment and extra kitchen stuff for my mom—a second freezer full of meat, sacks of rice so big I'm the only one who can carry them inside. We live in a town house, meaning that our house shares a wall with the house next door. I'll come in and sit down in the living room. Sometimes my sister-in-law Sofia will be over, playing with my little nephew, Ali, who's one. Ali will take a Tootsie Roll from the bowl on the coffee table and try to eat the wrapper as well as the candy; Sofia will reach inside his mouth and pull the wet paper out. Sofia and Ali and my brother Omar, a mortgage broker, live nearby. (I also have two sisters: Mariam, who's twenty-nine, and Zulikha, who's twenty-five.) Omar's thirty-one, fourteen years older than I am, and I've really looked up to him. Sofia says that when I was about eight years old, I would follow Omar everywhere—even to the bathroom, where I'd stand outside the door and wait for him to come out.

Omar's one of those people everyone looks up to. On his very first day at an American high school, a girl left a note with her phone number and the message "Call me" under the windshield wiper of his car. "This girl left me a note. What should I do?" Omar asked my dad. "Come back to Afghanistan over summer break," my father responded immediately. (It was more of an order than a suggestion.)

As a teenager, Omar sometimes traveled in Afghanistan with my father; one summer they went along with some rebel troops my father financed. We have a home video with footage of this trip and others. The beginning of the video is messed up—someone accidentally taped part of an episode of *Chicago Hope* over it. When the action begins, you see a line of mujahedeen—holy warriors—hiking up a mountain trail; Omar marches behind my father, grinning at the camera. His pakol is pulled over his eyes at a purposely odd angle, like a kid with his baseball hat on weird. When the mujahedeen come to a stop and launch rockets at the Russians, the sound explodes into our living room. A man prays that the missiles will hit their targets. In another scene men nibble at hunks of snow they cup in their hands. They ate a lot of snow, Omar says; it was a condiment for biscuits. Sometimes they'd be sitting there eating, and Russian helicopters would buzz overhead and everyone would drop his biscuit and just start running.

To regroup, they all might stop at a cave. "Like a regular room," Omar says, "but a room in a mountain." When you slice open some rocks, you find crystals inside; if you cut away these outcroppings, you'd find generators, refrigerators, and microwaves. One day Omar visited a cave in the province of Paktia outfitted with a sofa, maps for strategizing attacks, and flowered teacups.

"This Must Be Your First Time in Afghanistan."

That same day, Omar tells me, the mujahedeen captured a major Communist post. Their commander was Jallaluddin Haqqani, who was then a close friend of my father's, and had invited him along on this trip. (Haqqani now appears near Osama bin Laden and Taliban leader Mullah Muhammad Omar on the Americans' most-wanted list.)

The Communists captured that day were to be killed on the spot. At the time my father was reporting for Voice of America, and he had a tape recorder with him. Before the prisoners were killed, they were brought to my father to be interviewed. He asked them a couple of basic questions like "Why do you fight against the mujahedeen?"

The prisoners trembled. They said, "Could you please turn your recorder off? I just want to tell you something personally."

"I'm innocent," they said, the minute the tape recorder was off, the words tumbling out of their mouths. "I'm not guilty. So if they kill me, you're going to become guilty."

"I've never seen human beings like that," Omar told me. "In their eyes they were almost already dead."

Before the mujahedeen killed the prisoners, they gave them a banana. The minute they had eaten their last banana, the soldiers took them behind a rock. Then they shot them.

Haqqani tossed a gun to Omar. "Here," he said. "You want to kill one?" It was a hospitable gesture, like offering a guest tea and snacks at your house.

"No," Omar said.

"They are going to get killed anyway," Haqqani said.

Omar understood; he just didn't want to do it. Though he had a personal stake in the conflict—he'd grown up in Afghanistan, been uprooted by the war—it wasn't the same for him as it was for the mujahedeen, who had been fighting for years and had lost brothers, fathers, and families. As certain as Omar was that he didn't want to kill a Communist, they were certain that they did.

Conservative estimates of the Afghan death toll during the Soviet war hover around one million, but the figure is probably much closer to two million. During those years, approximately one third of the population (then between 14 and 17 million) fled the country; at one point half of all refugees in the world were Afghans. My family and I were among them.

My parents settled in Peshawar, Pakistan, not long after the Soviet invasion of Afghanistan on December 27, 1979. Among the Russian troops' targets that night was Kabul Radio, which was run by the government and was headed by my dad. Now, whenever I go to a bookstore, the first thing I do with any new book they have about Afghanistan is turn to the index and look up Kabul Radio. The books describe that first night and the ten-year war that followed. Peshawar became a sort of staging ground for the resistance, a place where people came and checked in and then went back into the country to fight. A baby photograph of me dressed up as a mujahed—a rocket launcher positioned behind me in our living room—embodies the spirit of the times.

Of course, I remember nothing of Peshawar; I left for America in 1987, when I was two. A young cousin of mine had been kidnapped, and though he was safely returned, my brother and I were at risk; the abductors had been after us. My mother wanted to get us out. Leaving my father behind to continue his work, we flew to the United States and moved into an apartment near relatives in Alexandria, Virginia. Many Afghan refugees lived near San Francisco, and we soon moved to the Bay Area, too.

My father came to visit when he could. I didn't like to be alone with him; he was unfamiliar to me. My mother and father both speak the Afghan language Pashto, but they grew up in different provinces, and there are regional variations. On one visit—I must have been about three—my father asked me to close the door. I was confused; I didn't understand the word he'd used for door. "Close the door," he said again. Then he thought I was ignoring him, and he got a little mad. "Close the door!" he yelled. I ran to my mother, crying.

Back in Peshawar, one of my father's closest friends was a famous mujahedeen commander named Abdul Haq. After Kabul Radio, the next thing I look up in any book about Afghanistan is Abdul Haq. If it means anything to say you have a hero, mine would be Abdul Haq. Most of the mujahedeen commanders weren't able to explain their struggle to the world. They were fighters, not great communicators. But Abdul Haq was a visionary. He understood both Islam and the West and saw how they could exist together. He met with President Ronald Reagan at the White House and with Prime

Minister Margaret Thatcher in London. His intelligence was equaled by his bravery. One night during the war he stumbled into a landmine. Hours later, with a knife and without any anesthetic, a doctor amputated Abdul Haq's foot. (Now, many years after the Soviet war, Afghanistan is still one of the world's most heavily landmined countries.)

In 1989 Soviet troops pulled out of Afghanistan in defeat, but for the next few years a Communist government still controlled the country. Then the Soviet Union collapsed, and the Communist regime in Kabul finally crumbled. My father assumed a diplomatic position in the new mujahedeen-led government. He was posted to the Afghan embassy in India and asked us to join him there. It all happened in a span of just weeks. "Sell everything," my mother told my aunt, giving her the keys to our apartment. But in Delhi we monitored the nightly radio broadcasts from Afghanistan with increasing despair. The Communists were gone, but now the mujahedeen were ruining everything by fighting among themselves. My father observed as much on his trips to Kabul: civil war was raging, and the prospects for a resolution were bleak.

When the Taliban emerged, my father sent us back to the United States. My mother and I returned to California and moved in with my grandmother. She lived in a home for the elderly, and we all shared a single room. I was about eleven years old and don't have good memories of that place. I was having a hard time in general. My cousin Yossef, who'd been my best friend when I left, seemed a lot different from me. He—and everyone else—now listened to this new thing called rap music. In school the teacher asked me to read aloud, and I embarrassed myself by standing up to do so, as was the custom in India. But I was so young that it was easy to adjust. Soon I was playing football, renting video games at Blockbuster, and trying out snowboarding in Lake Tahoe.

Meanwhile the Taliban were taking over Afghanistan. Though they at first seemed like a collection of upright religious students determined to restore order, their repressive ideology soon revealed itself. (So did the extent of their financial and military support from Pakistan, a country that has long been working against Afghanistan's best interests.) In this political climate, my father's life was at risk, and in 1996 he, like many of his peers, resigned himself to the fact that the long struggle for Afghanistan had, at least temporarily, reached a dead end. My father joined us in the Bay Area, and this time he was here to stay.

We moved into our house in Concord, a typical suburb with a Starbucks, a Safeway, and a Barnes & Noble. By the standards of the Afghan community here, my family is moderate—politically, religiously, socially. (For example, the women in our family do not cover their hair, but if I had a girlfriend, I wouldn't be able to talk about it.) At home our family speaks Pashto. My mother knows little English; my father taught himself during his years in Peshawar, and though he has a good grasp of the language, he underestimates his competence in it, often deferring to me to help him find the right word. (Though usually he will ignore my suggestion, or get impatient waiting for it, and decide to speak up himself.)

One day in the summer of 2001 I was up in my room, looking around for some live U2 concert tapes on eBay, when I heard my father calling me.

"Hyder!" he yelled. "Stop playing at the computer. Come downstairs."

Since it was my father, I hurried, running down to the living room. There was my father. And there was Abdul Haq.

I don't know how else to put it: literally, my jaw dropped. "Salaam alaikum," I said. *Peace be with you.*

"Salaam alaikum," Abdul Haq replied. He came forward and gave me the traditional Afghan greeting: a hug, a kiss on one cheek, then the other.

Abdul Haq sat on a brown couch facing the sliding-glass door. He was heavier than I'd pictured. He had a salt-and-pepper beard, with a lot more white than black, even though he was only in his early forties. He was wearing Afghan clothes, a baggy kameez partoog, and his prosthetic foot was just covered with a regular shoe. While he and my parents talked, I stayed very quiet, as if the sound in me had been turned off.

When my sister Zulikha came into the room, Abdul Haq stood up. "Hello, how are you?" he said formally.

My mother realized what was going on. "That's Zulikha!" she said. "Zulikha, you remember!"

"Zulikha! I thought you were Omar's wife," Abdul Haq explained. "Oh, Zulikha, I would never get up for you," he joked.

Abdul Haq had adored my sister as a little girl. "If I had a son your age, you two could get married," he'd say. Or, "When you grow up, you're going to be my secretary."

Zulikha had brought her cat into the room with her. It's a fluffy white Persian with green eyes, like the kind you see in a TV commercial. Now my mom was giving her a look like, *What are you doing? This is Abdul Haq! Couldn't you have waited a little to bring out your cat?* But Abdul Haq received the cat as graciously as if it were a member of our family. "It's really cute," he said.

In 1987, just weeks after his landmine accident, Abdul Haq came to the United States for surgery on his foot. It happened that my father was visiting us in Virginia then, and he drove to Pittsburgh to see him.

In his hospital room Abdul Haq told my father how much he had missed him and had been wanting to see him. "Be careful what you wish for or it might come true," Abdul Haq said wryly.

Abdul Haq looked over at Zulikha; she and Omar were with my father. "I don't have a gift for you," he said sadly. So he gave Zulikha the ring off his finger. We still have that ring, somewhere.

Actually, I think I was there in the hospital room, too. In fact, I'm a hundred percent sure of it. I was not quite three years old at the time. But when I brought it up, everyone said I was wrong, that I wasn't.

"No way, Hyder, you would never have spent even a day away from me at that age, much less two nights in Pittsburgh," said my mother.

"I don't really remember you there," said my brother.

"No, you weren't there," said my sister.

They knew how much it meant to me that I might have been there. I felt like they were really rubbing it in. "The hell with you guys," I whispered under my breath, and walked away.

I have this memory of walking into the hospital room, of seeing Abdul Haq sick: an untrimmed beard, curly hair. I remember feeling uncomfortable. But I was so young, and it's like all memories you have from that age: they're just flashes. They don't take place in fluid motion. I don't remember the ride to Pittsburgh, what happened first, second, next, an order. Just this flash in the hospital room.

I don't know, maybe I dreamed it. Sometimes you want to believe in something so much, you will it to be true.

In our living room my father and Abdul Haq started talking politics. Abdul Haq had just come from Washington, where he and others had hoped to interest President George W. Bush's administration in their plan to overthrow the Taliban. Abdul Haq was working in concert with a group that included Hamid Karzai; Zahir Shah, the former king of Afghanistan, who for years has lived in exile in Italy; and Ahmed Shah Massoud, the Northern Alliance commander. Massoud and Abdul Haq had a tense relationship that dated back to the Soviet war and encompassed both personal differences and broader regional and ethnic divisions. Their current partnership was a measure of just how seriously each of them approached this effort. Abdul Haq had come here today to try to convince my father to join them: he wanted him to move to Rome and take over operations for the king's office.

It became difficult for them to talk freely, so my father said that they were going to drive around a little. I wanted to ask if I could ride along, just sit behind them in the backseat.

Abdul Haq and my father got up to leave, and I followed them to the driveway. Abdul Haq limped a little as he and my father walked to the car. Then they got inside and I stood in front of the garage and watched them go down the street, the backs of their two gray heads through the rear windshield, until they turned left on Willow Pass Road and drove away.

A few weeks later I got into the same car around seven in the morning. I sat in the passenger seat, Abdul Haq's spot. My father was driving me to school, which was embarrassing: I was a senior and I didn't have my license yet. My friend Bruce was in the back. My father told me to put on the news station, and we heard the announcer say that all commercial airlines had been grounded for the first time in history. "This is breaking news," he said. Then he told about the two airplanes and the Twin Towers.

"Dad," I said. "Listen, there's some kind of attack." It was still so early that we didn't have any sense of what the attack was about, much less of what it would mean for Afghanistan. Even at school, where the teacher in my government class wheeled in a TV on a cart, I still didn't grasp the ramifications. I just kept worrying about Zulikha, who was visiting New York. On the screen, the towers cascaded to the ground. *I hope she didn't go there,* I thought.

When I got home from school, my mom told me Zulikha was all right, and that my dad had been glued to the TV since dropping me off that morning. I sat down on the couch with him in the living room, then ran upstairs to my room to look for more information online, then ran back down again. It was like that all week. Something big was going on, and I didn't want to miss a minute: my father was talking about going back to Afghanistan.

My father's first job after he arrived in America had been driving a taxi. Then an Afghan friend who owned a store in Oakland told him about a shop that did good business and would be easy to run. It turned out to be a hip-hop clothing store. My father bought it, but he never liked it. He'd sit there from ten till seven, bored out of his mind. He'd lock the door of the shop and take a nap, or decide to just close up early.

It's a familiar type: the exiled intellectual who comes to America and claims that things were better back home, who gets lazy and never adapts. That's not the impression I want to give about my father. If anything, he was the opposite of that: he would be the first to tell you that things are a lot better in America than in Afghanistan. He'd simply been subdued by his own lost hope. There had been all those years of struggle, and for what? In Afghanistan the people were tyrannized by an oppressive regime, and in America my father presided over racks of Fubu pants. Against the well-armed and well-financed Taliban, he and his peers were helpless.

But after September 11th, my father was energized. The United States was serious about toppling the Taliban, who for years had provided sanctuary for Al Qaeda. There was a chance for Afghanistan again. Abdul Haq called from Peshawar and told my father of his plan to undertake a mission into the country.

My father thought it was too soon; the Taliban were not weak enough yet. "Why are you going?" he said. "This is not the time."

But Abdul Haq was firm. "I am going inside and I will call you again, and then you will come join me."

Once Abdul Haq made a decision, nobody could change it. My father said that he had maybe too much self-confidence. In the 1980s in Peshawar, even the smallest commander would walk the streets inside a knot of body-guards. Abdul Haq had a driver, but other than that, he was just out there, all by himself.

The craziest thing for me was how everyone—*everyone*—was suddenly interested in Afghanistan. It was like somebody discovering a private family story, something that had mattered only in the small world of your house, and deciding everyone should know about it. Suddenly Americans were more familiar with places like Mazar-i-Sharif and Tora Bora than most Afghans. One night I watched a *Saturday Night Live* skit in which the actors announced, "They've taken Jalalabad!" They performed a whole song just about Kandahar. I sat there stunned. Yet sometimes the surge in attention to Afghanistan seemed to trivialize the place. At school I heard that one teacher showed the documentary *Beneath the Veil*, which depicts the oppression Afghan women suffered under the Taliban. I could picture the girls in the class making sad cooing sounds, the way they might during a video about animal rights.

I've had an account on AOL since seventh grade, and after September 11th, the Afghan bulletin boards got pretty crowded. People were posting all kinds of things—even typical Internet joke stuff, like a top-ten list of titles for movies. One of them was *There's Something About Sharbat Gula,* which was pretty good. Sharbat Gula was the girl on the famous *National Geographic* cover, the one with the haunting light-green eyes.

National Geographic published a new map of Afghanistan, and I ordered it and hung it on my bedroom wall. I'd look up at my father's home province, Kunar, and next to it my mother's, Laghman. Real places, bordering each other on a map, like California and Nevada, or Arizona and New Mexico. Those were places I could visit, and now suddenly Afghanistan was, too.

When my father began making plans to go back, I told him I wanted to go with him. He was opposed to the idea; he wasn't sure how he was going to get inside Afghanistan (a difficult project in the fall of 2001), much less what he was going to do when he got there. I'd be more of a hindrance to my father than a help. Then there was the matter of missing school. At the time all I knew was that I was determined to go to Afghanistan. I'd read a lot about it and felt like I knew my stuff; but even someone who couldn't hold a candle to me in an argument could still say, "Well, who are you to talk? You've never seen it." I'd always had to rely on other people for my opinions; I wanted to form my own.

One morning in late October I woke up early for school and, as usual, went to my computer to record an Internet stream of the BBC's Pashto service for my parents. The site was reporting that a major Afghan commander had been captured, possibly killed. I told my father.

"Dad," I said. "They're saying that some big commander might have died."

"Yeah," he said. "It's Abdul Haq."

It didn't hit me then; my dad's not the type to show his feelings.

"They're still speculating," he said. "Go to school. There's nothing you can do by staying at home."

While I was in class, my father decided that he had to tell my mother. He walked in and stared at her, but he couldn't say it; he left and came back. "They have captured Abdul Haq," he said. Then he grabbed the telephone and called Abdul Haq's eldest brother, Haji Din Muhammad, in Pakistan.

"What's going on?" my father said.

"There are two reports," Haji Din Muhammad said. "One of him being captured, one of him being killed. The captured part is true. But we don't know about the killing part yet."

When I came home from school that afternoon, my mother was crying in her bedroom. I had never seen her cry like that. I knew right away that Abdul Haq was gone. He had been shot dozens of times by his captors. When I wrote about the execution in my current events journal the next day at school, the teacher wrote a check mark and then, in red ballpoint pen, *Sorry.*

I read all the newspaper articles I could find about Abdul Haq. There was a lot of coverage: If he'd lived, he would have played a major role in Afghanistan's new government. Some blamed the United States for his death—when alerted that Abdul Haq was in serious trouble, America had sent only minimal support. The United States (the CIA in particular) had long viewed Abdul Haq as a reckless iconoclast; in their eyes, he was undermined by the very independence of spirit that was the source of his power.

My father was performing his own kind of analysis. "What am I going to go back to Kabul for?" he blurted out one day in the car. "I always dreamed we would go back together. What am I going to go back for now?"

For a while after Abdul Haq's death, my mother didn't want to hear anything more about my father going back. But I thought it should fuel him to go even more: I didn't want Abdul Haq to have died in vain.

The only thing I could see keeping my father in Concord was a doctor's appointment. Something in his eye had to be removed—he needed surgery. I tried to get the number of his doctor from him so that I could explain the situation to the receptionist and get the date changed. "I'm pretty sure if you talked to them, they would make an exception," I told him. But my father said that there was no rush; the end of the war against the Taliban was still nowhere in sight. Besides, the surgery had been scheduled a long time ago, three months, and he would be useless in Afghanistan without his eye.

Then in November, only weeks after Abdul Haq's death, the Taliban were—rapidly and surprisingly—defeated. Every Afghan exile had an opinion about what should happen next. My father dismissed all the talk. "Just talking in the U.S., this government is wrong, this government is good, that's not good for anybody," he said. "Anybody who's interested should prove this. The only way to prove this is to join the people, to help them." My father called up Karzai, who had undertaken a mission similar to Abdul Haq's in southern Afghanistan. "I'm coming back," my father told him. "What about your business?" Karzai asked. "I'm going to sell it," my father said. And that was that. My father pretty much hung up the phone, sold the hip-hop clothing store, and finalized his arrangements to leave for Afghanistan. (My father's old friend Karzai had been named the chairman of Afghanistan's interim government and was suddenly famous. "Hey," somebody said to my dad, "isn't that the guy you used to go swimming with at the Intercontinental Hotel in Peshawar every day?")

At last my father agreed to let me go to Afghanistan, too. I'd join him there over the summer break. He left in late December, and during the months he was away, I'd think about what he'd told me: "It's easy to talk about going back, but to do it is much harder." If anything, his words made me want to go back even more. Just to prove it—just to get the doubts out of my head.

I've always had an insecurity about being so privileged. If I wasn't so fortunate, I could have easily been growing up in Afghanistan, in a generation that doesn't know anything but war. After what Afghans have been through, I think almost anything could happen to me and I would try not to complain about it.

The summer after my sophomore year I got an excruciating stomachache. Finally my mother dragged me to the emergency room, where I downplayed the pain. Then I went to the parking lot to lie down in the car. When they finally called my name, they rushed me into surgery. It turned out my appendix had burst. The doctors said I was an hour and a half from dying. I was in the hospital for two weeks, and when I came home, I was in my room for a long time, hooked up to an IV.

Then during junior year I discovered a little cyst on my back. Again, I minimized the problem. But the cyst grew and grew, and eventually they had to operate, dig down the length of my middle finger to get it all. At home every night my dad had to fill the wound; he was the only one who could stomach it. But complications arose, and I had to have a second surgery. I was out of school for three months. I grew apart from my friends—I missed a lot of hang-out time. But I'd always been a little different anyway.

In the months before I left for Afghanistan, school seemed increasingly irrelevant. I wished I could fast-forward to the end of the year. I did my best not to talk too much about the trip around my friends; I didn't want to be overbearing. Besides, when people asked, "Why are you going back?" I'd find myself unable to answer. The thing I spent all my time thinking about seemed impossible to explain.

One spring morning in a darkened English classroom, we watched the end of the movie *Frankenstein*. Then the lights came up, and our teacher told us to write an essay describing three differences from the book. But instead everybody was just talking. We discussed whether our friends would ditch school and go snowboarding in Tahoe. We laughed about how another friend had tried to spit a loogie out the passenger window of someone's car, not realizing the window was closed. A girl got up and announced she was going to the restroom, and one of my friends observed, "Yeah, the restroom at Burger King." One guy hid another guy's cell phone and we waited for him to notice.

Then we started talking about my trip to Afghanistan. My friend Omar said that he might go back in July with his dad, an engineer. (There are maybe ten Afghan kids in my senior class of three hundred.) "But if I don't go with him," he said, "there's partying at my house, you better believe it. I'm worried about partying, not about Afghanistan." Then he added, "I'm only kidding."

"How are you going to keep in touch with us?" someone asked me.

"I'm not," I said, and everyone laughed.

"I'm telling you, bring a laptop," my friend Alec said. Alec isn't Afghan, but we call him Halfghan, because he can recite his cell phone number in Dari. "Wireless Internet," Alec joked. "Hey Hyder, how's Afghanistan?" he pantomimed his question, and my response: "I met the greatest girl."

"But I haven't seen her face yet," Omar broke in. It was a good joke, and there was a moment of hysteria.

"Were you always planning on going back, or was it because of nine-eleven?" someone asked.

"Before nine-eleven, there wasn't anything to go back for," I said.

An Asian American girl sucking on an Everlasting Gobstopper asked the hard question: "How come you're going?"

"It's a long answer," I said. "I really can't summarize it in a sentence." I was sort of stumbling.

Then Alec jumped in. "He's really deep with his roots," he said. "He's going to get his education here, and then he's going to go back to Afghanistan and help rebuild it."

"Really?" the girl said.

I nodded.

"I'm his manager," Alec added. "Ten percent."

"Well, that's a good summary," the girl said.

It was a good summary, but there was so much more. How could I explain how much I had riding on the trip? If Afghanistan didn't work out, I worried I'd have nothing. My old plan—community college, then Berkeley, a degree in business or finance—seemed irrelevant. I wasn't sure if anything in America could ever mean enough. I'd lie in my bed at night, unable to sleep.

My brother joked that I couldn't sleep because of my diet pills. Before my father left for Afghanistan, he'd made a deal with me. He'd buy me the ticket to go if I lost weight. My health-conscious father has offered me incentives to lose weight my whole life, but this was the first one that worked. I'd go down to the garage after school, where I had a treadmill and a punching bag. I'd wear a sweatshirt, plus another shirt, plus a garbage bag, to help me sweat more. I restricted my diet to vegetables and chicken from the grill, and by the end of two months I'd lost nearly my goal, sixty-five pounds. My mother started to worry about me.

My mother wanted me to go to the doctor and get shots before leaving for Afghanistan, but I didn't want to take them. It seemed like something a foreign tourist would do, take shots to make sure you didn't get malaria, or diseases from the water, or whatever. *It's my own country,* I told myself. *Whatever is in the air or water, I can take it.*

I talked to my father only a few times during the months he was away; his best time to call coincided with the hours during which I was at school. (Depending on seasonal time changes, Afghanistan is eleven and a half or twelve and a half hours ahead of California.) Once my mother mentioned to him that I had been talking about staying in Afghanistan for longer than just the summer, until maybe November.

My father laughed. "He has not been here yet," he said. "He will get bored. He will want to come back before even three months."

That stung a little. I was plenty insecure about not being Afghan enough without my father rubbing it in.

Then there was just a week left. It was so busy: I was taking my finals early, missing prom and graduation and the senior trip to Cancún, all so that I could make it to Kabul in time for the loya jirga, the meeting at which Afghans would convene to choose their new government. (The Karzai-led interim government appointed after the fall of the Taliban had controlled Afghanistan for the past several months; the upcoming loya jirga would establish a more permanent body.)

My father called and said he wanted me to bring some things he couldn't get in Afghanistan: dress socks, Tylenol PM, and Krazy Glue. "A lot of Krazy Glue," he said. I had to laugh about that. In America my father used that stuff for everything. Now he was going to use it to repair Afghanistan, the whole broken country. Then he told me to shave my goatee, so I went ahead and did that.

I packed my books about Afghanistan, a sport coat, new headphones for my Discman, and my collection of U2 CDs. Fifteen years earlier my brother had taken his own U2 tapes along with him to Afghanistan. (Omar had discovered the band when "Pride (In the Name of Love)" came on one night during his shift at Pizza Hut.) One day a mujahed asked Omar what he was listening to, and Omar removed the headphones from his ears and put them on the fighter's head. After only a few seconds, the man ripped them off. "Why is that guy screaming so loud?" he said. "Why is he so angry?" It was funny; coddled teenagers all over the West "identified" with Bono's outrage, yet a man who'd actually lived through the experiences evoked in the music found it inaccessible. The mujahed who had every reason to be frustrated and angry had no desire to hear his emotions reflected back to him in song.

I also packed a bunch of recording equipment—a microphone and a cassette recorder and dozens of D batteries. A reporter who'd spoken to my father about Abdul Haq's death had wound up interviewing me, too; afterward she'd asked if I might be interested in taking a tape recorder to Afghanistan and making a documentary about my trip for the public radio program *This American Life*. Though I had no experience doing this kind of thing, I liked the idea; privately I knew it would give the summer a focus if I started to feel like things were going awry.

At my brother's I watched a videotape of a speech Karzai had made a few months earlier at Georgetown. To the young Afghan-Americans in the audience, he said, "Work hard. Learn well. Study well. And make money. Bring it to Afghanistan." He urged everyone, "Whatever passport you have, come back. Come back to Afghanistan."

It was hard to imagine anyone as young as I was going back. Even if they wanted to, they might not have the opportunity. I was a special case; my father was already there. I might be the first one: the first teenager to come back to Afghanistan from America.

I'm coming back; I'm going back. That's how everyone says it, even if you've never been.

2

OUR CAR WAS IN THE driveway, ready to leave for SFO, but there was a momentary panic: I couldn't find my ticket and passport. They finally turned up in my sister's room. I had a long trip ahead of me, and at this rate I wouldn't make it through even the first leg. My first stop would be London, followed by a flight to Dubai; then another plane to Peshawar, where I'd stay with family for the night before crossing the border into Afghanistan the next morning. My itinerary had been patched together by a travel agency in Los Angeles; for an ordinary civilian, this was still an extremely difficult trip to arrange.

We made it to SFO in time. There we were surprised to run into several of Abdul Haq's family members. Among them were his nephew's wife, who, it turned out, would be traveling on my exact same flights; and his sister, whom I'd met just a few weeks earlier with my mother. She'd cried, telling us how she'd gone and gathered up her brother's clothes. To Kabul, she had carried a few small posters of Abdul Haq to hang around the city, but those she put up were immediately torn down—presumably by loyalists of the assassinated Northern Alliance commander, Massoud. Today at the airport she said she had a message for me to deliver. She was upset that Massoud had been officially proclaimed the national hero of Afghanistan. "Chairman Karzai, your father, Hedayat Amin Arsala—these were Abdul

Haq's friends," she said. (Arsala, Abdul Haq's cousin, is a cabinet member.) "Ask them, Where were they when this happened? Did they just forget about Abdul Haq?"

I understood her grief and outrage, but I didn't know how to respond. "Okay," I said uneasily.

Then I checked in, and it was time to leave my family behind. Standing at the top of an escalator, I turned and waved goodbye to my mom, then glided down out of sight. It didn't quite hit me how much I was going to miss her. I can admit that I'm a little bit of a mama's boy. I've grown accustomed to being separated from my father, but I've never been apart from her, and it will be harder.

The takeoff was intense. The plane tilted up off the runway, and in that instant I felt myself being rocketed into my future, striking out for the new world and leaving the familiar one behind. My mind was racing a thousand miles an hour. I had loud, brand-new headphones, through which I was listening to U2. I was getting really pumped up. Then I got up to go to the bathroom, and when I came back, I managed to break the little plug you stick into the jack on your CD player. That kind of killed my mood.

The old lady beside me said that she and her husband, seated across the aisle, were going to London. "What are your plans?" she asked kindly.

"Actually, I'm not going to London," I told her. "I'm just traveling through there. My final destination is Afghanistan."

"Oooooh," she murmured, with undisguised shock. She said not another word to me during the entire trip.

The farther east I flew, the darker the planet got. Europe was all lit up, but by the time we neared Iraq, deep black empty sections dominated the view, with a scattering of village lights here and there. But Dubai, the Arabian city in which I landed, had a luxurious sheen. Its airport made London's look shabby. At a McDonald's I ate a Big Mac. It tasted pretty much the same as it did in California. *This is probably the last time I'll eat a Big Mac for a while,* I thought.

I finished my hamburger and went to the gate for Peshawar. The area was crowded with people speaking Pashto, like it was just a regular language. That blew me away. It's a very disorienting experience to have the thing that has always made you different all of a sudden make you the same.

During the flight, I watched our progress on a computerized map. Then we landed in Peshawar, and I walked off the plane thinking, *This is it. I'm here.*

At the baggage claim I suddenly forgot the color of one of my suitcases. It belonged to my mother, and I hadn't gotten a close look at it before I left. Then a brownish-reddish bag came by that looked right; flustered, I tried the lock, which thankfully worked.

Then I was in a crowd of people, all of us waiting to have our luggage inspected. From where I stood, there was no way to see who might be waiting for me outside. I knew it wasn't my father, who was busy in Kabul. Instead he had sent a relative to meet me. But I didn't know my family here, and now I panicked, wondering how we would recognize each other. I felt like a lost child in the grocery store. *Why did I come here?* I despaired. *I should have stayed in America. What the hell was I thinking?*

I went through a gate. The whole airport was filthy; it smelled, and everyone had a beard. It felt like it was 115 degrees. Then I heard, "Hyder! Hyder!" There was a zap of relief, as if my mother had called my name from the other end of the cereal aisle. Here was my uncle Rauf Mama, whom I'd known as a child in India and whom I'd seen in recent photographs. *Mama* is the Pashto term for a maternal uncle. In this case it's confusing, because Rauf Mama is actually related to a female ancestor on my father's side. But even in cases where there are no blood ties, there is an Afghan custom of referring to close friends by such an endearment. (There are lots of people about whom I find myself saying: "So, my uncle—actually, he's not really my uncle, but we call him that.")

Rauf Mama was a major commander in the Soviet war and was wounded too many times to count; he lost an eye to a landmine, and now the empty socket holds a little ball, the immobile iris always staring straight ahead. He's a small muscular guy with a bushy beard—like an Afro growing out of his chin. He's the same age as my father, fifty-seven, but he has the stamina of an ultramarathoner. He had literally walked thirteen hours to be here to pick me up today, hiking over the mountains up in Kunar, then making his way down the hot edge of Pakistan.

Rauf Mama told me later that when he first saw me, he was confused; I was talking to a woman. *If Hyder got married, I'm pretty sure I would have known,* he thought. But I was just saying goodbye to Wazhma, Abdul Haq's nephew's wife.

In the small airport, I hugged Rauf Mama and greeted several of my family members—I didn't recognize them, but they all leaned in to kiss my cheeks—and then we went out to the car. Everyone made a big show of me sitting in front, and I slid in and grabbed for the seatbelt. It didn't work, and then it dawned on me: "People don't really use seatbelts here, do they?" I said to the driver. He laughed, confirming: "Nobody wears a seatbelt." Then we set off. I'd forgotten that the driving here would be like it is in India: cars cutting each other off, honking, no lanes—no rules, for that matter. Just being a passenger in these dense, hectic streets made me feel a certain satisfaction.

Soon we pulled up before the house where I would spend the night. I knew I'd officially arrived when I walked into the living room and saw an AK-47 propped up against a cabinet, fully loaded, ready to go. Rauf Mama showed me how it worked—the safety trigger, and the switch that let you choose to shoot machine-gun style or one bullet at a time. Then my cousin Habib from Los Angeles popped up. Habib, who's a little older than I am, looked like he'd seen a ghost. His face had lost all color. "Did something happen?" I kept asking him. It turned out he'd had an adverse reaction to Afghanistan. Habib had planned to stay in Kabul with his father for the summer, but he had lasted only three days. Now he intended to go back to California. He showed me the designer jeans and bootleg DVDs—*Look, I got this for five dollars, this for two dollars*—he'd bought at the bazaar in Peshawar.

The phone rang. It was my mom, telling me to make sure I brushed my teeth, took a shower, and put on clean socks. Then Rauf Mama and I went out to the bazaar ourselves. I bought three pairs of kameez partoog: baby blue, sand-colored, and dark brown. Afterward we went to the house of one of my aunts for lunch. "I haven't seen you since you were two and half!" she exclaimed. Even if I don't recall anything of Peshawar, it was nice to meet people who remembered *me* here—who could confirm that I'd once been a part of this world. After we ate, my uncle said I should get some shut-eye, so I changed out of my clothes—jeans and a red Banana Republic shirt—and into one of the new kameez partoog and lay down on the bed. I realized I'd traveled for thirty hours without even a wink. The clothes were so loose, the house so cool, the bed so comfortable—I closed my eyes and went to sleep right away, without even trying.

In the morning Rauf Mama woke me early for the trip to Kabul. Rauf Mama couldn't come, but he was sending his son Salaam along with me. We'd drive from Peshawar up the Khyber Pass to the border crossing called Torkham, where we'd hire a taxi to take us the rest of the way to Kabul. All in all it would be an eight-hour trip. In the car I told Salaam about my radio documentary and asked if it would be okay if I made some recordings. Then I took out the microphone, which was over a foot long, with a big foam cover. It attracts attention, and at a checkpoint, the police held us up: *What's going on?* I let Salaam do the talking. "He's an Afghan, going back to his country," he said.

"Who's he?" the police asked, and I had to give my name, the way you do out here: *Hyderakbar, son of Fazelakbar.* Afghans don't have last names; you're the son of whoever. Only people who engage somehow with the wider world adapt their names to fit the other convention. (Sometimes the foreign press decides upon a last name for you, interpreting a compound name, like Abdul Haq, as two distinct entities. "Haq was an Afghan hero," reporters intoned in the days after his death. It was the equivalent of referring to a Peterson as "Mr. Son.")

Then we were crossing the Khyber Pass. I knew from my reading that it wasn't so much physically spectacular as symbolically resonant. But it looked pretty good to me—a rugged road between mountains—and at least for a moment I felt like, *It's really happening.* I was along the same stretch once traversed by an army of Alexander the Great's; by Babur, the founder of the Moghul empire that ruled India for two centuries; by the British invaders; and of course by my father and Abdul Haq and countless mujahedeen.

We soon reached the border station at Torkham. It was dusty and hot. There was a small gate not even the size of one you would see at the entrance of a gated community in America. We joined a long line of cars, and when we got toward the front, we paid a little kid, maybe eight years old, to carry our bags to the other side in a cart. There were a whole bunch of these kids running around. I started to notice that nothing happened without a bribe. People who had the disheveled look of returning refugees had to pay the guards off before they were allowed to cross. But when it was our turn, the guard took one look at my American passport and said, "Yes sir, go right through."

On the other side of the gate, Salaam and I stood outside, and he began to search for a taxi. "Is this Afghanistan?" I said. It seemed like he didn't hear me, so I said it again: "Is this Afghanistan?" I literally had to ask him four times before he paid attention.

"Yeah, yeah, yeah, yeah," he said, glancing at me distractedly. "This is Afghanistan."

I looked around. Before me a little kid headed back toward the Pakistani side; instead of letting him cross, a guard stopped him, then beat him. I turned away from the sight and into a crowd of beards and burkas. This moment had been the focus of so much longing. But now I was here, and there was no shivery sense of recognition. I didn't have that sense of *Wow, this is my country*; none of that kiss-the-ground stuff.

Salaam found a comfortable-looking taxi, the '99 Toyota Corolla, and settled the price. We put our bags inside and headed off. Everything out my window was destroyed: walls, buildings, even the ground itself. It was as though a giant wrecking ball had swung from one end of the country to the other. Old Soviet tanks were marooned here and there, wasting away on the side of the road. I'd seen pictures of this stuff, but there's just no way anyone could get it from the slow pan of a video camera, or single images from the newspaper. You just can't understand the scale of the destruction until you're actually moving through the endless, barren, three-dimensional space.

The driver put a tape in the deck: Shakira. "This is your people's music," he laughed.

So we were driving through the ruins, listening to Shakira, the windows down because the car might break if we tried the air conditioner. There was lots of honking; the system here is organized around horns instead of traffic laws. The air was heavy with dust, and my right eye was completely red, I was sure; I scratched it constantly.

I knew we would soon be in Jalalabad, one of Afghanistan's five major cities. I was anxious to see the place. But when we got there, I just saw a bunch of bombed-out structures that had been partially rebuilt with mud and rocks, which seemed to be the top choices for building materials here. There were a bunch of shacks selling tomatoes, watermelons, Pepsi drinks, sugarcane juice. The driver exchanged currency, and then we began the last leg of the journey to Kabul.

All through the drive Salaam had been telling me: "If you want to get some sleep, get it on the road to Jalalabad. The road to Kabul is horrible— it's really bad, it's really been destroyed." I was thinking, *Okay, fine— probably potholes here and there, have to slow down, go around them, etc.* But what Salaam should have said is, "From Jalalabad to Kabul, there is no road." The Corolla jerked over rutted, busted ground. I must have hit my head against the ceiling about thirty times. I started to feel dizzy; I was sure I was going to throw up. I was sick from the ride and with regret at what I had done. With growing apprehension, I thought, *Maybe I wasn't ready for this.*

We descended a rocky, windy stretch and soon arrived at the checkpoint where the guard searched my U2 CDs. And then we were off, and the journey was nearing its end.

Now we are finally entering the city. There are German peacekeeping troops, and destruction that rolls off the road for miles, and a blur of streets as the driver makes his way to Kabul Hotel, where I'll be staying with my father.

When we pull up, I see that the hotel is really something else. There's a huge hole in the building from where a missile once hit. It's an unfixed, multistory crater. *Wow,* I think. *I can't believe I'm staying here.*

"Hyder!" I hear from a window up above.

"Dada!" I yell, which is the way we say it in Pashto. Then I climb up to the room—the hotel is four stories, and there are no elevators. He gives me a big hug, and we shake hands and talk a little—*Hey, how are you*—and

like everything else it is anticlimactic—not at all as grand or dramatic as I expected.

"Want to wash your face?" he says, and I go into the bathroom. There is an old stained sink and a mirror, and when I look at my reflection, I see that I am caked in dust from our journey. Everything about me is completely white, even my hair. I turn on the faucet and close my eyes, splashing water on my face and wondering what will happen next.

3

THREE NIGHTS LATER I'M IN the same bathroom, cleaning myself for evening prayers. The tile floor is soaking wet, as always. We don't have a working shower, so instead we fill a bucket with cold water—the only kind there is. We warm it with a long stick that turns bright red, then pour it over ourselves with a mug. Now, as I finish, I hear an explosion outside—then another, then more—maybe five in all. *Were those rockets?* Quickly, I note the time—a quarter to six—and run out to my father.

"Isn't this a pretty big deal?" I say breathlessly.

"Sort of," he replies mildly. "It's a kind of welcoming for the loya jirga." The conference to choose the new government is set to begin in about a week; there may well be attempts to disrupt the proceedings.

I run to the balcony—it's just a small space where three or four people can stand—and lean out into the air. It's as if nothing has happened. Everybody is still walking at the same pace; the cars continue their loop around the traffic circle. Except for a couple of people, nobody is searching the sky, or pointing and shouting "Heads up!"

"The whole city seems to be functioning pretty normal," I report to my father.

"Yes," he says. "Everybody's just going about their own business."

I stand there for a second, considering this. *They've seen plenty of rockets here in Kabul.* It's hard to imagine that I'll ever become so desensitized. And not just to rockets—to all of it. So far the place has been one relentless shock to my system.

"Do you want to see the rebuilding or the destruction?" my father asked me two days ago, on my first morning here.

"The destruction," I said. Coming from America, I figured I wouldn't be that impressed by the good parts. I wanted to see what had gone bad.

We were sitting in my father's car, a Mitsubishi Pajero SUV paid for by the Afghan government. (No matter what their make, Afghans call all SUVs "jeeps.") The currency here is so inflated—one dollar equals about forty thousand *afghanis*—that when my father went to the bank to pick up the money for the jeep, they presented him with four enormous sacks of bills, like in a cartoon. He couldn't fit all the money into a single taxi; he had to make two trips.

We set off from the hotel for my tour. In places the city had been leveled to the horizon. You'd see the ragged front wall of things and then a blank space behind. Westerners sometimes think of Afghanistan as backward; it's important to realize that the country's twenty-three years of war were anything but old-fashioned. These battles were fought with Stingers, not muskets. Very modern warfare has reduced this country to a very primitive state.

I stared out the window as the city zipped by. Most of the cars on the streets were cabs, painted yellow and white. (Ordinary people in Kabul aren't wealthy enough to own private vehicles, and the international aid agencies and diplomats now arriving seem hesitant to invest in anything permanent. The situation is still unstable; maybe they'll be here for only a few months.) There were no sidewalks; people walked at the edges of the road. Two dingy white horses pulled a cart loaded with several men and one woman. She was wearing a burka, like all of the women I saw.

We passed a junkyard of rusted-out buses; a mountain up which people carried water for their daily use; and the bed of the Kabul River, which was dry due to drought and lined with a marketplace of shacks. (Because rain messes the whole thing up, the location is known as the Titanic Bazaar.)

Every now and then we'd see a green flag flapping, marking the spot on which a martyr had been killed and buried.

That evening we went to a wedding party held by a prosperous land-owning family. They lived in green fields on the outskirts of Kabul. We parked at the edge of a long driveway and walked through a gate. The house's sand-colored façade was peeling off in patches, and you could see the bricks underneath. Music tinkled in the distance, and as we approached, it grew louder, increasing in volume as I walked up the stairs. Outside an open doorway was a pile of shoes; I removed mine, stepped inside, and the music exploded.

Several men were seated in a circle playing instruments—I recognized a sitar. The melodies were joyful, strumming; the scene was almost miraculous when you considered that for the last several years, music was banned by the Taliban. People were seated in a square around the room, as is the custom here, crammed together on thin cushions with their backs against the walls. There were a mix of those in traditional dress and those who seemed to be recently returned exiles: a woman with uncovered hair and dark lipstick, men in button-down shirts. A couple of people dangled cigarettes between their fingers. There were also two massive, uniformed international peacekeepers, present as guests.

The windows had been thrown open, and the thin curtains blew a little; one fluttered against the side of my father's face. He told me that the singer, Bilton, was one of the most famous musicians in Afghanistan. There was another famous guy in the room, an artist with a silver ponytail. He is at work on the project to restore the massive sculptures known as the Bamiyan Buddhas. The Taliban attempted to destroy the Buddhas, which were carved into a sandstone cliff west of Kabul in the third and fifth centuries; the statues violated their ban on idolatry.

At one point I went out to the car. As I sat there talking to Salaam, the light began to fade, and by the time I got out, it was completely dark. Salaam left the headlights on for me, but once I got a little ways from the car, I couldn't see anything. I held my hands before me, and they were swallowed up by the night. Finally I found a wall and crept along that back toward the music inside.

Before dusk we had walked around the fields—there were 180 acres—
and seen the owner's crops. He grew a special kind of mulberry—*tut*, in
Pashto. I grabbed the fruit from the trees and ate it, without washing it or
anything.

By the next evening I had gone to the bathroom at least twenty times and
thrown up twice. I lay on the bed in the hotel room, thinking of the senior
graduation trip to Cancún. *Why'd I pick coming here?* I thought.

In the days since, I've been here in the hotel room a lot. My father leaves
for meetings, and I sit inside, the traffic sounds from the street rising up
through the open window. I count the bugs flying around the room (fifteen) and my mosquito bites (seven on my left arm, four on my right), all
the while doing my best to dismiss a nagging feeling that I should have
taken a malaria shot. I'm having a hard time sleeping at night—my father
snores—and my eyeballs ache with fatigue. There's nothing to do except
listen to music on my Discman or on a radio station that seems to cater to
the German peacekeeping troops (*Nine-ty-nine red balloons . . .*). I pine
for standard forms of entertainment the way someone in a teen movie
might pine for love. *Even if I just had the Internet or something,* I despair.
I can't even go out for a snack, since everything makes me sick, including
French fries. *Don't eat those. The way they fry them isn't healthy,* my father tells me, but of course I don't listen, and throw up all over the place.

Every day seems like something just to endure. I think about cutting my
trip short, staying for just one month. *One month.* Even that seems crush-
ingly long.

So this is my glorious homecoming: sitting on a bed in a run-down hotel
room, staring out the window at a mountain in the distance, waiting. Not
even for something to happen, but for the whole thing to end.

I'm not sure whether I'm confirming my father's expectations or disappointing him. The last time my father stayed here at Kabul Hotel was a decade ago, in the heady days following the collapse of the Communist
government. Much as they are doing now, Afghans then returned home in
joyous droves to begin the work of rebuilding their country. Back then the
other bed in my father's room was occupied by Abdul Haq.

Abdul Haq and my father were full of hope when they arrived here. But almost immediately things begin to fall apart. Now that their common enemy was gone, various mujahedeen commanders began to lash out at one another. Soon the city was divided into little fiefdoms; it was not possible to cross from one to another without the equivalent of a municipal visa. Abdul Haq was the security director, and at night he and my father would lie in their beds, talking. "This is not possible," Abdul Haq would say. "You see how many governments are in Kabul right now? I cannot keep the security. I don't know for which government I should work."

Then one day Abdul Haq went to his office and found himself blocked from entering. "You can't come here," the men said. They were members of Massoud's troops.

Several commanders tried to convince Abdul Haq to retake the office by force. But he'd had enough. He told my father, "The Russians have left. The Communist regime has collapsed. There is no reason to fight. We should not be spilling blood. I've decided to give up. I'm very sad that we brought such a system to Afghanistan, that we ourselves don't even want to work in it." Abdul Haq resigned his position and left the country.

When I was a newborn baby in Peshawar, Abdul Haq whispered the Azaan—the Muslim call to prayer—in my ear. It's a tradition roughly equivalent to a Christian baptism; it sort of makes you officially Muslim. Often a family or religious elder does it, and Abdul Haq chuckled that my parents had picked him. But they'd selected him on purpose; they hoped I would follow in his footsteps. I've made my mom repeat this story a million times. "Hyder, I just told it to you three weeks ago!" she'll say.

Now, brooding in my hotel room, just two floors up from the one in which my father and Abdul Haq stayed, I wish that he were here with us in Afghanistan, gently initiating me into this world.

One day I leave the hotel room and go with my father to the presidential palace. It's a short drive, so close that we could have walked. We go through a large gate set between stone columns. The gate has huge locks and seems like it must weigh a thousand pounds; a guy strains to push it open. The palace—or the Arg, as it's called here—is not just one building, like the

White House, but an entire complex from which Afghanistan has been ruled since the nineteenth century. Walking on the paths outside, we can hear the shearing sound of manual mowers being pushed across the lawns.

Inside, we sit in a waiting room. There are expensive carpets on the floors and paintings on the walls. We drink a cup of coffee, and soon we go to see Karzai. I notice immediately that his bald head is as shiny in real life as it appears on television. "Salaam alaikum," he greets my father.

"Salaam alaikum," my father says. "This is my son Hyder."

I get kind of nervous—it's hard not to be, meeting him. My heart rate goes up, and there's a queasy feeling in my stomach.

"This is the one you made cry in Virginia," my father tells Karzai. Once, on a visit to our home there, Karzai had joked that if I were looking for a girlfriend, he had a niece my age. I was about four years old at the time, and I started crying.

"Oh, I see," Karzai smiles. I would never mention it, but I've heard that his niece has gotten really pretty.

We all go to pray at the mosque. Coming toward us, I see someone I recognize, a warlord named Rashid Dostum with a ruthless reputation. He's pretty up there, even by Afghan standards—he would tie his prisoners to tanks, then crush them. His forces were once known as the *gilam-jam,* or "carpet-snatchers." *Gilam-jam* is an Afghan way of saying "stripped down to the floor"; Dostum's forces were *gilam-jam* because they looted everything in sight, including, literally, the carpet.

Today Dostum is wearing a dark suit and a shiny tie. The outfit doesn't do much to professionalize his image. He's backed by a beefy entourage, and the way he moves is cave-mannish. He gives me a huge smile and a hearty handshake—he must think I have something to do with Karzai. Over the years Dostum has switched sides so many times that basically everyone is his enemy. The flip side of that is that basically everyone is also his friend. His presence in the palace underscores the ethical muddiness of this time. Even the most outrageous characters are trying to curry favor with the new government, and it isn't clear whether anyone is going to discourage them.

Later my dad asks if I want to get a picture with Dostum. "Yeah," I say. *That's definitely something you could show off to people,* I think.

"Okay," my dad says. Dostum and I sit on couches in Karzai's office, a vase of pink flowers between us, and my dad gets the shot.

This is like Lollapalooza, I decide—like going backstage and getting to meet all the rock stars.

Now I begin to have days more like the ones I imagined, where I get to meet the people I wish I was old enough to have known before. (I often feel as if I was born a generation too late—I missed both the jihad and the *Joshua Tree* tour.)

One day my father and I go to see a famous mujahedeen commander named General Rahim Wardak. Wardak is an imposing figure; he looks to be over six feet tall and is heavyset. Someone brings out tea, and Wardak turns to me and asks if I'd prefer something else: Coke, Fanta, Sprite?

"No, no, I'll have tea, too," I say.

"No, no, be honest," he says.

"No, no, I'll have tea," I say.

"Oh, don't try to be Afghan," he tells me. "Say what you want."

Don't try to be Afghan. I feel as though I've been pricked.

Wardak starts giving me advice. I tell him I'm interested in coming back to Afghanistan for the long term, that I think I'll study engineering. He thinks that would be good. He has experience raising sons: one was a Rhodes scholar, and another played soccer in Brazil. Then I sit quietly as he and my father talk politics.

"It's a dirty business, no?" Wardak sighs to my father, then turns to me. "You should stay away from it," he advises.

I have only the barest glimmer of what he's talking about. But in the weeks that follow, his meaning will become all too clear, as the good days begin to alternate with bad ones of an entirely different kind.

4

I'M JOGGING IN KABUL, WEARING a kameez partoog and Nikes and circling the garden in front of our hotel. The baggy outfit takes some getting used to: the shirt dangles, and the pants flap around my legs. My headphones are on, my Discman in hand. I do this a few mornings a week. I pass people out walking, but I've never come across anyone else out for a run.

My father has been appointed the governor of Kunar, and sometimes he will hold meetings out here on the grass. The grass doesn't look too bad, maybe a little unhealthy and unmowed. My father will sit behind a scratched-up folding table, and bearded men from Kunar will gather around on mismatched chairs. The chairs will be too small for them. They'll start talking politics: what's going on in Kunar, what my father should do when he finally gets up there and moves into the governor's house after the loya jirga. Everyone in the group will express their support for my father, but everyone knows just as well that this cooperative front is not the whole story.

There will be people here who want to kill my father, not so much for who he is as for what he represents: stability, government, the rule of law. There will be people here who've killed others over less. Yet everyone will be unfailingly gracious and polite. To put it mildly, I'm having a hard time getting used to the dissonance.

Take this guy up ahead here—I'll call him Ahmed—whom I often see when I'm jogging. I've heard enough about him to know that he's someone I'd like to avoid. He's killed a man over a woman. Now Pashtunwali—tribal code—dictates that a member of that man's family must kill Ahmed or one of his relatives in revenge. This is just one of seven or eight vendettas Ahmed has on him, yet here he is in the garden, completely unconcerned.

"Salaam alaikum," Ahmed says spiritedly to me now. I stop jogging and stand before him, a little sweaty. Ahmed regards my Discman curiously and asks if he can listen. The weird etiquette here dictates that I can't show any reluctance, so I take my earphones off and put them on his own head. Ahmed listens to "Where the Streets Have No Name" and hands the earphones back to me, seemingly not knowing what to say.

Then I take off again, a surge of discomfort propelling me back toward the hotel.

At the hotel there is often a line of people from Kunar waiting to speak to my father. Karzai has asked my father to stay in Kabul until after the loya jirga, and though my father's supporters want him to start governing from the capital, he is unwilling to do so. "I can't be acting like the governor of Kunar in Kabul Hotel," he tells them. "You will have to wait."

But the tribesmen will not be discouraged. They have no sense of time; once they showed up at five in the morning. "We just want to come inside," they said to my father. "Sure you can come inside," he replied. "In four hours." There are certain tribal elders who visit each day, and I'm touched by the affection they show me. They're these burly guys from a lawless outback, and they make me feel like one of their own.

Since the fall of the Taliban, there has been basically no government oversight of Kunar. Several factions have a furious interest in keeping it that way—which means keeping my father out of the province. The most infuriating of these antagonists is a man named Ruhullah.

Ruhullah's uncle Jamil Rahman was one of the people who laid the foundation for Al Qaeda in Afghanistan. He brought hundreds of Arab fighters into Kunar during the Soviet war. In 1991 he was assassinated, and once he was gone Ruhullah—a suspect in his own uncle's death—pretty much took over the "family business." During last fall's American bombing campaign, he is said to have smuggled Al Qaeda operatives out of Tora Bora. This summer he is an official member of the Kunar delegation to the loya jirga.

One day we meet with Ruhullah and a couple dozen others at a dormitory in which many of the delegates are staying. We're in a small room. The beds—twin-size metal frames with thin mattresses—are pushed against the walls, and people lean against them. My father rests his elbow atop the coverlet, and Ruhullah sits cross-legged next to him. Both have their satellite phones out in front of them. Ruhullah has a medium-length beard the airy texture of cotton candy. He is wearing a khaki-colored kameez partoog—the same as my father—and a gray vest.

Ruhullah immediately takes command of the meeting, acting like he is in charge instead of the other way around. My father indulges him, then begins his introduction. He explains how he initially refused the governorship of Kunar; how he then refused the governorship of the province called Wardak; how he said no to Ghazni; and how he was presented with yet another offer: "They came to me and said, 'What about Laghman?' And I said, 'I can't be the governor of Laghman; I can't control Laghman.' And they asked me, 'Why wouldn't you be able to control Laghman?' And I said, 'My wife is from Laghman. She's just one person and I can't control her. Since I haven't had any luck with that, I think it would be hard for me to control all of the Laghmani people.'" Everyone laughs, and my father shifts to the serious part, explaining that he decided to accept the job in Kunar when Karzai told him that everybody was coming to Kabul, complaining about the troubled provincial areas, but that few people were willing to back up the talk with action.

"So I'm here just to be of service to you," my father says now. "I don't have any other agenda. If I wanted money, I'd go to America. If I wanted a comfortable life, I'd go to America. Everything was in America. I came from there to here to try to help."

47

Ruhullah listens, tugging at his beard, then pulls his hand away from his mouth and begins speaking himself. "There are a couple things we need to discuss," he says. "Kunar was the first province to stand up against the Russians. You were a part of that." He nods to my father. "You know that very well. Against the Taliban, we kept the resistance." Ruhullah revisits the turmoil of these years: "In Asmar, when there were three hundred houses destroyed—"

"Six hundred!" yells another man in the room.

"—in fighting between Taliban and anti-Taliban," Ruhullah continues. "How did this happen? Who's responsible? Who needs to be punished for this? I can tell you in front of all these representatives, and in front of anyone else, that Mullah Rauf was the one who did all of this."

Mullah Rauf is Rauf Mama, my uncle; he is also a longtime rival of Ruhullah's. Now Ruhullah is framing Rauf Mama as a Taliban lackey— *He was the Taliban's this and the Taliban's that*. Rauf Mama was not a member of the Taliban. But he never actively fought them—for the common reason that a personal enemy was anti-Taliban, and it would have been unthinkable to affiliate with his adversary's side. The destruction in Asmar to which Ruhullah is referring was not Rauf Mama's fault—oh, but the details don't even matter. Ruhullah is simply trying to inflame old wounds.

Now Ruhullah names three of my father's strongest backers and explains, "We are opposed to them, not you." Of course, Ruhullah's opposition is to anything that will curtail the benefits he reaps from chaos. In early fall, for instance, it will be reported in a British newspaper that Ruhullah failed to distribute millions of dollars provided by the European Union to compensate farmers for eradicating their poppy crops.

With no real structure around, it's easy to claim authority and hoodwink newcomers. But it's mind-boggling that Ruhullah fools anyone for even five seconds. When, months later, the Americans at last arrest Ruhullah and ship him off to Guantánamo, the *New York Times* writes that he "could stand as a metaphor for the uncertainties they face. . . . [H]e might, in effect, have been a sort of double-agent, keeping contacts with the Americans so he could pass information to fugitives in the mountains." The language bothers me: *double-agent*. Where did they get the "double"? Ruhullah is so obviously simply an "agent" that the only appropriate use of "double" here would have been as in "double-blind"—to indicate either ignorance or will-ful oblivion. Military spokesmen and reporters tend to suggest that the sit-uation in Afghanistan is incredibly complicated and difficult for outsiders to grasp. Sure, that's the case sometimes; but I don't know how much more obvious you can get than Ruhullah. His ties to Al Qaeda are glaring.

Now, in the dormitory room, my father listens calmly, even to Ruhul-lah's defamation of Rauf Mama. Finally my father says, "We're all brothers here. If we go into this blame game, there's going to be nobody left. Unless there's something substantial, like a warlord who's committed crimes on a mass level—we can't focus on personal differences right now. If we stick to trying to figure out, *Is this the right guy?*, this will take ten years on its own. We should draw a line from this day on. If you look into the past, no-body's clean."

Instead of responding to my father's remarks, someone Ruhullah proba-bly bribed speaks on his predetermined topic. "Your great respected family name and your own name are being misused by the people around you," he warns my father. "They are using your name to put forward their own agendas."

As the man continues, Ruhullah stares at my father, trying to gauge if his strategy is working. Finally my father whips around and gives Ruhul-lah a wide-eyed, mocking look, head-on. Ruhullah's eyes dart away. It's one of those moments that makes me just love my dad: a guy who proba-bly has Osama bin Laden's number programmed into his satellite phone wants to kill him, and my dad responds by making fun of him, right to his face.

But despite all of the backstabbing, many people are still full of hope for the loya jirga. After all, malice and vendettas are the status quo. There's an earnest belief that Afghanistan is on the eve of a real transformation. The loya jirga will deal a blow to the warlords, set a course for reconstruction, and institute a strong central government. People are carrying around papers, trying to join movements, collecting signatures, and nominating candidates. I feel like I'm living through the Federalist Papers. The mood in Kabul is anticipatory: there's a sense that even daily life as we know it will change after the big event. The conversations go like this:

The fruits aren't growing yet.
Of course not. They're waiting for the loya jirga!
The flowers will blossom once the loya jirga comes.
I was going to shave my beard, but I decided to wait for the loya jirga.
We must settle this now.
No, no, wait for the loya jirga. We'll deal with this then.

The loya jirga is being held at the old Polytechnic Institute on the outskirts of Kabul, and the night before the proceedings officially begin I sit parked outside with our driver, Sartor. It's dark and from our seats inside the jeep, we can barely make out the white tent in which the event will be held. My father is inside that tent; I'd hoped to be there, too, but I couldn't get past security. Now Sartor and I sit waiting for him to come out.

Sartor is a member of Rauf Mama's tribe. He's in his early thirties, and he's known me since I was born. He was sort of our full-time helper when our family lived in Peshawar. I don't want to say he was a servant, because the relationship is much closer than that. My father sometimes calls me Sartor, in the way that a parent will inadvertently substitute one sibling's name for another.

Now, straining to see the people grouped around the tent's entrance, I try to imagine what will happen tomorrow, when the proceedings have begun and everybody is inside. "Do you think it's going to work or not?" I ask Sartor.

"I don't care," he shrugs.

I ask my question another way: "Do you think that after this the country's going to get more destroyed, or stay the same?"

"More destroyed," he says. His pessimism is founded on recent history; many similar ceremonies have come to naught. Even when, for example, a group of prominent mujahedeen leaders traveled to Mecca, the heart of Islam, during the civil war, and swore there that they would unite, their agreement quickly dissolved into more strife.

"But what's left to destroy?" I joke now.

"Well, they just made this tent right here for the loya jirga. They can destroy this," Sartor proposes. "They can take the tent apart and rip it up meter by meter and divide it among themselves." Sartor leans back in his seat, both of us laughing.

"It doesn't even matter that nobody can go in there with a weapon," Sartor continues. "These are Afghans. They will find a way to fight. They will use slippers if they have to. They can have a war of slippers!" He flicks his hand forward, like he's batting at an invisible enemy with his shoe.

"You're not missing anything in there," he tells me. "I'll gather a bunch of kids around for you, and I dare you to ask them to pick themselves a leader." It's easy to picture the scenario: the screeching and bickering, the shoving and the storming home and the tears. "There you go," Sartor says. "There's your historical loya jirga."

It shouldn't come as a surprise to me when he turns out to be right.

5

ON A LATE AFTERNOON IN JUNE my father and I and about two thousand other people are seated in an arena-size tent, waiting for the king. Lights have been rigged from the lofty ceiling. Before me stretch rows and rows of heads, wrapped in turbans or covered in filmy white chadors. The audience ends at a stage, above which hang two gigantic monitors on which the week's speeches will be displayed. Eager visitors like me hold digital video cameras slightly above our heads, our little viewscreens aglow with the empty podium.

The king—Zahir Shah, who ruled Afghanistan for forty years—will soon take the stage and officially open the loya jirga. But he is late, as is everything in Afghanistan, by almost an hour. Now the space echoes with the sound of hundreds of conversations as people stride up and down the aisles, leaning into the rows and greeting friends.

Even I've seen familiar faces. When I got to my seat, I borrowed my dad's satellite phone to call my mom in California. "I'm at the loya jirga," I told her. Across from me I recognized the writer Ahmed Rashid. He's been reporting on Afghanistan for about twenty years—his authoritative book *Taliban* was on the front table of probably every bookstore in America in the weeks following 9/11—and he sometimes appears as a guest on cable news shows. "Mom," I said excitedly, "Ahmed Rashid is right here!"

Rashid turned and looked at me strangely. (I guess it was his first encounter with his teenage fan base.) Then I saw a little man with a sturdy white beard. "Ismail Khan is passing me," I told my mom through my teeth. "He's passing me right now." Ismail Khan's odd magical-creature-of-the-forest facial features belie his reputation as one of the most obstinate warlords in Afghanistan. He sees himself as "the emir of southwest Afghanistan," exempt from any outside authority, especially that of the central government. The presence of warlords here at the loya jirga has prompted questions about strong-arm tactics and intimidation. Just seeing them skulking around the tent is frustrating, stoking fears that this will be a new government in name only, a big-budget remake featuring the same thuggish cast of characters. (The production even has a hair-raising title: "The Emergency Loya Jirga.")

Now there's a quick hush, then a rustling, then thunderous applause. Here, finally, is the king. People cheer, photographers storm the aisles, and everybody stands in their seats. Finally I turn off my camera because I am going to waste literally ten minutes of tape on just the clapping.

King Zahir Shah is probably the most unifying figure who exists in Afghanistan. His reign—which technically began in 1933, when he was only nineteen years old—is remembered as a peaceful time. In 1973 Zahir Shah was deposed by his cousin, Daoud Khan; this coup was the first event in a domino-series that led to the Soviet invasion and the twenty-two calamitous years that followed. But affection for Zahir Shah arises out of more than nostalgia for a bygone era. He is not associated with any of the outsiders who have attempted to impose their systems upon Afghanistan—he has nothing to do with Communism, or radical Islam, or even democracy. Zahir Shah inspires such an outpouring of support because he is seen as endemically, organically Afghan—like the loya jirga itself.

The loya jirga is an old tribal tradition of Afghans. A jirga is a council or an assembly: people getting together on a local level to, say, sort out a land dispute, or resolve a death vendetta. A *loya* jirga is a grand assembly and is convened to decide matters of national import. In this case, representatives of all of Afghanistan's provinces and ethnic groups have come to Kabul to vote for president. The representatives, selected with varying degrees of fairness, include religious and tribal elders and perhaps 160 women. (Absent are several supporters of my father's who are being held hostage by Ruhullah's men.)

Plans for the loya jirga were laid out in December 2001—just weeks after the fall of the Taliban—at UN-sponsored talks in Bonn, Germany. The participants agreed on the composition of the interim government that would preside over Afghanistan during the six months until the loya jirga could be held. The dominance of that government by a group of several people from a single small valley has been a sore point ever since. These are the Panjshiris. They hail from Massoud's home, the Panjshir Valley, and were his close colleagues in the Northern Alliance. Panjshiris are ethnic Tajiks; among the other ethnic groups in Afghanistan are Hazaras, Uzbeks, and the largest, Pashtuns. (My family is Pashtun, as was Abdul Haq, as is Hamid Karzai, as are the Taliban, as is the king.) Pashtuns, who have traditionally dominated Afghanistan's government, were incensed that the Panjshiris were handed control of several critical bodies, including the army, the interior ministry, the foreign ministry, and the intelligence service. But to ascribe all of the bad feelings to ethnicity, as the Western press often does, misses a larger point. The interim government lacked a popular mandate. When the Taliban lost Kabul, the Northern Alliance steamrolled on in and laid claim to the city as their own. I remember my father sitting in California, watching the scene on TV. One factional power had been displaced only to be immediately supplanted by another. He was astonished that the Americans had failed to stop their advance. "Mark my words," my father said. The Americans had let the Northern Alliance get into Kabul; their next problem would be how to "take them out."

But now, with the king in the arena, all the discord seems momentarily forgotten. As he nears the front, I restart my recorder, in time to catch him taking his seat behind a cloth-covered table. King Zahir Shah is eighty-seven years old and nearly bald. Tonight he is wearing a dark suit. At the time of the 1973 coup, he was in Italy, receiving medical care for an eye problem. He remained there in exile, returning to Afghanistan for the very first time just two months ago. A high-profile delegation traveled to Rome to escort him back.

The king sits at the highest point of the stage; Karzai stands at a podium below him and to the right. *"Bismallallah Rahman-e-Rahim,"* Karzai starts. *In the name of Allah, the benevolent, the merciful.* So many non-Muslims believe Islam to be a religion practiced by crazy militants; yet this is a faith in which important words are prefaced by a phrase invoking a gentle God.

Karzai's face appears on the two giant video monitors. They magnify a tic he has, an involuntary twitching around his eye. My brother recalled Karzai from his childhood in Peshawar as soon as he saw the flutter on TV. "Now I remember this guy," Omar said. "He used to be at our house every day."

Karzai bestows an honor on Zahir Shah, naming the king *Baba eh Millat:* Father of the Nation. He gives the usual martyrdom speech about Massoud—and then he mentions Abdul Haq. A little rush goes through my body. Karzai says that Abdul Haq's story brings tears to his eyes, and soon the audience is clapping. I'm making more noise than anyone, and when the applause dies down, and there's just one guy left clapping, that guy is me. Abdul Haq's brother Haji Din Muhammad is sitting nearby, and now he looks over curiously. He stares at me blankly, then sees my father and turns back around.

What I feel is a mix of everything: joy that Abdul Haq is finally getting his due; hope that such acknowledgment promises a shake-up in the government; and sadness that Abdul Haq is not here in the tent with us. I feel my eyes fill; my father looks over and notices. It's embarrassing to be so exposed before him. There is a certain formality to our relationship—it's like that in Afghan families. But my father puts his arm around me. Then he does something which he hasn't done in years and probably won't do for years again: he kisses me on the cheek. Now, as the speeches continue, we sit here side by side, in silent acknowledgment of the momentousness of the night's events.

Afterward I run out to Sartor, who is near the jeep. "Were you listening on the radio?" I say. "Did you hear the cheers for the king?"

"What cheers?" says Sartor. "That must have happened when things went dead."

I'm astonished. People outside are saying that at the moment of the king's entrance, the radio broadcast of the loya jirga ceased. It came back on when Karzai began to speak. Nobody is sure what happened—whether it was a coincidence or, likelier, not—but it doesn't matter anyway. The path for the loya jirga has already been set. Things went dead at the moment when hope was most alive.

Despite the crowd's warm embrace, the king is largely sidelined from the remainder of the proceedings. In the days before the loya jirga opened, more than eight hundred delegates had signed a petition supporting his nomination as head of state. Under this scheme Karzai would have been the prime minister. But some observers believed that the division of power would weaken Karzai's authority; as well, the Northern Alliance might refuse to deal with the king. On the day the loya jirga was set to begin, the U.S. envoy to Afghanistan, Zalmay Khalilzad, met with the king and some of his closest supporters. Hours later Zahir Shah appeared at a press conference and, through a spokesman, expressed his full support for Karzai. The possibility of the king playing a more politically active, less ceremonial role had been extinguished.

At some point Pacha Khan Zadran, a warlord from southern Afghanistan, approached Khalilzad and began yelling: *Why did you bring the king back if you won't let him do anything? He should have stayed back in Rome. What's the difference?* A crowd gathered; delegates staying in the Polytechnic Institute dorms heard the commotion and looked out over their balconies. Though Khalilzad tried to explain the situation, the damage had been done. Many now believed the loya jirga to be controlled by a foreign power; Karzai was weakened by association.

At one point during the jirga I head outside the tent with my father. A car crosses before us; to my surprise, Karzai is in the driver's seat. The king sits in the rear; Karzai is escorting him away like a chauffeur. "Give me the kingdom, and I'll carry him on my back," someone nearby comments wryly.

So what goes on at a loya jirga? Mostly people make speeches. One of the early speakers is a fundamentalist with a wild bushy beard. He looks like a caricature of his type, and watching him, I recall a story my father once told me about another extremist—I'll call him Mahmud. My father met Mahmud during the resistance, when both were based in Peshawar. In

1984 Mahmud, my father, Karzai, and several others traveled to America. In California they met with government officials; they also visited Disneyland. Back home in Concord, we have a snapshot of a clean-shaven, twentysomething Hamid Karzai standing next to Goofy (or perhaps one of the Three Little Pigs). But elsewhere in the United States there are family albums that show children standing next to a bearded, turbaned character their parents have probably never been able to identify among Walt Disney's creations. The whole day people kept approaching Mahmud with cameras, clearly assuming he was a theme park attraction. Mahmud was happy to oblige, believing that the American children just wanted to have their picture taken with a real, live freedom fighter. Nobody spoiled the fun by filling Mahmud in.

Now, as the speaker blabbers on, I stare up at his enormous beard and his puffy turban, and I understand exactly how someone could have mistaken Mahmud for a cartoon character, making an unintentional mockery of him.

The loya jirga sometimes seems to be making an unintentional mockery of itself. There are organizational gaffes, like when all of the "white beards"—elders—are invited to come forward to receive honorary medals. A crowd of white beards rushes toward the stage. "Sit back down," someone announces, clearly unprepared for a group this size. "We'll do it tomorrow." The men continue forward. "Okay, never mind," the announcer tries again. "Back to your seats!"

Then there are deliberate attempts to derail the events. Reports begin to circulate that people have been removed from the jirga and jailed for their remarks. These are delegates who spoke out against the warlords, or decried the way people misuse the name of Islam to advocate their own political agendas. (At one point my uncle Naim Majrooh, who as the elected secretary of the jirga is responsible for coordinating the speakers, runs into one of these men. "I loved your words. Where have you been?" my uncle asks. "I was in jail," the speaker says.)

Others make less provocative yet equally inflammatory statements. At one point Gul Agha Shirzai, a slope-shouldered warlord whose hair and beard make a dark, continuous ring around his face, suggests that the word

"Islamic" be struck from the new government's official name. "We should take the Islamic out of Afghanistan," he asserts. Shirzai has a point; religion has not traditionally been one of the central government's organizing principles. Afghans are devout people, but the locus of their spiritual life has always been the village mosque, not the presidential palace. Yet the wounds of the jihad against the Soviets are still too raw to eliminate an acknowledgment of the faith for which millions of Afghans fought. As Shirzai speaks, people far back in the arena start yelling, crisscrossing their arms above their heads, as if saying no in the air. By the time he leaves the stage, everyone is riled up, and it's Abdul Haq's brother Haji Qadir who calms everyone down.

Up on stage Haji Qadir is the physical opposite of Shirzai. He is tall and slim, with a close-cropped white beard and white clothes. Now he raises his arm, one finger outstretched. "We have already decided that this is going to be the Islamic government of Afghanistan," he declares. "We're an Islamic nation; the country is going to have an Islamic name. We should not ruin this event by arguing over that." There are cheers; the mood has brightened. "You all agree? Okay, then," says Haji Qadir, and sweeps off the stage.

Usually things are not settled so quickly. A guy wastes a half-hour saying stupid stuff to incite the crowd (e.g., "The king is not my father! He's an absentee father!"); by the time he finishes, people are approaching the stage for a rebuttal; one of the organizers is saying, "Please, everybody sit down. Calm down"; and, in, the audience, there's a growing weariness. On the floor delegates engage in their own battles. A group gathers around two men locked in even the most inanely repetitive argument. "Death to Russia!" "No, death to Pakistan." "Death to Russia!" "Death to Pakistan!" (The exchange is comical but rooted in one of Afghanistan's deepest problems, foreign interference. After the Soviet war some of the minority groups in the north cemented an alliance with the Russians; some Pashtuns in the east and south were forced into a relationship with another previously reviled country, Pakistan. One of the first tasks of the new government must be to break these ties, which do more harm than good; the outside powers are more invested in furthering their own interests than Afghanistan's.)

The commotion on the floor naturally diverts attention from the speakers up front. When Sibghatullah Mujadeddi, who was a leading figure in the resistance, takes the stage, he waits for the audience to get quiet. When they don't, he assumes the mic doesn't work. "Hey, hey, what's going on?" he says. His voice booms to the end of the tent; clearly the sound system is not the problem. "Please be quiet!" he exclaims. "Come on, I'm an elder, you guys. Why aren't you listening? I have the right to get on stage and talk to you and have you pay attention to me. I'm a jihadi leader, I've defended the Afghan name." The ruckus continues, and Mujadeddi regards the crowd in exasperation. *"Chee gap ast!"* he exclaims. *"Chee gap ast!"* It's the Afghan equivalent of "What is going on?"

When an announcer reads off the results of the presidential election, for once everyone is quiet. But as soon as it becomes clear that Karzai is the winner—with 1,295 votes out of 1,575—the silence explodes, and people rise from their seats. I see my father staring, from a distance, at Karzai; Karzai looks him in the eye and nods his head. Now a crowd fills the front platform, pressing against a railing that corrals them in. There is a constant rhythmic clapping; Karzai raises his palms in the air, and the obstinate elfin warlord Ismail Khan grins beside him.

There are so many people on the platform that they tell them to get down; it's about to collapse. Everyone moves onto the floor. Now I'm swallowed up inside the crowd, trying to make a little pocket of air for my video camera. One of Karzai's bodyguards—a man named Qudrat from my father's home village—takes me under his wing and helps me along. "Make way, make way," someone says. We leave the tent and stumble outside. There are cameras here and there, but mostly there are warlords and power brokers and politicians, all trying to be the closest person to Karzai. I'm pushing right alongside them; at one point I near Dostum (the guy who ran over his prisoners with tanks) and elbow his bodyguard out of my way. Then Karzai reaches his car, a black Mercedes S600 with tinted windows. "Get in the car," he says to Gul Agha Shirzai. "Let's go for a ride back to the palace." Shirzai controls Kandahar, Karzai's home province; still, many people believe he's an all-around bad guy, with ties to the opium trade. It's disappointing to learn that he's Karzai's guest. They get in the car, the taillights flicker, and the two are carried off into the night.

After they leave, everyone gets quiet. Suddenly I have a bad feeling; I'm here in this dark alley, alone with the men who'd trailed Karzai like groupies. Politics seems very weird at this moment. I'm glad my father was not among those who shoved their way to Karzai's side.

At the end of the jirga, Karzai is scheduled to announce his cabinet. There's still hope that the body will be filled with qualified professional people rather than with warlords and others picked to satisfy various factions. The jirga has not gone badly, all things considered; dozens of enemy camps have banded together to set a course for their country without breaking out into battle, the plain fact of which counts for a lot.

Karzai stands at the podium, flanked by two Afghan soldiers in brown uniforms. The tent is packed and brightly lit.

"I wish this were like Bonn again where the cabinet was ready for me," Karzai had joked earlier. "When I came to Kabul, we just got to work. It was easier."

And now apparently it is easier just to stick to the template that was laid out back then. There are no major changes. Karzai even keeps the intractable former Northern Alliance commander Muhammad Fahim as his defense minister. For months Fahim has been using the post as an umbrella for his own militia. Now he is also appointed as one of Afghanistan's three vice presidents, and he is first in the group, which is understood to mean that he will lead the country if something happens to Karzai.

One of Fahim's associates, a politically savvy man named Yunus Qanooni, is shuffled to a less influential position. About a week ago, Qanooni announced that for the betterment of the country, he was going to make a sacrifice and step down from his powerful post as interior minister. You had to wonder what calculations lay behind the move. Now, from the podium, Karzai announces that he doesn't have an education minister. "Why don't you become the education minister?" he proposes to Qanooni, looking down at him in the front row. "Good, he accepts!" Karzai says.

But most people at the jirga can't see what happens next. Qanooni leans forward, yelling up at Karzai, "No! I don't want the education ministry.

Don't give me that. Education is not my specialty. I don't have any knowledge of that!" Karzai ignores him, brightly announcing Qanooni's "acceptance." Qanooni tries to get up and has to be restrained. As Karzai continues, Qanooni sits back, shaking his head. (Qanooni's disappointment is probably short-lived. He will soon be made a "special presidential security adviser," vaulting him back up to the top of the heap.)

So much for the fruits growing and the flowers blooming: it's the end of the loya jirga, and the world has not been transformed.

Except there's a hole in the world now, someone who is gone. As the proceedings wind down, Karzai announces the death of Said Shamsuddin Majrooh, one of Afghanistan's most famous elder statesmen. He was the architect of Afghanistan's 1964 constitution, which will serve as the basis for the constitution the country will adopt in the coming months.

I knew Said Shamsuddin Majrooh simply as Baba: *Grandfather*.

6

I'M SITTING ON THE FLOOR of a helicopter, flying east toward Kunar for Baba's funeral. His coffin, covered with a rug and bouquets of flowers, lies before us. One of my uncles, Walid Majrooh, points out the window—a round porthole of light behind his shoulder—and yells something at me. The helicopter is so loud, it's almost impossible to hear anything but the sound of our flight; nobody else is even trying to talk. "That's your mother's village," my uncle tells me. I nod gratefully. The truth is that everything below us looks the same to me: desolate.

Our day began at the Kabul airport, where one of my cousins arrived with Baba's body on a flight from Dubai. He'd begun his journey in Atlanta, Georgia, where Baba had lived for a little more than a decade. Baba was ninety-two years old and died of a mild stroke. Technically Baba was not my grandfather—he was my father's great-uncle. When my father was an infant, his own father, still a teenager, died of an illness; when he grew older, his mother sent him from Kunar to Kabul to live with Baba, who became both a father and a grandfather to him.

At the airport we assembled on the cracked tarmac to pay our respects. The crowd was a Who's Who of Afghan politics: Karzai and other members of the new government, warlords, and former jihadi leaders, including a man named Sabbawoun. Sabbawoun was currently under house arrest for his role in an aborted coup, and perhaps he was taking advantage of a special exemption for funerals. My uncle Walid Majrooh eyed him warily; during the resistance, they'd disliked each other so intensely that they'd once pointed Kalashnikovs at each other, face to face. Rounding out the group was a random Japanese guy who'd gotten off the flight from Dubai, noticed me with the video camera, and decided he'd might as well stick around for the show.

Soon the coffin was carried to a waiting helicopter. The shadow of the propellers spun around and around on the cement. Several men hoisted the coffin up to the door; it barely fit through the narrow opening. Then the few of us—just family members and security—who would be continuing along to Kunar climbed inside. The helicopter rose, and we began our deafening procession across the sky. Then we turned and headed back to the airport. It was too loud to ask why. "This helicopter is too heavy. It was about to fall," the pilot said casually when we'd landed. "We'll take another helicopter that's better than this."

So now here we are, inside the second chopper. Of course I'm sick: I coughed all last night, and now when I turn the video camera around for a self-portrait, I capture a sweaty, pasty face. I throw up four times before we even land in Kunar. Everyone gets worried I have malaria.

My father came only as far as the airport; he is not traveling with us to Kunar today. After the burial he would have had to return to Kabul, and his "retreat" would surely have been used against him: *Did you hear? Fazel Akbar came to Kunar, but he chickened out and went back to the capital.* As well, his presence would have placed us all at considerable risk. There remains in Kunar a small but powerful opposition to the establishment of law and order. My father would have had to enter the province with military support—a convoy of perhaps a thousand men packing machine guns and RPGs (rocket-propelled grenades). "I'm a *dushman dar*," my father joked, trying to make light of the situation as he helped the rest of us make our preparations. *A man with enemies.*

Oddly, my father's absence is the reason I am here. "You have to go," he told me. "There's no way around it." If I stayed back, he explained, people would be sure to notice: *His son wasn't there, either. They must be really scared to come to Kunar.* This is the first situation in Afghanistan in which

I'm more than just an observer—I'm a participant in these events. It's strange not to have my dad here, especially on a day when I actually feel connected to this place. Looking around the ring of dignitaries at the airport this morning, I felt like I belonged more than others: *Baba was my relative, and this is my family history.*

Baba was born in a small village in Kunar in 1910. As he grew into young adulthood, he gained a reputation as a leader and modernizer; the central government made him a sort of congressman and moved him to Kabul, as much to keep an eye on him as anything else. Eventually he became the justice minister, which was the position he held in 1963, when he was asked to head the committee charged with writing a new Afghan constitution. The constitution they designed—in daily meetings over the course of nearly a year—was heralded as the best in the Islamic world. Its balance of democratic and Islamic principles seemed to perfectly suit the modernizing state. Baba was asked to become Afghanistan's prime minister, but he declined the position. He said it was time for young people with fresh ideas to run the government. At that moment it seemed as though Afghanistan genuinely had a chance of entering a new era. But over the next several years, as the Afghan Communist parties gained power, Baba and others became increasingly disillusioned with the nation's course.

By the time of Daoud Khan's 1973 coup on Zahir Shah—carried out with the help of Communist party members—Baba was no longer part of the government. But he was still a well-respected figure, and the Communists worried about his influence. One day a leading Communist named Nur Muhammad Taraki came to visit Baba at his home. Baba was praying, and while Taraki waited for him, he noticed several books on Communism atop the coffee table. When Baba joined him, Taraki said, "How can you be praying and still have these books on your table? You must not understand what these books are saying."

"No," Baba said. "I understand what they say. That's why I'm praying. It's you who don't understand what they say."

In 1978, Daoud Khan and his family were killed in a Communist-orchestrated coup, and Taraki became the president of what was renamed the Democratic Republic of Afghanistan. Not long afterward, Baba got sick, and his daughter and her husband went to visit him in the hospital. Baba's manner was impulsive and erratic; there was definitely something wrong with him. They later learned that Taraki's men had tried to poison him.

Baba was far from the only person Taraki's regime tried to subdue. It's hard to get across just how brutal this era was. The government arrested, tortured, and killed its opponents. In one year-and-a-half period, twenty-seven thousand men were executed at a prison on the outskirts of Kabul called Pul-i-Charki. *Twenty-seven thousand.* It's a figure that might rush past your eyes unless you really stop to consider it. One book I read drew this comparison: more people died at Pul-i-Charki—a jail—than in the 1973 Arab attack on Israel—a war. The stories from this place are wrenching: broken Fanta bottles used as instruments of torture; prisoners machine-gunned down in the courtyard; others drowned in a cesspool, and their wives told to search for their bodies with long sticks.

The systematic elimination of its opponents did little to boost the faltering Communist regime, which had been severely weakened by infighting. Meanwhile an armed resistance movement was gaining strength in the countryside. The Soviet Union, which had long goaded and supported the Afghan Communists, now found itself unable to talk sense into its protégés; basically its quarter-century of influence and 2.5 billion dollars in economic and military aid had created a monster. Eventually the USSR decided that the only way to save Communism in Afghanistan was to invade the country. They started rolling into Kabul on December 24, 1979. Later it was surprising that many people had not suspected a thing. "The Russians are bringing in a lot of aid," the minister of information commented to my father around this time. "We should pump up the propaganda." But on December 27 the Russians launched their attack, and the war was off to its official start.

I've heard the story of this night all my life. Things began normally. "When are you coming home?" my mother asked my father on the phone. My family was then living in an upscale apartment complex called Micro-rayon that had been built by the Russians. That night some relatives were over for dinner, and my mother told my father, "Everybody's waiting for you."

"I'm running late," my father said. "I'll be home in an hour."

One of my uncles said, "Tell him I'll go over there to meet him, and we can come back here together."

"No," my mother said. "We're comfortable here, just leave him be. He'll be home in an hour anyway."

But then he wasn't, and my mother started to worry. She tried to call my father back, but the phone didn't work. "What's going on?" she wondered. She went to a neighbor's apartment; their phone was dead, too. She went downstairs, across the street. Lines were silent all through the city.

Then lights flashed up, and from the windows my family watched as the city came under fire. "Look, they're attacking Kabul Radio!" my mother said.

Her brother tried to comfort her. "No," he said, "I think that's the Ministry of Health."

My mother said, "No, it's Kabul Radio. I know what it looks like from here."

It was very late that night before anyone went to sleep. In the weak light of the early morning, my mother put on a big fur coat and, trying not to wake the others, crept toward the door. When she opened it, she found another relative standing before her in the hall, on the verge of ringing the bell. "What are you doing?" he said.

"I'm going to see what's going on," she told him.

The talking woke everybody up. "You can't go by yourself," my mother's brother said. "I will come with you."

"No," my mother said. "My husband is there. I can't have you hurt, too."

My mother walked alone through the deserted streets, and outside Kabul Radio, she saw the Russian soldiers.

During the past decade Afghanistan's deepening ties with the USSR had had an impact on the careers of citizens like my father, who'd lived in Moscow while at work on radio projects. Now my mother used the little bit of Russian she knew from that time. "Moosh," she tried, saying the word for husband and indicating the station. The soldiers took her inside.

For some time she was ignored. Then a Russian soldier approached and said, "We have a problem. We speak English and Russian, and the people on the street speak Pashto and Dari. People can't understand what we say, so they keep getting shot. Will you tell the people that they will be shot if they keep walking on this street outside?"

At last someone brought out my father.

"Are you okay?" my mother said.

"I'm fine," he told her. "Some people were killed. But they just took us inside a room, and we played chess all night to pass the time. We're really hungry. If you could bring us some biscuits, or anything? And some people need cigarettes."

Then other people came out: the television director, the technical director, more. "Oh my God," they'd say. "Will you please tell my wife I'm here? Please tell my family I'm here."

Around noon the following day my father was released, and when he got home, he filled in the outline of what had happened. Two days before the attack some Russians had come by Kabul Radio and announced that they needed to service the tanks parked outside. (In those days Kabul Radio was heavily secured; the flailing government constantly showed up with new rules to announce or fresh propaganda to disseminate.) But on the evening of the attack the newly serviced equipment did not work. It was a scene that must have repeated itself elsewhere in the city; the Soviets had arranged for the methodical removal of batteries from the engines of tanks.

My father explained that the Soviets had planned to seize Kabul Radio and replace the regular evening news program with a broadcast of their own, one that would report the ouster of the old regime. They had carefully coordinated their plan so that the same news would play on a transmitter out of Termez, a city in the USSR. But something went awry, and they did not arrive at Kabul Radio in time to execute their mission.

So out of Kabul, the evening news went something like this: *Today the president met with so and so and did this and that.* Out of Termez: *The old president is gone. He is no longer here. I am Babrak Karmal, and I am now the president of Afghanistan.*

Because both broadcasts were picked up by radios in houses and apartments around Kabul, calls started coming into the station. "Which broadcast should we believe?" callers asked my father. But at the end of the program the female announcer in Termez made an error. Instead of saying, "This is Kabul," as she'd probably been instructed, she said, "This is Termez." To the people listening at home, it was an ominous blooper.

When Soviet soldiers seized Kabul Radio, high-ranking ministers were summoned to the station, and while some were savvy enough to stay away, many did in fact arrive. They were herded into an empty studio in which they were left sitting for hours. At one point my father walked past and saw that the ministers had begun playing a modified volleyball game. They were using cushions as balls, bopping them back and forth across an imaginary net.

The mood darkened when a Soviet soldier came into the room in which my father was being held and said that several engineers had been killed. These men were flipping out, running from the soldiers instead of following their instructions, which were delivered in a language they couldn't understand. "We want a translator to come right now," the soldier said. "Who knows Russian?"

A bunch of people pointed at my father, who played dumb. He was lucky that night; the soldier believed him. But he knew he would not be so fortunate in the months that followed, and after talking with Baba, he began to orchestrate a plan. My father announced that he wanted to return to Moscow and work there as the director of Afghan radio programming. Under that guise, he and my mother began to sell their belongings, including their blue Fiat and their furniture.

One night in February, in an early act of popular resistance, people all around Kabul climbed upon their rooftops and chanted, simultaneously and defiantly, *Allah-u-Akbar*. It's the Muslim call to prayer: *God is Great*. Though the words were spoken by people in winter clothing who'd crawled up from their living rooms, they must have seemed to come from something far greater; they must have resounded as if they'd been spoken by the sky. My mother always starts crying when she talks about this night.

Soon a Communist friend of my father paid him a visit. "Give me a break, I know you're not going to Moscow," the friend told him. "I know you're going to Pakistan. If you're going to leave, you better do it quickly. I'm not supposed to tell you this . . ." he said.

My father had been incorrectly identified as an organizer of the rooftop protest and officially blacklisted. Now there was no time to waste. As soon as the snow melted in the mountains, Baba and my parents and my brother and sisters—between three and nine years old at the time—sneaked into Pakistan, by mule and on foot.

My family settled in Peshawar. At first my mother was unhappy there. Before leaving Kabul, she had pared down her clothes and tied her favorites into three bedsheets. My father hadn't had the heart to tell her she wouldn't be able to wear any of her fashionable boots and dresses in Peshawar, a dusty, conservative frontier town. No sooner had they arrived when people began to talk: "Fazel Akbar is a good mujahed," one man said, "but his wife goes out without the chador."

The man who made that comment was Yunus Khalis, the head of one of the seven Islamic parties of mujahedeen fighters. (Think of it this way: instead of one army fighting the Soviets, there were seven.) The parties were all headquartered in Peshawar. There commanders received their weapons from Pakistan's intelligence service, the ISI, which was supplied by the CIA. The CIA didn't have a special interest in Afghanistan, other than that this was the cold war, and the United States saw everything through the lens of a battle for supremacy with the USSR. Determined to prevent a Soviet victory in Afghanistan, but unable to directly assist the mujahedeen, the CIA decided to use the ISI as a middleman.

But the CIA made the mistake of allowing the ISI to take control. The ISI made no pretense of equitable distribution. It preferred commanders whose agendas it could direct. Their favorite jihadi leader was Gulbiddin Hekmatyar, the head of a fundamentalist party called Hizb-i-Islami. Just as the Soviets created a monster by doling out aid to a country they thought could be harnessed to serve their global interests, so too did the Americans, by their careless enrichment of the wrong mujahedeen. It is a misconception that U.S. funding created the Taliban; the relationship is more indirect. By affording Pakistan so much control, the United States created the conditions under which the Taliban—and eventually Al Qaeda—could flourish. The disastrous repercussions of this policy will continue to reverberate for years to come.

At one point in the 1980s a group that included my father, Baba, and

Karzai's father, Abdul Ahad Karzai, attempted to form a national shura, or council, composed of tribal leaders from each region. Their efforts ended when Baba received a death threat at his home. It was common knowledge that it had come from Hekmatyar and the ISI. The event was a sobering foreshadowing of the tragedies to follow. In the years to come, Karzai's father would be gunned down in Quetta; Baba's son Said Bahauddin Majrooh would be assassinated, too.

In Kunar today the plan is to bury both father and son. Majrooh's coffin will be arriving from Peshawar, where he has lain in a temporary grave since he was killed in 1988.

Now, as we near the end of the flight, I peer out the window. The scenery below us is amazing: lush green mountains. As we shudder to the ground, I feel like I'm about to enter a fantasy park.

The door opens onto scrub of dirt and pebbles. I stumble down the little steps and follow the crowd that has gathered to meet us.

At the burial ground some of the men press up alongside. "Are you his son?" they say, referring to my father. I'm a little taken aback that they know who I am. I keep my eye on the video camera, trying to tape everything for my family in the States, half-listening to what the men say: "Your dad should come to Kunar. All the people are backing him. He should not feel like there are problems here. There's nothing going on in Kunar."

"I know, I know," I mutter.

"Tell him there's nothing wrong in Kunar. Why isn't he coming? Tell him everything is safe."

Another man tells me his name. "Tell your father hi," he says. "Tell him that I am in Kunar."

Baba's daughter, Parwin Ali, shrouded in black, approaches her brother's newly carved grave. Someone kneeling beside her speaks softly, then cups his hand on the back of her head. She's crying. Her husband, wearing a charcoal sport coat over his kameez partoog, approaches. As he turns her away from the grave, I hear a sob catch in her throat. I imagine that this brings everything back, that she's remembering her brother's death, all the scenes.

* * *

Said Bahauddin Majrooh was once the dean of the literature faculty at Kabul University. He'd been educated in France and spoke six languages; he wrote philosophy and poetry and was worldly and urbane. In Peshawar, Majrooh ran a nonpartisan press organization called the Afghan Information Center, and he became a magnet for Western journalists and scholars eager to understand the war. Barnett Rubin, one of America's foremost experts on Afghanistan, called Majrooh a "peaceful and brilliant intellectual" and "my teacher and mentor."

At first my father and Majrooh worked as a team. But my father soon broke off to run his own information center. My father, who was less at ease with Westerners, was more interested in being in contact with the mujahedeen on the ground than the journalists sent to cover them. He felt that the real story of the war wasn't getting told, and to that end he began to make his own trips inside, combining his own reporting with information from a network of commanders.

Toward the end of the war, as focus shifted to the aftermath of the probable Soviet withdrawal, Majrooh conducted a survey to find out what version of the future Afghans preferred. Then, as now, King Zahir Shah's supporters were promoting him as a unifying figure. Majrooh himself wasn't a huge fan of the king. "To be honest," he'd say, "I think he's a lazy man. He's not as dedicated to Afghanistan as I would like a king to be." But the results of Majrooh's poll showed that more than seventy percent of Afghan refugees favored Zahir Shah's return; they wanted him to come back and lead Afghanistan.

Majrooh's report created a stir—not least with the ISI and Hekmatyar, whose power would have been threatened by the king. On a February evening in 1988 Majrooh came out to greet someone at the front gate of his compound; there he was shot and killed. As Rubin later wrote, Majrooh had been "assassinated with weapons U.S. taxes may have purchased, weapons that were supposed to defend our security."

One time I asked my mom how many countries held funeral services for Majrooh. "Anywhere there were Afghans," she said, "they had his funeral."

The coffin in which Majrooh was buried was made of wood, and over the years thin gaps have spread between the planks. Standing before the box in

Kunar, my uncle looks down and sees Majrooh's face inside. But the sight isn't gruesome; his face is intact.

In the Koran it says that if you're a true martyr, your body will never decay. Take a step back from martyrdom's current associations—set aside your belief or disbelief in any religion or god—and consider the essence of what it means to sacrifice yourself for the truth. I'm sure that when my uncle looked inside that coffin, he saw something pure.

Then the burial ceremony is over, and we're back on the helicopter, flying toward the capital. (I throw up twice on this leg.) As the mountains flatten into sheets of brown dust, I think about the last time I saw Baba. It was my junior year in high school, and he'd come to visit us in California. He slept in my room, which made me proud. One day Baba asked my father what I was majoring in at college. "He's a junior in high school," my father said. "He's not in college yet."

"Really?" said Baba. "Are you sure?"

"Yeah, I'm pretty sure," my father laughed. Baba wasn't senile; Afghans don't celebrate birthdays. For whatever reason, they're just not something you keep track of. When we immigrated to the United States, my mother had to stop my father from fabricating dates on our paperwork. "No, no," she told him, "I know the real birthdays."

"He has to be in college," Baba said to my father now. "He's too smart. He has to be twenty; twenty-one."

It might be one of the biggest compliments I've ever received; I imagine I will still be talking about it when I am a Baba myself someday.

Usually my father doesn't go out of his way for people; it's just the way he is. But in the middle of the night, if my father heard Baba's door cracking, he'd leap out of bed and show him to the bathroom or help him fill a glass of water. Baba wondered if he could come and live with us. But he was ill, and increasingly feeble, and would have needed someone at home with him all the time. It would have been too hard.

When Baba got back to Atlanta, he gave us a call. "I think I left something there," he told my dad on the phone.

"What?" my dad said.

Baba replied, "I left my heart."

7

Just over a week later I'm at Baba's old house in Kabul with my uncle, who's trying to fix the place up. For a while there was a guy living in the basement who didn't want to budge; now that my uncle has finally convinced him to leave, repairs remain. We follow a couple of workmen with hammers in and out and around the yard, talking here about a new paint job, there about a broken door. It goes on like this for three hours, by the end of which I am hot and irritated.

Back at the hotel I step out of the taxi, preparing to—I'll be honest—complain to my father about my frustrating morning. He's walking back from the garden, and I hurry over, ready to launch into my story. But his solemn demeanor stops me. "Something's happened," he says. "Haji Qadir has been shot."

"Haji Qadir has been shot!" I exclaim.

"Be quiet." My father almost cringes at my outburst. "It's not appropriate to yell it like that. Calm down. We should go back up to the room."

Inside we turn on the radio and wait for news. We hear a report that doesn't add much to my father's information: Haji Qadir has been shot and his condition is serious.

"There's really nothing we can do right now," my father announces after that. "So we should just take a nap." Napping is my father's default mid-afternoon activity; it's because, unlike a lot of people, he doesn't go back to bed after rising at dawn for morning prayers. But this afternoon I don't think he can sleep. I certainly can't. I keep thinking about Haji Qadir.

Haji Qadir and his brothers are perhaps the best-known set of mujahedeen siblings to emerge from the resistance. Though Abdul Haq was the only one with truly international renown, Haji Qadir and the eldest brother, Haji Din Muhammad, were famous in the region. Din Muhammad spent the 1980s as a top figure in one of the seven parties, and Haji Qadir commanded an area in the family's home province of Nangarhar.

When the mujahedeen took over Afghanistan, Haji Qadir became a member of his province's governing body, the Nangarhar shura. In the years since, most of the shura's members have been killed in feuds related to the internal power struggles that then engaged them. It's certainly possible that Haji Qadir's shooting is an act of revenge for events stretching all the way back to this rancorous time.

Haji Qadir was the nominal head of the shura, but all of its members were on a fairly equal plain. Nangarhar was an important place over which to exercise control; the American equivalent would be presiding over the entire Eastern Seaboard. As a border province, Nangarhar functions in this land-locked country like a port. There customs are collected for goods entering from Pakistan. During the years of the Nangarhar shura's stewardship, the province also had the dubious distinction of producing much of the nation's opium. Unsurprisingly, members of the shura vied for control of these two highly exploitable markets. (Haji Qadir has always denied accusations that he pocketed customs or dipped into the drug trade.)

Throughout this period Afghanistan was in a civil war; more than fifty thousand civilians died in Kabul, and at least a million fled as their city was reduced to ruins. Those displaced found little relief in the countryside, which was the domain of warlords and bandits. When, in 1994, the Taliban appeared on the scene, it seemed as if they might actually be able to put an end to the violence. Yet their identity was a mystery: all anybody really knew for certain was that they were religious students, that they had pledged to bring peace, and that they had emerged from Pakistan.

In 1994 Baba, Abdul Haq, my father, and several other prominent national figures made plans to gather in Kandahar to discuss the Taliban's increasing power. But before they could get there, the Taliban captured that city, which became their base. (My father now speculates that the ISI, which backed the Taliban, got word of the planned meeting and speeded up its plans to take Kandahar before he and the others could arrive.) The group met instead in Quetta. There a representative of the king expressed Zahir Shah's support for the Taliban movement, but my father wasn't so sure. "I personally do not trust them," he said. "These people just came out of nowhere."

Abdul Haq got a little mad at my father, who is known for his skepticism. "Give them some time," he said. "Don't be so cynical about everything. You never know. This might be a good movement."

"Okay," said my father. "I'll take your word for it. I'm just letting you know that these people—there's no way of figuring them out."

Sometime later my father visited Haji Qadir at home in Jalalabad, Nangarhar's capital city. On his way in he ran into three young men on their way out. My father recognized one as a nephew of Rauf Mama's. They exchanged pleasantries, and then my father went inside. "Who were those kids leaving the house?" he asked Haji Qadir.

"Oh, them?" Haji Qadir said. "That's the Taliban."

"Seriously?" my father said.

"Yeah," said Haji Qadir. "Why?"

"I don't know," said my father. "I was just curious."

My father was surprised. This was the mighty Taliban? A bunch of kids who'd grown up in Pakistan? The profile seemed unlikely, but it turned out to be right. Many in the Taliban's ranks had been educated in religious schools called madrassas, which were often funded by Arab extremists. There the boys were taught a radical interpretation of Islam.

The Taliban grew in strength, financed in large part by Pakistan. According to writer Ahmed Rashid, it is rumored that in the summer of 1996 the Taliban offered Haji Qadir $10 million to surrender and leave the country. Like many powerful mujahedeen, he spent the next five years in exile.

When Haji Qadir returned to Afghanistan, he was one of the first prominent Pashtuns to join up with the Northern Alliance. But he walked out of the 2001 Bonn talks in anger as his new allies wrangled to keep all the plum positions for themselves. Karzai was eventually able to woo him back, and by the end of the loya jirga Haji Qadir held three important positions: governor of Nangarhar, minister of public works, and vice president.

I met Haji Qadir not long after I arrived in Kabul. In Pashto your mother's brother is *mama* and your father's brother is *kaka*. My father didn't introduce him to me as Minister Haji Qadir; he said, "This is your *kaka*."

"He's the one from Pittsburgh?" Haji Qadir said, shaking my hand. It was a pleasant surprise—here was someone who could perhaps at last confirm my recollection of standing there in Abdul Haq's hospital room many years ago.

"No," said my father. "That was the older one."

Haji Qadir was charismatic—he had a glow to him. He was light-skinned, with a distinguished face. Apart from his traditional Afghan clothes, he might have passed for a British aristocrat. People said he'd long appeared older than his years; now that he was nearing fifty, Haji Qadir's age was finally beginning to catch up with his looks.

My thoughts are interrupted when my father's phone rings. "Hello?" my father says. It's a short conversation. He tells me to get ready; Karzai has asked to see him, and we're going to the palace right now.

Karzai has become increasingly reluctant to send my father to Kunar. While political calculations underlie his reasoning, I also get the sense that something more personal is at stake. Karzai may underestimate the strength of the support for my father in Kunar; he doesn't want to see his friend fail. Then there's the probability that my father is among the few longtime associates in whom Karzai can trust. He wants my father to stick around the presidential palace and be his chief spokesman.

"If I stay here, you'll have a well-run press office. But if I go there, you'll have a strong province," my father countered last night. He asked Karzai to sleep on it and reconsider. "Then if you still want me here, I'll stay."

So now, as the jeep enters the palace, my father is pretty certain of Karzai's decision. On a day like this, you don't need a briefing from the governor of a rural province; you want your head of press.

* * *

"This Must Be Your First Time in Afghanistan."

We sit in the waiting room. The doors to Karzai's office are closed, but we can hear him inside, talking to a bodyguard of Haji Qadir's. It's almost like an episode of *Law and Order,* with Karzai playing the detective: *What happened? What did you see?* The interrogation feels inappropriate, like President Bush battering a witness with questions moments after an assassination attempt on Vice President Cheney, as if he's going to solve the case himself. Then the bodyguard bursts into tears. I've never heard a man cry like that.

We learn the basics. Haji Qadir was shot as he was leaving his office. He was in his car with his bodyguard and son-in-law. As they departed, they were fired upon by gunmen with Kalashnikovs; the car crashed into a wall.

And soon we know the end of the story: Haji Qadir is dead.

After Karzai calls to my father, I stay in the palace for a few moments, ill at ease. I imagine someone approaching: *Hey, who's this kid? Get him out of here!* I decide to go wait in the car with Sartor.

Outside in the passenger seat, I call my mom. "Do you already know, or should I tell you?" I say. I'm leaning out the window, so that the satellite phone will work better.

She says, "No, I don't know, tell me." I tell her that Haji Qadir has been assassinated, and she immediately replies, "Tell your dad to come home."

"He can't come home," I say rationally.

"If he can't come home, you can come home," she insists.

But I can't come home either. It's just my mother's gut reaction; I realize that it's five-thirty in the morning, California time, and I'm probably waking her up.

Sartor and I stare out the windshield until we see my father. It's official, he tells me, when I meet him across the lawn: he's the presidential spokesman now. As if on cue, his three satellite phones start ringing all at once. He tosses me one to answer, and I tell the reporter to hold on. We stand outside like that, taking the calls; my father jokes to a passerby, "This is my secretary." Then we walk together to a garden in which Karzai and several others are seated around a table.

"Stay back," my father says. "It's not appropriate for you to come." It's the first time in all my weeks here he's told me not to follow. I stand there, feeling conspicuous, and when a bodyguard beckons to me, I join him gratefully. He's seen me around with my dad, he says. Now he and his buddies start talking about how they'll miss Haji Qadir, who was a flamboyant presence in the palace, somebody a little fun.

Soon I see my father get up to take a call, and I excuse myself to join him. I notice Karzai staring at me, and I seize up a little. I glance over my shoulder at my father, and when I turn my eyes forward, Karzai is pointing at me. *Me?* He nods his head. I indicate my father: *Do you want me to get his attention?* Karzai mouths, *No, no!* I point at myself, seeking final confirmation—*you mean me?*—and Karzai nods and waves me over.

When I talk about Karzai and the others from a distance, I assume the persona of an insider or a peer. But face to face the dynamic changes: they're the geopolitical superstars, and I'm their seventeen-year-old fan, torn between asking for an autograph and trying to exude maturity. Now, on the walk across the courtyard, I literally feel the air around me, the absence of my father at my side. It's humbling to realize how much I rely on him; when he's next to me, I'm never worried, as I am now, that I will do or say something wrong.

At the table Karzai smiles and asks, "Why are you hiding all the way in the corner? Have a seat. Do you want some tea? There are cookies, too."

All I can think is: *God knows what kind of stress you are under. So many people—including me—had such outsize expectations for the loya jirga, thinking you'd be able to reverse years of history in one nine-day council. Now you've just found out that your vice president got gunned down, and you're asking me what I'd like to drink?* I stare at the little tea cups and cookies before us on the table and mumble, "No thanks, I'm fine, thank you."

He smiles and says, "Are you sure?"

"Yes," I say. "Thanks."

"How about a glass of water?" he asks, holding up his own bottle.

"No, no, that's okay," I decline. Immediately I regret it: I should have told him yes. Then I could have said, *The president of Afghanistan poured water for me.*

But soon I start to feel comfortable with Karzai. The conversation is like one I'd have with a friend of my father's who'd stopped by the house. "What do you plan on doing here?" he asks. I try to answer as intelligently as possible. An aide who handles Karzai's papers and letters joins in; he's come back from Berkeley and he jokes that we're neighbors.

Soon Karzai gets up. I watch him pace back and forth across the garden. He's wearing a plain kameez partoog. It's strange to see him out of his customary emerald cloak, almost as if he's taken off his costume. He doesn't look like a president; he looks like an ordinary guy, walking around in white pajamas.

Karzai and his advisers have decided, for better or worse, that the best way to loosen the grip of a handful of powerful Afghan warlords is to bring them into the central government. The idea is to lure them away from their fiefdoms by offering them desirable positions in the capital. Now it's possible that the other warlords will use Haji Qadir's death as an excuse not to come.

Haji Qadir was supposed to be a test case, an example. Though he was still technically the governor of Nangarhar, it was understood that eventually there must be a successor. For a while it seemed like that successor would be my dad. It got to the point where we were even discussing the possibility of bringing gym equipment to the governor's house. But the plan fizzled for various reasons—among them Haji Qadir's reluctance to relinquish the post.

The loss of a regional base had prevented, for one, Ismail Khan of Herat from agreeing to a deal. He'd been offered the interior ministry, which has far more prestige than governor. He said, "Sure, I'll be the interior minister— as long as I also get to be the governor of Herat." Rumor has it that then they went back to him and offered him an even better position, vice president.

"Sure," he supposedly said. "I'll be the vice president and the governor of Herat—but I'm not leaving Herat."

People in Afghanistan know where the nation's true power and strength lie, and it's not in the presidential palace; it's in the countryside.

Soon my father and I leave the garden and walk across the palace grounds to his new office. His phones have hardly stopped ringing; government officials have been instructed to refer calls to him. But there's no one telling my father what to do, not a single adviser. It isn't how you imagine it working at the White House: Ari Fleischer sits down, they come up with a consensus about what they'll withhold and what they'll reveal. It's just me and my dad in an empty office, all by ourselves.

So we kick around a couple of ideas. (Or more accurately, my father makes suggestions, and I sit there and nod my head.) My father decides to tell reporters that it's too early to say how serious this is. Its import depends on the motives: was Haji Qadir killed by a personal rival, or was his assassination a political act?

Phone to his ear, my father pulls out a pad and scribbles notes. A lot of reporters want to speak directly to Karzai. Even when told he isn't taking any calls, they persist. *We know him personally,* they say. *Just tell him it's so and so, and I'm sure he'll talk to us.* I watch my father bounce from *Newsweek* to *Time,* from Reuters to the AP; among callers from England, Japan, Iran, Pakistan. The journalists try to corner him: *Isn't this a failure of the government? Doesn't this make people feel unsafe in Kabul?* But my father is completely smooth, switching from Dari to Pashto to English, not giving an inch. It's a crazy day to start this job. I compare it to walking into your new school during finals week and finding out you're not excused. My father's composure never wavers; you might forget that he is also dealing with the death of a friend. When, this winter, my father arrived in Jalalabad, Haji Qadir was the one who escorted him from there to Kabul. Out of all the old friends and relatives, he was the one who took him back.

Eventually it grows dark, and we leave the office. We run into a friend of my father's, a Kabul security chief named General Fazel Azeem Mujadeddi. He's a tall guy, and you can tell that when he was young he probably had a track runner's body, but now that he's older, he's got a little bit of a gut. He and my father have an affinity for each other, in the way you do when you really connect with someone you see only over summer break: despite the time apart you always slide effortlessly back into the friendship. The security chief has had some difficult years—one of his sons died of an illness and another drowned. My father has sympathy for him; once he gave him a Gucci cologne set as a gift.

"Do you want me to take you to see the body?" the security chief asks.

"Yes," my father replies, and looks over at me. "We're going to take him, too," he says.

I sit between them in the backseat of the car. I've been thinking about Baba's funeral. Haji Qadir was the one who arranged for a helicopter to fly us up to Kunar; he stood there with us at the airport and prayed. Now, little more than a week later, he's the one who's dead, the one whose body we're on our way to see.

My father says, "Hey, check out this car." It's a brand-new Land Cruiser, fully loaded. I nod, to let my dad know I appreciate the car as much as his efforts to keep me entertained. We rarely interact with anyone even close to my age. Sometimes I can tell my father still worries about how I'm doing here.

Kabul has an eleven o'clock curfew, and the streets are always almost completely empty at this hour, but tonight they are so still and dark that it's eerie. The road to the hospital is surrounded by trees; I feel as though we're going deep into the woods.

We pull up in front of the Charsaad Beystaar, the Four Hundred Bed Hospital. The simple name matches the interior. It isn't like an American hospital, with a big brightly lit lobby, an atrium, and a man at the desk to help you find your family member. This hospital is dark. I follow my father through the hall. My mood is anticipatory, different than it would be at a funeral. In California several months ago, my best friend's brother died in a car accident; viewing his body was a bleak and solemn experience. But this has the quality of something historic: a gunned-down vice president, a whiff of political intrigue.

At the end of the corridor, someone opens a door. Inside it's damp, cold, and dim, and the floor feels like clay. Before us there are two boxes. Not coffins: just two boxes on the floor of an empty room.

"Which one is Haji Qadir?" my father asks. Several men have joined us; one says that Haji Qadir is in the box on the left. (The other box holds his son-in-law, the car's driver.)

My father walks up to Haji Qadir's body and reaches for the towel that covers him. I squint, trying to make out his face. It's completely scratched up, almost unrecognizable. Suddenly I want to get in there really closely, but not in front of the others.

My father touches Haji Qadir's face. "Oh, I see, he's been wounded here, and here," he says. Then he asks, "He wasn't shot in the face at all, then?"

"No, sir," someone replies. "He was shot in the heart."

My father unwraps the towel to reveal Haji Qadir's chest, and I see the hole where the bullet entered his skin. My father touches this, too.

"They've done a good job cleaning up the wounds," he remarks.

Now I can barely stand to look at the body, but I try to keep from fidgeting, or from turning my head away. My father's touch is clinical, and the mood in the room is calm. I do my best to look experienced, but my only frame of reference is secondhand. *It's not like how it is in the movies,* I repeat blankly to myself. I try to summon up some kind of feeling, but the only one that arises is complete emptiness. I tell myself, *I guess it's too real to be dramatic.*

My father seems not to be contending with any of this, and it occurs to me that for him, the situation is routine. My uncle Rauf Mama lost his eye fighting the Soviets—it's easy to see how the war changed him. My father's marks are less visible; it's taken me all these years, and standing here in this damp room, to register their existence. It's like I've finally spied my mild-mannered father in his superhero clothes.

Now he says a little prayer, and we leave Haji Qadir's room.

The city seems to have been placed on high alert, and on our way back we are stopped at several checkpoints. The soldiers have no idea who's behind our tinted windows; they stop the car, we roll down the glass, and then they see the security chief—their boss. He tries to be patient, let the soldiers do their job, but eventually he tells the driver, "Put your foot on the pedal and just go."

The driver accelerates, and my father and I whiz forward without stopping, flying unimpeded into the dark night.

8

OUR DAYS SETTLE into a pattern. We rise at five in the morning, are out the door by eight, and, after navigating the crowd that still gathers at the hotel for my dad, we drive to the palace and get to work. We often don't return until late. On the day Pakistan's ambassador visits, it's eight-thirty by the time I'm back at our room, inserting my key in the door.

Across the hall a guy is talking to a hotel worker, struggling to make himself understood. "Are you asking for the time?" I say in English.

"No, no," says the man gratefully. He's Indian, small and round-featured. "I'm asking for a fan. I told him I needed one a couple of hours ago." *Good luck,* I should probably tell him. We have a fan in our room, but we had to go buy it ourselves.

I explain the man's request to the hotel worker. "Oh, I already went looking for the fans, and I couldn't find any," he sighs lazily. "I'll try to find one, and if I can't find it—oh, well," he shrugs.

I translate his response, shining it up with a hospitality-industry veneer: "He's trying to find a fan but it's very difficult. His supervisor is in a meeting right now, and he doesn't have access to the room where the fans are located."

"It's not possible that this big, huge hotel does not have one fan," the Indian man says indignantly. Then he seems to crumple. "I can't sleep at night without a fan, and I have a headache."

"I can't find it. Oh, well," the worker repeats unapologetically.

We go our separate ways, and as the Indian man walks down the hall, I yell over my shoulder, "This must be your first time in Afghanistan."

"Yes," he says.

"You better get used to it," I advise.

"Okay," he responds, "I'll try."

I turn back to the door and enter our room. It's taken three months, but finally there's someone in Afghanistan who's even more out of place here than me.

With my father's new job, my mood improves. It makes things easier, having a schedule, someplace to go every day. The palace does not lose its sheen. The windows of our office look directly upon Karzai's; his are tinted, but sometimes you'll catch a glimpse of his bald head. Even at my most cynical about Afghan politics, I never stop feeling as though history—or at least a diplomatic thriller—is happening around me. Then there's the fun of being inside the media instead of on the receiving end. I get the news at the same time reporters for CNN, the *New York Times,* and the BBC do. Sometimes we even get the news *from* them.

One day I answer the phone, and a reporter asks for a statement about an explosion in Jalalabad. "Yes," I reply. "Can you hold on?" I turn to my father. "There's been an explosion in Jalalabad?" I say quizzically. It's the first we've heard of this.

"I have no idea," says my father. "Just tell them, 'No comment.' "

The communications infrastructure in Afghanistan is virtually nonexistent; its absence adds a degree of difficulty, and occasionally comedy, to my father's work. We decide to call a warlord named Hazrat Ali who might know about the explosion. Before the Taliban fell, he was a little-known, mediocre commander; then the Americans tapped him to help at Tora Bora. He's presided over Jalalabad ever since. Today Hazrat Ali doesn't pick up; my father, who is writing a report, tells me to keep dialing until somebody answers, then to say, *Hold on,* and pass the phone to him.

Meanwhile we try everyone we can think of; then my father suggests that we call Haji Qadir's old satellite phone. One of Karzai's advisers is in the room with us, and he says now, "What are you going to do that for?"

"You never know," my father says. "His son might have it or something."

And wouldn't you know, it actually works. If that doesn't say it all, I don't know what does: our best source of news is a man who has been dead for over a month.

Then there are incidents straight from the pages of a spy novel. Among the employees of the press office is a man whom no one seems to know much about; everyone calls him "doctor." Finally my father approaches him. "What are you doing here?" he asks. "Do you have a background in journalism? Or are you a doctor?" The conversation does nothing to clear things up, and at the end of it my father dismisses him.

About an hour later the man returns to the office and makes a phone call. I'm sitting at a nearby desk. "It's over, it's not going to happen anymore," he says to the person on the line. "Go to Plan B. I'm telling you, it's over."

That's the last time I see the guy. Who knows how many infiltrators lurk around the palace, hanging around offices, nodding their way through meetings, taking notes.

My father has a lot of private meetings from which I'm excluded, but whenever something big is happening, I get to come along. One day I attend a welcoming ceremony for the president of Iran, Muhammad Khatami. Khatami is Iran's first head of state to visit Afghanistan in forty years; soldiers and cameramen line the walkway along which he and Karzai will make their grand entrance. The two pull up in a black car and stand waiting at the edge of a long red carpet. The carpet does not spool out in a continuous roll. Rather, a series of red rugs have been placed end to end. Sun glints on the stripes of Karzai's emerald cloak. Next to him Khatami looks especially dour. He wears a severe black cape and a long gray dress that extends to his ankles.

An Afghan soldier yells welcoming remarks, and a military band begins to play. The musicians stand in a row, their pants ballooning slightly over the tops of their black boots, their conductor waving his white-gloved hands up and down. It looks good, but it doesn't sound right; the horns lurch and whine through the hard parts. But then the men recover, plodding cheerily through a rousing refrain, and the band makes me proud. They seem like a symbol of determination, of the whole country starting over back at square one—putting their lips to the mouthpieces and their fingers to the keys for the very first time.

There are other ceremonies to fumble through anew as the country regains its footing. One is the Independence Day celebration, which commemorates the end of the last of the three Anglo-Afghan wars. At one time, this celebration lasted eight days—it's the decorous event depicted in my 1968 issue of *National Geographic*. But the recent history of public executions in this stadium is probably closer to everyone's mind on the afternoon we pack the stands, and the festivities, simple as they are, provide a real measure of progress.

Athletes from Afghanistan's fledging national sports program parade around the track. There are men, maybe wrestlers, with bare, shiny torsos; soccer players with striped shorts and shin guards; helmeted cyclists wheeling their bikes alongside them; and bodybuilders who strike familiar grunting, curled-armed poses. There's a man on stilts, and a version of baton twirling involving something sharp. At one point a group of martial artists takes center stage. They work in pairs, one holding an object, the other trying to break it. One guy holds a clay bowl near his chest; his partner throws himself into a *hi-yah!* kick and shatters it. The pieces fly into a nearby crowd. An Afghan soldier covers his eye with his hands, writhing as the karate-choppers merrily continue around the field.

A pack of men carrying rifles appears, doing a little jig with their weapons in time to the music. They are meant to be mujahedeen. As far as I can tell, this isn't a traditional Afghan dance; the men, including some white beards, are just bobbing around.

Then out of nowhere, someone starts shooting. Smoke rises swiftly toward the stands. I've been videotaping; now my grip shakes, and the field jerks. Are they aiming for Karzai, who's sitting just a few feet away from me? One American soldier grabs his radio; another ducks back. But then the audience begins to whistle and clap. Seemingly encouraged, the men fire their rifles again. The ministers nearby me are applauding, too; even Karzai joins in, grinning and leaning forward over his china teacup and saucer. It's as if everyone is responding to a resonant symbol, like the final notes of an anthem or a rippling flag. The men shoot toward the stands with abandon.

* * *

Most of the days have a more typical office rhythm. There are no copy machines in the palace, so Sartor and I are often sent out into Kabul to make Xeroxes. He and I leave the grounds so frequently that finally the guys at the huge, hard-to-open gate ask us to go around another way. We go out, get lunch, come back to the palace, and sit in the car, eating our food, watching people pass by, making comments, and cracking jokes.

Our favorite lunch—or mine, at least—is called *shami* kabob, a delicious mash of ground beef and spices. We buy ours from a guy who cooks on the sidewalk outside a little restaurant. He slides the meat off of the kabob stick, wraps it in bread, and bundles the whole thing in a newspaper, then sticks it in a plastic bag. Sartor finds my passion for *shami* kabob hilarious; it would be like somebody coming to America for the first time and falling in love with a delicacy called the Big Mac. He would prefer to stay away from *shami* kabob, whose quality is notoriously suspect. One day I notice that my meat is totally red in the middle. *Oh, well, screw it,* I think, *I've already eaten half of it now.* I gnaw my way through to the end. Within twenty-four hours, I've thrown up three times and gone to the bathroom eight or seven. (Such are the statistics I keep this summer, like notations on a stomach doctor's chart.) Lying in bed the next day, I try to be honest with myself. *I eat this stuff on purpose.* It's the same as my preference for unbottled water; the same as refusing to get vaccination shots. I've been hoping to force my body to become Afghan—to adapt. Its violent response makes it hard to ignore that I'm a little bit American. Okay—*a lot* American. The admission makes my mind feel a little better, if not my stomach.

The hotel is a lonely place to be ill; it never starts to feel like home. Our quarters are increasingly cramped. At the beginning of the summer we had an extra room for our frequent visitors, and when it was empty, I could go in there for a little privacy. But then the hotel got crowded and they gave the room to another guest. I don't understand why they couldn't have assigned the newcomer to one of the vacant rooms down the hall instead. I've never seen a single person go in or out of there.

One day I'm walking past as a hotel worker opens one of these doors. But the door he uses doesn't open into a room—it opens onto the sky. Across the threshold there is no floor, just nothingness. It's the place where the rocket hit, the location of the big, fat four-story hole. If you took a step forward, you'd plummet into the rubble. I almost start laughing. I half-expect to hear the *meep-meep* of the Road Runner, careening down the hall and catapulting through the open door, yet somehow avoiding the trap set for him by the smirking Wile E. Coyote.

The lighter episodes are a welcome distraction from my mounting fears about my father's safety. (For some reason I don't worry too much about my own; I can picture him being attacked, but not me.) A friend in a position to know tells him, "We're getting a lot of information about your security. You need to beef up your security people." My anxiety intensifies when an associate of Ruhullah's asks Sartor for information about me and my father. "How many people are with them at night, sleeping?" he says.

"Oh, eight or nine men," Sartor lies gravely.

"You guys have any weapons?" Ruhullah's man wonders.

Soon—thanks to him and other factors—we do. Now we sleep in easy reach of an AK and a small pistol. When we leave the room, we throw the weapons in the backseat of the car. Still, I worry. How can we possibly prevent someone desperate for money—a giant demographic in Afghanistan—from accepting five hundred bucks to wait outside the door of our room and kill my dad?

Rauf Mama teaches me about the guns, and though I wish for shooting practice, I have to settle for learning to dismantle and reassemble them. I sit there in the hotel room, the parts of the Kalashnikov arrayed before me. I slide the piston in, replace the spring, and pop the top back on. My hands look cool, all greased up and dirty, and I move onto the clip, emptying the bullets, listening to them jingle into a pile. I click back and forth from single-fire to automatic, which releases all your bullets at once. I cock the gun, make the famous sliding, quick *chunk-chunk* of a thousand movies. *Chunk-chunk, chunk-chunk.* I really like that sound.

We have two clips for the AK; each clip fits thirty bullets. Then there are eight bullets for our little pistol, for a grand total of sixty eight. Still, Sartor thinks we need more ammunition. "How many people do you plan on killing?" my dad jokes.

Sartor takes note of my interest in the weapons. "Your mom said to learn Pashto," he tells me one day, "not to learn how to take apart a Kalashnikov." Though I speak Pashto fluently, I cannot read or write the language, which uses a variation of the Arabic alphabet. "You have to learn Pashto," Sartor says.

"I am learning Pashto," I say. It's a joke: a reference to a defining feature of Pashtun culture, the love for guns.

Once I use my father's satellite phone to call my friend Matin on his cell phone in California. "I'm at the palace," I say. "Right behind Karzai's office."

Matin is in a car with our friends, driving over the Bay Bridge to San Francisco. He seems weirded out to hear from me. I feel weird, too, as though I've placed a phone call to another location on the timeline of human experience, some future dot that history has yet to hit. We hang up, and my friends zoom even farther forward, across a bridge that links them to a city that seems at this moment the apex of the civilized world.

At the end of August Karzai and a horde of government officials, soldiers, and reporters prepare to leave for a three-day trip to three northern provinces: Kunduz, Takhar, and Badakhshan. My father says I can come, but I'll have to pack light; there will be a lot of frantic dashing from event to car and a very real chance of being left behind. "Don't think someone's going to come and tell you to go in a car," he warns me. "Just start running."

I wonder if I'll even make it out of Kabul. Our plane holds only forty people, and it's overfull. Before we take off, someone stands pointing: *You come out, you come out.* "Space is tight," I say to my dad. "Maybe I shouldn't go." But he tells me just to stay sitting down. It works; I'm far enough on the fringes of consciousness that the Afghans think I'm part of the Americans, and the Americans think I'm part of the Afghans. In the air people look miserable. The plane—a British military aircraft manned by an American crew—is horrible, and so is the weather; four people throw up, and had the flight been five minutes longer, I would have, too.

In Kunduz there are kids handing out flowers, an official army welcome, and another inexperienced band. Before us a soldier walks along a red carpet, kicking his legs straight forward like a wind-up toy. On the roads we can see nothing in front of us except dust, which seeps through even our rolled-up windows. Then suddenly the cars in our convoy stop, and everyone races out, eager to cover Karzai's first stop on the trip, a girls' school. (Girls are finally returning to school after years of being denied education under the Taliban.)

One of the journalists on the trip is a BBC television correspondent named Kylie Morris. The little girls are more interested in this tall, skinny Western woman and her cameraman than they are in their country's new president, on whom they have literally turned their backs. "Look at Karzai, look at Karzai," a man admonishes them in Dari. "They're not going to film you here, you have to stand there. I swear to God! They're going to film you over there, not over here." The girls ignore him and continue to stare up at Kylie, who regards them helplessly.

In every other place Karzai is received like a superstar. At one point we walk down a wide, dusty street, trailed by villagers. People watch from the tops of houses, not just standing still but actually following along from roof to roof. On another stop men peer down from high branches of trees. When we drive, people line the roads.

People embrace Karzai with more than just their curiosity; after he speaks, they line up to tell him their problems. Karzai seems to take these encounters to heart. At one stop he tells a shopkeeper, "Hopefully your store will prosper."

"If all of Afghanistan prospers, then my store will prosper, too," the shopkeeper replies. "I want all of Afghanistan to prosper first." Karzai likes the anecdote so much that he repeats it in a Council of Foreign Relations speech I later see broadcast on C-SPAN.

In another crowd someone asks Karzai if the government could increase the salaries for teachers. In fact, such a plan is in the works, but the news has yet to reach this region. In most other countries communications have transcended—even conquered—the landscape. But in Afghanistan mountains and other topographical features still slow information's passage. Then there are political issues. At one point during the summer, a man from the American government organization USAID meets with my father to discuss how to extend the reach of Karzai's voice across the nation. The project would involve more than just wiring networks. In the north, for instance, Rashid Dostum has his own television channel, as does Ismail Khan in the west. They are unlikely to devote bandwidth to the views of the central government when they can flood the airwaves with their own propaganda.

At some point we're flying again, this time in a helicopter with open windows. Dust streams in, and everyone looks uncomfortable—except for Karzai. His eyes are obscured by wraparound sunglasses given to him by an American soldier, and his head rocks meditatively against the wall. His ears are stopped up with tiny yellow earplugs. (The propeller spins at the deafening pitch of close-range gunfire.) The shades make Karzai look like a rock star—or like a skydiver in a Mountain Dew commercial, about to hurtle down into the atmosphere and *Do the Dew!*

Most of us are less composed. The wind ripples our clothes with real force—like when you see a newscaster broadcasting from the site of an approaching hurricane. One man pats at his turban, which you could picture just unwinding like a snake. The lone woman on the helicopter, the minister of health, clamps a hand to her chador. (She is notoriously tough. During the Taliban times she is said to have pulled a knife on a soldier who ordered her to cover herself up.)

When we land in Badakhshan, the country's northernmost province, we're escorted into a Russian jeep. The windows don't roll down, and my clothes get drenched with sweat. We drive with a door open just so we won't boil to death. *I'm going to hate this place,* I think.

On top of everything I'm sick, which is never fun when you're traveling but is even worse when you're in a country where a public restroom is likely to be a hole in the ground. I squat and think, *Damn, I miss toilets.* (Men here squat even when they pee; it's considered inappropriate to do so standing up. Thus there are no male-superiority jokes about that aspect of human physiology in Afghanistan.)

The stifling drive seems worth it when we reach our destination, Burhanuddin Rabbani's house. Rabbani, the leader of one of the most powerful of the seven parties during the resistance and later the president of Afghanistan, lives in a mansion practically cantilevered over a wide, rushing river. There are multilevel patios with mountain views, planters filled with flowers, and red carpet stretching up the outdoor stairs. Even the weather has improved; it's nice and cold here.

We're staying for dinner, but my stomach is killing me, and I'm not in the mood to eat. Slightly miserable, I wait for the meal to begin, guessing that I'll probably be placed with the journalists and all the other extra, unimportant people like myself.

Then somebody comes outside looking for Fazel Akbar's son. "I'm right here," I say.

I'm led to a door manned by security guards. Inside I see Rabbani, Karzai, my father, and several others seated around a table. Next to my father is an empty chair.

"This is our real guest," someone welcomes me. "He came all the way from America."

I sit down next to my father. It's like having received a dispensation from the king to move from the scullery to the head table. There are so many people who probably wanted this seat; I feel a little guilty. The food is awesome, kabobs and rice and chicken korma. I think to myself, *I'm going to be messed up tonight anyway, so I might as well eat.*

I listen to them talk about reconstruction, about Afghan politics. Karzai jokes with Rabbani, who is known to be unhappy about his current position on the sidelines. "Wow, this is a really beautiful place," Karzai tells him. "It's really amazing. If you give me your place here, I'll let you have my place in Kabul."

Somebody at the table whispers, "Karzai better be careful what he says. Rabbani might do it." An Afghan poet once wrote a verse about Rabbani's reluctance to step down from his failing presidency, focusing on the piece of furniture on which Rabbani sat each day of his term. It went something like: *My beloved chair. I've worked so hard for you. I've fought a holy war for you. My beloved chair, I'll take you to the mountains of Badakhshan. I'll take you everywhere.*

Tonight beside the river I feel a sense of completion. This is the kind of scene I'd imagined—sitting at a table with the current president, a former president, and my father. There will be experiences this summer that change me more, events that will be more deeply meaningful. But this is a special kind of pinnacle. Here I am in Afghanistan, playing myself in one of my own dreams.

9

I'M LYING ON MY BED AT around three-thirty in the afternoon, trying to fall asleep. My headphones are clamped around my ears, and I'm listening to the U2 song "Mysterious Ways." The opening guitar riff is so explosive that my bed actually shakes.

I open my eyes. *My bed is shaking?* The phenomenon seems beyond the reach of even U2 guitarist The Edge.

"Dad?" I say. He's napping. "What is that?"

"Probably just another bomb explosion," he mumbles.

I get up and run to the balcony. A cloud of smoke rises by the building across the way, and people are running through the streets. The urgent *whee-whoo, whee-whoo, whee-whoo* of an ambulance siren swells, then fades and is quickly followed by another.

I find Sartor, and together we head toward the scene. The bomb has exploded in the middle of a marketplace—probably one of the most crowded places in Kabul at this hour. Just days ago I was there with my father, who bought some freshly cracked almonds. Now, on our way, Sartor and I see someone we know. "Don't go there," he warns us. "You don't want to go there—trust me. You don't want to see it. There are bodies and people injured everywhere. They'll probably block it off before you can get there."

Sure enough, there are barricades, a huge crowd. I get only a quick glimpse. Witnesses are saying there are hands and arms over there, unrecognizable pieces of human flesh. *Were those things I saw limbs?* It's too hard to process. On our way back to the hotel, I see the ambulances. A pair of headlights is smeared with blood. A driver we know from Karzai's presidential convoy appears. "How many deaths?" we ask. "How many injuries?"

The driver just shakes his head. "It's too numerous to count," he tells us. Blood pools inside the open doors of the ambulance.

It's Thursday, September 5, almost my last day in Kabul. I'm leaving this weekend for Peshawar, where I'll spend a couple days with my relatives before returning to California. I think of my mom and hope she's not watching the news right now: the BBC is reporting that a bomb may have exploded in Kabul Hotel.

We have a TV in our room now, atop a table at the end of our beds, and when I get back, my father and a couple of others are gathered around the screen. Kylie Morris describes a "scene of complete panic and chaos"; crowds of people, many of whom were on a lunch break or shopping for dinner, fled into the streets after the blast. Apparently it was a car bomb; now police are breaking into nearby vehicles in search of others. A correspondent named Joe Phua reports that "parts of human beings" and "shoes covered in blood" sit before him on the ground. The segment is punctuated by an anchor's closing words—"an explosion in central Kabul, some reports say at least twenty-two are dead"—and a signature BBC techno beat that ends with what sounds like crashing cymbals. It's strange to see the packaging of the news, to hear a soundtrack already applied to events that are taking shape just outside our window, perhaps a couple hundred yards away.

We get in the car, and my father tells the guards at the cordoned-off area that he's Karzai's spokesman and needs to check out what's going on. We step out into the marketplace and are approached by a French reporter he knows. The reporter has long wavy hair and is wearing a blazer and a dress shirt. "I'm sorry about this," he says. "I hope it is the first and the last. I hope really deeply in my heart."

"I hope so," my father replies quietly.

There aren't many people around, and nobody stops me when I go and stand right in the epicenter, next to the car itself. Much of it has been destroyed; nearby I see a piece of the engine and tire treads. I kick some of the metal, which makes a clanging sound. There's the chiming of glass being gathered up—the ground is covered with shards. I step gingerly around pools of water, tinted red; they've been trying to wash away the blood.

As we leave, we drive past crowds gathering, people being beaten away with sticks. We're going to see one of my uncles, Abdullah Ali, who replaced Haji Qadir as the minister of public works. Security checkpoints are in force at almost every intersection. Because we're traveling in a government car, we bypass most of them, but one guard peers at me suspiciously. I'm recording for my radio documentary, so I'm wearing big headphones, holding a mic by my mouth. "Is that a foreigner?" the guard says.

"No," my father tells him. "That's my son."

We reach my uncle's—and then there's a phone call that there's been an assassination attempt on Karzai.

The car bomb takes on a chilling significance; the two events seem more than coincidentally linked.

Nobody knows whether Karzai is all right. He had traveled home to Kandahar for his brother's wedding. My father was supposed to go along, but he stayed behind to be with me. The phone rings again. This time the man on the line is crying.

Back at the hotel we call my mother. "Please come home," she says.

For hours my father has tried unsuccessfully to reach Karzai. We're beginning to think that he really is dead but that for tonight the news will be kept secret, giving the government time to formulate a plan. The move would not be without precedent. After Massoud's death, the Northern Alliance stayed tight-lipped, fearing that the truth would incite chaos.

Finally the BBC shows an interview with Karzai. "I'm fine," he declares. "I expect things like that to come across the way."

Meanwhile my father's phones are ringing off the hook. Networks ask him to talk live, and reporters request comments. But he simply doesn't have enough information. He tried both of Karzai's satellite numbers, neither worked, and that's that. I'm the one screening the calls, and the reporters won't take no for an answer. The *New York Times* is exceptionally rude; the caller clearly does not realize he's on the line with a fluent English speaker. "Oh my fucking God," he mutters to himself, when I can't accommodate his request. "What the fuck is wrong with this guy? What the fuck is wrong with this country?" I hang up on him.

This stuff is real to me, and it's just a job to them. The reporters go to bed cursing me out because they won't be able to file good stories; I go to bed having realized how easy it would be for it to all fall apart.

The next morning I wake on the balcony, covered with blankets; the air at night is autumnal now, pleasantly cool. I'm sick, of course, and I groan in complaint. The call to prayer is being broadcast over a loudspeaker. When it ceases, the bright chirps of birds fill the sky. It almost fools you: *Rise and shine, good morning!* It doesn't fit the moment—it's such a peaceful sound.

In the room my father is watching the BBC's footage of the assassination attempt. Karzai leans out of his car window to greet a young boy; as he does so, a would-be assassin—a local-government security guard—begins to fire. He gets off just a few shots—a quick *dot-dot-dot*. A young man throws himself on top of the gunman, who falls to the ground. Then the American bodyguards assigned to Karzai spring into action. They leap from their jeep and return fire in a thick hail—*dadadadadadada!*—apparently killing the shooter, a bodyguard, and the young man. An image of a bullet hole in Karzai's headrest shows how near he came to death.

At the palace Sartor stops the car in front of Karzai's office, and my father jumps out, taking nothing with him, not even a folder. But Karzai hasn't arrived yet, so we proceed to our own office. The adviser minister of culture shows up; he was in Kandahar with Karzai. The minister is unshaven, and his hair is messed up. He tells my father that the man who knocked the gunman to the ground sacrificed his life for the country and should be declared a national hero. He also tells my father that the shooter's Kalashnikov was set to single rounds, not automatic fire. The mistake almost certainly saved Karzai's life.

There's a pause to take this in, then a flurry of activity as everything starts up again, at triple the usual speed. My father organizes a press conference, and I watch as reporters from around the globe fill the designated room. I recognize Russian, French, and Japanese. In English BBC correspondent Lyse Doucet, who was in Kandahar with Karzai, rehearses a report. "It's clear the assassination attempt has changed the rules," she says, then repeats the sentence.

Today I'm carrying my big foam-covered microphone and my tape deck. "If you want to record, you can record up front," a guard offers. He's the same guard who asked me to join him in the garden on the afternoon of Haji Qadir's death.

The area he's indicating will be whispering distance from Karzai. "No, I can't stand there," I protest. "I'll be on all the cameras and stuff. It'll look really weird."

"No, come on, come up here," he urges. Suddenly I'm in front of just about everyone—in front of the front row—and then Karzai enters, and it's too late to go anywhere else. When Karzai spots me, he does a double-take; it's the first time he's seen me with the microphone. He addresses Lyse Doucet.

"Lyse, I saw your footage this morning," he announces.

"It's your footage, sir," Lyse replies. The crowd chuckles.

"My footage, your filming," Karzai shoots back. Then he describes the video, focusing on the role of the young man who died. "That is the man who actually saved my life," Karzai says with wonder. As he tells the story, he combines his own perception ("the next thing I knew is that he is pushing the gunman down") with the details he's gathered from the tape ("he was about twenty-two years of age—that's how I see it in the footage").

Karzai speaks briefly about the marketplace explosion (it's estimated that thirty died and 170 were injured), but talk soon turns back to the events in Kandahar.

"Sir," a male, British-sounding journalist begins, "it has inevitably raised again the whole question of security in Afghanistan. And as you know, it comes at a time when the government of the United States has changed its position on the expansion of ISAF." The reporter is talking about the International Security Assistance Force, a peacekeeping coalition stationed in Kabul. For some time Karzai has advocated for ISAF's expansion into the unstable countryside; the United States resisted the expansion until just days ago. (Within two weeks it will have changed its mind again.)

Karzai tries to separate the issues: "ISAF is not supposed to prevent assassinations," he points out. "ISAF is supposed to provide general security to the country."

"Would you like to comment on the proposal that ISAF now be expanded?" the reporter presses.

"I have asked for it long, long time ago," Karzai says vehemently, "mostly as a security measure that would indicate to the Afghan people that the world community is not going to abandon Afghanistan again, like they did after the Soviet Union left." Cameras snap, and Karzai turns to the next questioner: "From you!"

A local journalist speaks up in Pashto. "A few days ago the leader of Hizb-i-Islami, Mr. Gulbiddin Hekmatyar, announced a jihad on this government. Do you think these incidents have any connection to that announcement?"

"I don't know if Hekmatyar's announcement has anything to do with these attacks or not," Karzai starts. "But Hekmatyar should look into his conscience. What has happened to Afghanistan? Who destroyed this country? Who killed the thousands of people?" Karzai continues: "If he wants to be Osama's friend, he should go and proclaim jihad where Osama wants jihad." It's a point that is often overlooked: Al Qaeda isn't waging war on behalf of Afghanistan. They see the country's land as cheap real estate, its people as savages. They care about other citadels of the Islamic world—Palestine, Saudi Arabia—not this place here.

Now Karzai looks straight into a television camera, as if speaking directly to Hekmatyar himself. "You already destroyed Afghanistan for one foreigner. Now you're going to destroy it for another foreigner?"

My father hands Karzai a piece of paper; Karzai glances down at the note, then back at the audience. "Who killed Abdul Haq? Who killed Massoud?" he says. "And now you're going to destroy Afghanistan again? Were you *zigwali*"—brought into this world by your mother—"to destroy Afghanistan?"

I've never seen Karzai so emotional. Yet the English-speaking reporters receive his Pashto words blankly. They are missing what to me is the most important exchange of the press conference: the one in which Karzai reaches into the heart of the country's long difficulties, telling a story that matters for more than just today.

"Mr. President," says Lyse Doucet, "do you agree that you will now become a prisoner of your own security?"

"No, ma'am," Karzai bellows. "No way."

"But it now seems that it's extremely dangerous for you to move out of Kabul among your people."

"It was always dangerous, Lyse!" Karzai explodes. "Come on! I've been through this before. I've been hit three times when we were fighting the Soviets. Did that stop us from fighting the Soviets? My father was assassinated in Quetta by the Taliban and terrorists. Did that stop me from fighting?" he asks. "I will not stop. I will continue."

At his words I feel a little thrill. It's a rare thing for someone my age to be genuinely inspired by a leader of any nation.

"I am more concerned about the loss of life yesterday in Kabul than I am about the assassination attempt against me," Karzai concludes.

"Is there any review of your security under way, any additional precautions—"

Karzai cuts the speaker off. "Well, I will be more careful," he allows. "I will not be as reckless as I am." Perhaps this incident will put an end to freewheeling processions like the one down the dusty street in the north. "And we will have to really improve the recruiting procedure in the provinces. The provinces' recruitment procedure is very lax—anybody that comes in is accepted. That has to be changed." It's hard to imagine an American official admitting the existence of such a deep flaw—in part because of the unlikelihood of a quick fix. Karzai's charisma dissolves such practical concerns. But later, when you think about it, you always wonder how he is going to follow through on such impossible tasks.

Eventually Karzai becomes irritated with the tone of the questioning. "I think the press is taking things in a reverse manner," he protests. "There are governments—I'm not going to name them—who are established governments for centuries now. They cannot stop bomb blasts. Why would you expect us to suddenly do, you know, wonders? Does Afghanistan have—what is that thing called?" he asks crossly. He waves his hand in the air like a wizard.

"Magic wand?" someone suggests.

"Magic man?" Karzai says, tacking it right on to the end of his other sentence. "It happens," he says. "It happens all over the world."

Soon my father is leaning in to Karzai, reminding him to thank everyone, and the press conference is over. Right when it ends, Karzai looks at me and nods. He's good at that—the little gestures that give the impression you're important or special seem to come naturally to him. I feel the hopefulness about Afghanistan I always do when I hear him speak. I go to the window and look out at the mosque, where Karzai will probably soon go to pray. It's about six-thirty, and the sun is beginning to set. Days from now I'll be in California. *California*. It seems so far away.

The next afternoon I find myself in a helicopter, heading north to the Panjshir Valley. We're on our way to visit Massoud's grave. It's September 7, two days before the anniversary of his assassination, but Karzai is making his official visit now because of a scheduling conflict. He'll soon be on his way to New York City for the UN General Assembly.

Yesterday after the press conference, I went to Karzai's office with my father. "Hyder's leaving the day after tomorrow," he told him. "So he wanted to say goodbye."

"Leaving?" Karzai asked. "Where is he going?"

"I'm going back to America," I said. "Hopefully I can come back and help the country some more."

"Oh, very good, very good," Karzai said. "I hope you have a safe trip to America, a safe stay there, and a safe return to Afghanistan." Then he turned to my father. "Why doesn't he come to New York with us?"

The prospect of the trip glittered like the gold dragon studded with rubies that sat just a few feet away.

"He already has a ticket from Peshawar, and he's going to go from there," my father said.

"I could go through New York—" I jumped in.

"No, it's okay," my father said.

"Yeah, that's good," Karzai agreed. "You'd probably get bored with us anyway."

Still, my hopes had been raised. But when I spoke to my dad about it, he said that Karzai was just being nice because I'm his son. The New York trip would be hectic, and I probably wouldn't even be able to go to a lot of the official events. Karzai hadn't thought it through, but my father had, and the answer was no, and that was that.

Now our helicopter takes a hard turn and lands in Panjshir, the narrow valley that was Massoud's home. We drive along a river to his hilltop shrine. There are dozens of us on this trip, including government officials and the media. We all stand before a freshly painted white dome with a green top. The news crews all try to get a good shot.

Massoud's veneration has continued unabated. Vendors sell Massoud T-shirts and Massoud rugs. His name is constantly invoked by those in power to justify their position at the top, and his acolytes plaster his posters on lightposts, trees, and buildings. One day an official from the Saudi Arabian embassy came to see if my father could stop the practice. The Saudi Arabians had tried to explain their position: *We're sure Ahmed Shah Massoud was a good person and a tremendous leader, but you have to understand, we're an embassy. This is Saudi Arabian property in Afghanistan. We can't be supporting one commander over another, or having posters on our wall. You have to respect this.* But the request was ignored.

"We take the posters off, and they're there the very next day," the official told my father. "They'll come at night and make sure it's on again." (The act is a sort of comeuppance; Saudi Arabia was one of only three nations to formally recognize the Taliban.)

The trip rushes by—CNN correspondent Christiane Amanpour asking Karzai a question, Massoud's young son reciting a memorized speech—and before I know it I'm climbing back into the helicopter. It's a short ride back to Kabul. As we approach, the sun is setting, casting the city in gold. There is a layer of haze; it's the cliché of "the exotic East." Still, the picture-postcard view is magical. I'm glad for the parting shot.

The next morning I sit in the hotel lobby, ready to go. I told my father that the last thing I wanted to do before I left Afghanistan was visit Abdul Haq's grave. At first he was against the trip, which would require a detour near Jalalabad; but he finally agreed, sending me along with a letter I can show to the warlord and security chief Hazrat Ali, who can help arrange the visit.

My departure, like my arrival, is anticlimactic. Sartor and I cram into a taxi with another guy who is also headed to Jalalabad. I take a last look at the beat-up hotel, which will soon undergo renovation—investors are anxious to exploit Kabul's growing population of diplomats and foreign aid workers. As we drive off, I speak into my microphone—*It's become home now, so it feels weird, looking at all of this around me. It's a lot different from America. And I think when I go back to America, everything there is gonna be a litle weird for me*—and before I know it, we've climbed out of the city to a checkpoint, and somebody is giving me a hard time about the microphone. Not just somebody—it's the guard from before! The same guy who searched my U2 CDs on the way in is there to witness me on my way out.

Now we drive through high, jagged mountains. We pass a destroyed Toyota 4-Runner that has toppled down a cliff. One of the guys in our taxi knows the story behind the accident—all four passengers in the vehicle died. I just sit there casually, looking out the window, taking it all in.

In Jalalabad we seek out Hazrat Ali at a place called the Winter Palace. The palace was once the king's seasonal retreat, and I'm hoping to get a glimpse of it, but Hazrat Ali isn't there. We're told we might find him at the local military base.

Two soldiers guard the base's entrance, and I can tell that, like Hazrat Ali, they're Shalai. It is, to say the least, a source of irritation that Hazrat Ali, the biggest commander in this Pashtun region, is not himself Pashtun. The Shalai—as they are known to Pashtuns; others call them Pashai—are a distinct ethnic group with their own language. Many come from a small valley north of Jalalabad called Darinur. "Is Hazrat Ali here?" I ask.

"Do you know who Hazrat Ali is?" one replies disdainfully. "To just walk up to the base and ask for him? Do you know who Hazrat Ali is that you're just asking for him like that?"

"Well, go ahead and assume that I must be somebody, to be asking for him like that," I tell him. I'm feeling untouchable, like an Afghan pro. "I have a letter," I say.

"Can I see it?" he says.

"Can you read?" I say. It's the only way to do it, to shame them a little bit. Otherwise they'll just keeping telling me no.

"No," he replies.

He stands there staring at the letter blankly. "Are you reading it?" I nudge.

"No, I'm not," he admits.

I grab it back. "So do you know where Hazrat Ali is or not?"

"He left the compound forty minutes ago," the man says. Then he gives me the names of several places where he might be. Hazrat Ali is itinerant by design; if he stays in one spot too long, his enemies will show up and kill him.

We set out in renewed pursuit of Hazrat Ali, but we soon realize that we could wind up wasting the whole day on the wrong search. Sartor and I decide to find Abdul Haq's grave by ourselves.

I've been thinking about Abdul Haq all summer, but especially in the days since the assassination attempt, which underscored Karzai's vulnerability. Unlike, say, President Bush, who is the public face of a group project, Karzai seems utterly alone. He hasn't managed to surround himself with a group of like-minded advisers. How can one man rein in the warlords? Or force the regional militias to disarm? For all of Karzai's strengths, he lacks the muscle of Abdul Haq. They would have made a perfect team: one the diplomat, the other the warrior. It will take a long time for someone new to acquire the legitimacy Abdul Haq already had.

I've seen only a few posters of Abdul Haq around Kabul, and their scarcity seems to confirm his sister's observation that any put up are immediately torn down. Still, I find myself returning to the saying, *History is written by those in power.* I hope that someday I will see a statue of Abdul Haq in Kabul, along with the one currently planned of Massoud.

Of course, I also recognize that I am engaging in a certain amount of hero worship. It's impossible for me to see Abdul Haq's flaws. He died young, and for me he was immortalized before any blots crept into the frame. There's so much this summer that has disappointed me about Afghan politics; it's nice to hold on to something pure.

"Do you know the Surkh Road area?" I ask a taxi driver.

"Yeah, I know Surkh Road," he says. Sartor and I bargain over the price and get into his car.

Before we pull away, a bystander sticks his head through the car window. "Can I ask you a question?" he says to me.

"Sure," I answer. "Go ahead."

"What was Abdul Haq's relation to you?" he says.

"Family friend," I say tightly. The question disappoints me. It's as if filial obligation is the only plausible reason for my visit. I'm sure nobody asks your relation to Massoud when you stand before his shrine and honor his memory.

About forty-five minutes later we reach a dirt road that ends at a barren field. Sartor and I step out of the taxi and begin to look for the grave. We pass a couple of piles of stones that don't look official enough to be right, so we keep searching until we come across a villager who tells us to go back to the spot we dismissed.

There are two graves there, one for Abdul Haq and one for his nephew Ezatullah, who was captured alongside him. Both graves are raised mounds of dirt into which light-colored stones have been pressed. I sit on the ground. The stillness of the place is its own presence, an actual full sound. Every now and then there is the buzzing of a bug. I'm covered in dust. At Massoud's shrine there were news crews, an entourage of dozens. Here it's just me, crouching by Abdul Haq's head, staring down at the little pile that is the earthly presence of this legendary man.

I stand; I'm tired, unable to make sense of my feelings. Sartor and I walk together through a little low wind back to the car.

The driver leaves us in Jalalabad, and from there Sartor and I walk to the home of one of his friends. We are welcomed to his guesthouse, which does not connote wealth; it's a simple room that most people have for visitors. (It's called a *hujera,* and is separate from the main structure, where the women and young girls would be.)

Sartor's friend is nowhere in sight, so instead we hang out with the friend's younger brother. Eventually we get a little worried about the older brother, and we are relieved when he finally shows up sometime after midnight. For the past several hours he's been stuck with Hazrat Ali's Shalai forces. They'd stopped his car, climbed inside, and forced him to chauffeur them around as they looked for people to apprehend. "Those Shalai," the brother says to us resentfully.

Homemade food is brought in, and while we eat, the brothers tell stories. The younger one is a scrawny, class-clown type, and I'm surprised to learn that he owns an arrest record that stretches around the globe. His crime is that he's been trying to flee Afghanistan for the West.

During the Soviet war it was relatively easy for Afghans to obtain international asylum. By the Taliban era, things had changed. Germany, for instance, decided that since the Taliban were not a recognized government, the Afghan state effectively did not exist. A state that did not exist could not commit human rights abuses upon its citizens; therefore, Germany argued, they were not obliged by international law to accept Afghan refugees. Germany's action against Afghans was just a single instance in a broader pattern in which the Western world tightened immigration restrictions against people of many nations. (The situation worsened after 9/11.)

So asylum seekers with the means to do so turned to smugglers. The younger brother explains how—sometime in 2001, it seems—he traveled to Karachi, where he met with a man who agreed to provide him with a fake Malaysian passport. (A Malaysian national would be able to enter England without a visa.) The younger brother paid the smuggler and flew to Kuala Lumpur. The doors were about to close on his plane to England when an official began asking questions about his passport. He was deported back to Pakistan.

From Pakistan he and a companion made their way to Rwanda. Once there they arranged to travel to London. But as they were waiting to leave, 9/11 happened. They were thrown into a Rwandan prison and held for four months.

"I couldn't speak the language or anything," the younger brother says. "They would call me 'Al Qaeda' and say bin Laden's name, and that's the only thing we could understand. Whenever we heard bin Laden's name, we'd be like, 'No, no, no!'"

The prison was dismal. They slept on bare cement floors, and their meals consisted of mushed banana. "For the first three or four days, I couldn't tell what it was and I wouldn't eat it," the younger brother remembers. "And then finally I couldn't move around anymore, and I started eating it."

A Rwandan security official approached the younger brother and told him that he could get him out of prison and into Germany within a year. All he had to do was marry his daughter. "Sure, sure," the younger brother agreed. "I'll marry your daughter." He had no intention of staying with her; as soon as he could, he would run away. But then another man came and said, "He's saying you're going to marry his daughter, but you know you're going to have to sleep with him, right?"

This is not the brothers' only story. Their attempts to escape have taken them to Kenya, to Tanzania, to Singapore, to Dubai. They describe floating on a small boat for eighteen days in the ocean between Indonesia and Australia. We begin to discuss other ways to get out—Sartor mentions a trip through the mountains of Ukraine that will lead you into Europe. (In Afghanistan escape routes are standard conversational fare.)

The younger brother is jokey and upbeat even when describing his travails. "Now I'm just chilling in Afghanistan," he shrugs, as if his presence here is only temporary. He has resolved to try again; he is determined to get to the West. *And here I am,* I say to myself, *traveling there the day after tomorrow.*

As if reading my mind, the younger brother says curiously, "You're just going to go to America."

"Yeah," I say.

"And they're not going to say anything," he continues.

"Yeah," I confirm.

"So when you live in America, people just let you live the way you want," he says.

"Yeah," I say. The brothers shake their heads, fascinated. Out of anything in the whole night, this is what interests them most.

We go to bed late, and I lie under a rattling fan. I thought by coming to Afghanistan, by trying to help, I might feel less guilty. But now I'm not sure of what I'll feel back in California—knowing that while I can get away from here, other people can't.

10

THE HIGHWAYS ARE TOO quiet. That's one of the first things I notice, driving away from SFO in the car beside my mom. I've grown accustomed to horns being used with abandon. But here there's barely a bleat. All the traffic laws are being followed, and the road is smooth. The pavement whizzes beneath our wheels.

The last leg of the flight went on forever—we'd been routed over Canada, which made the ground we'd yet to cover seem even more vast and interminable—and I had a sinking feeling when we landed. I'd declared that I wasn't carrying any foreign fruits or other agricultural products. The truth was that my bags were stuffed with groceries that my mother and aunts had requested from Peshawar. But the customs agents let me by with barely a glance, and my mood lightened.

I disembarked without hassle in Dubai, too, though that incident aroused more complicated feelings. There we were herded into two lines, one for U.S. and European passports, the other for everyone else. The employees were gruff with the Pakistanis who'd arrived on my flight from Peshawar: *Go there, that line, leave me alone.* To the Westerners, they'd apologize for the inconvenience: *I'm sorry, sir, form a line here, please.* I looked scraggly—I hadn't shaved, having forgotten my razor in Kabul—and when I approached, I could tell the agent was ready to tell me to get out of his face. Then I pulled out my passport—my blue American passport.

The agent's features warmed: *Oh, I'm sorry, sir, that line over there. Oh, and you have a long layover? You are guaranteed a hotel room. It's this way to the shuttle.*

I walked away. If you went by paper, I was American, but if you went by instinct, I was Afghan. I could spend years deciding which was the real me, but nothing would ever change that fact.

From my mother's Saturn I exchange a couple of cell phone calls with my brother, who is somewhere near us on the road. We're both so keyed up and excited to see each other that my mother takes an exit just out of the Caldecott Tunnel, and I run out of her car and into Omar's.

At home, as I have requested, my mother has pizza waiting for me, but I go straight for the VCR instead of the table. I connect a cable to the digital video camera and slip in my tapes of the summer. I narrate the events on-screen; whenever someone reminds me of the pizza I say, "Hold on, hold on," and keep going. When I finally grab a plate, I'm surprised to find that I can eat only a slice and a half. Pizza seems like an unpleasantly heavy meal.

I stay up late with my mom, telling her stories I've had to keep secret all summer. (My father and I revealed little during our phone conversations, which were probably monitored.) It's one in the morning when I finally get in bed, and I don't wake up until one the next afternoon.

For a few days afterward I just enjoy being comfortable. We all watch my videos a lot. (It's a reversal: my family has always told me the stories about Afghanistan, and now I'm the one recounting the tales.) In Kabul I'd visited the apartments where my brother grew up, and he watches this part intently. The once upscale complex is still standing but has decayed. The buildings are set in a wide, empty plaza scoured by warfare. The camera zooms in on balconies, on the corrugated façade, on curtains edging out of open windows, on a blue blanket flapping on a clothesline. My brother's gaze is searching, as if he might discover in one of the building's bullet holes a tunnel to the past.

My mother's least favorite part of the videos is the loya jirga. "Why didn't you record any of the women?" she asks, genuinely irritated. "What's wrong with you? This was such a historic moment—women were finally able to give their opinions. They said so many good things, and you haven't even recorded one."

Until she points it out, my omission hasn't occurred to me. She's right to be upset; women were among the most outspoken delegates to the loya jirga. They reminded those assembled, for instance, that the Taliban were not the only ones in Afghanistan to commit atrocities against the female population; that distinction also lay with previous regimes, including some of the mujahedeen who were seated here among us. For their part, the men made jokes about the women's bravery. "They haven't been inside political prisons," they would say. "This is their first taste of freedom. They're inexperienced, so they say whatever they want. They'll figure it out soon enough."

At the end of the jirga, the women protested to Karzai that they were not properly represented in the new government. "You women are really something," Karzai marveled. "Six months ago you couldn't go out on the street. Now you're not satisfied with two ministries in the new cabinet?"

The fact is that Afghanistan isn't ready for women to go from zero to sixty. In public, most women still shield themselves with burkas. One evening I sat in the car with our driver in the marketplace. We were waiting for my father, who was making a purchase nearby. There were hundreds of people streaming around us, bicycle bells trilling, a kid carrying maybe ten gallons of water on his back. There were men in skullcaps, men in pakols, men in turbans. But every woman I saw was wearing the exact same thing, a burka. I decided to time it, see how long it would take before I saw a woman's face. It was now five-seventeen. *Burka, burka, burka,* I ticked off. Maybe eight women passed for every hundred men. *Burka.* Then a woman wearing a ninjalike mask approached; you could see just her eyes. It was five-twenty-three. After six minutes, I had seen a pair of eyes, but still no face. *Burka, burka, burka.* It was like a never-ending game of duck, duck, goose. *Burka, burka. Burka begging.* I pointed the beggar out to my dad, and he handed her some *afghanis.* And then I saw my first face. Her hair was covered, her neck, her body, everything else. Five-twenty-six. Nine minutes.

Obviously, my mother has identified a larger gap in my summer. With the exception of the Western journalists, I rarely found myself in the company of a woman for more than a few minutes. The quality of their absence was so extraordinary that it's hard to even define. Other men we worked with returned at the end of the day to wives and daughters. Our summer was rough enough around the edges as it was; I missed the gentleness of a feminine presence.

Unfortunately, because of the loya jirga videos, my mom isn't exactly lavishing me with TLC. She digs into me a little bit, not the way she would if she were really mad but enough so I get the point. "I'm kind of hungry," I'll announce. "What is there to eat?"

"Go look in the fridge yourself," she'll say.

Just days after I get home my father comes back, too. He flies in from New York after the UN General Assembly. This is his first visit in almost a year. Our lives feel oddly normal: my father goes with me to the DMV, and he pays credit card bills. He gets a temporary membership at the gym and goes over there to run and swim and sit in the Jacuzzi. He makes me change the oil in the car, and he talks about what to do in case of various problems. "I don't know when I'm going to be back, so you have to really learn this stuff," he says.

Some friends and family members give my father a hard time for his decision to go to Afghanistan; perhaps they criticize him just to make themselves feel more secure about their own choice to stay in the United States. Pashtuns are full of complaints about the direction their country is taking. "If you don't go back to represent Pashtuns, who will?" my father says, trying to sell them on it. (At times it's almost as if he's doing marketing for the Afghan government.) "We can't have America fixing that problem, too. The Pashtuns have to do it themselves."

The visit flies by. He's with us for a month, and then he's gone again. Now that I've gotten so used to seeing him every day, it's hard to go for long stretches without communicating. Four weeks might pass between our conversations. My mom, with whom he speaks more frequently, gives me the updates. They begin renovating Kabul Hotel, so my father switches to the Intercontinental. Traffic is insane, and his new commute to the palace takes over an hour, meaning he no longer has as much time to exercise. He worries about the reduction in his activity, and he speaks to Karzai, who suggests that he walk around the palace with his cell phone. "I'll call you when I need you," Karzai tells him. My father has always been fitness-minded, but especially so since developing high blood pressure. During Ramadan, the holy month when Muslims fast from sunrise to sunset, he tells my mother that he's not taking his medication. She's concerned about his health and is seriously considering joining him in Afghanistan. She could help him with his diet; now he just eats whatever is served. It's a manageable problem, unlike many others.

By the time I returned from Afghanistan, the first semester at community college had already begun. It's too late for me to enroll, so I have a lot of time on my hands. I work for my brother a little bit, trying to get the hang of the mortgage business. A friend who works at a collection agency sets me and another one of our buddies up with a job there. (One of the rules is that you have to be nice to the people who bounced checks at Whole Foods.) It's a lot the same as before I left, in terms of me trying not to talk too much about Afghanistan around my friends. They mostly want to hear about the crazy stuff: about taking apart Kalashnikovs, or the bloody scene of the car bombing. When my radio documentary airs, a couple newspapers do stories about me. My friend Matin tells a *Los Angeles Times* reporter, "When he came back from Afghanistan, he had no fear. He was overconfident." I tease him about the quote. "I was trying to say really confident," he maintains. "And she put overconfident. Or maybe I was just nervous to be talking to an *L.A. Times* reporter."

I wouldn't say I have no fear; maybe it's just that after Afghanistan, it's easy to adjust to America. The harder thing will always be going from here to there.

Though I still follow the news from Afghanistan, my avidity is now coupled with the knowledge that there's more to the story than whatever I read. I scan the articles online, then occasionally click over to the Afghan message boards on AOL. The quality has gone down, but every so often I come across something interesting. One day I find myself reading a post by a girl named Salma, who's just returned from Kabul. We get to chatting on

IM, and I learn she actually stayed at Kabul Hotel. I wonder if I might have seen her. One morning I'd gone out front with Sartor. A family clearly returning after years in the States was stepping out of a taxi. The daughter, who looked to be about my age, was crying. I was curious about her but couldn't stop to talk; the next thing I knew, people would be whispering, *Fazel Akbar's son is chasing girls in Kabul.*

On IM we go over the dates of her visit. "Did you come in a taxi?" I type.

"Yes," she replies.

"Were you kind of crying?" I ask.

"Oh my God, that's me," she writes.

"And are you really tall and lanky?" I continue.

"Yeah," she confirms.

"I saw you," I tell her. "I even pointed you out to my driver: 'Look, these people are here from America.' "

Salma is from Los Angeles, and she'd been shocked by Kabul. She hadn't come with any traditional clothing, and people harassed her for wearing jeans. Her family had stayed for only two weeks. I probably would have hated the place after a stay that short, too. You need longer to adjust.

Salma and I stay in touch, and the funny thing is, she starts talking about how she wants to return to Afghanistan. It's as if she's forgotten all the miserable times. I have an idea how that works. After only a couple of months of comfort, I actually miss Kabul's volatility. *Life there was just more interesting,* I think. Then there's the corollary: *There I was more interesting.* And the tone of the place: *Over there, people are so simple, more real.*

When I begin having thoughts like these, I know I've already been away too long. When you start idealizing Afghanistan, it's time to go back.

Part Two

Both Sides Speaking in Code

Summer 2003

Nothing in life is so exhilarating as to be shot at without result.

—Winston Churchill, *The Story of the Malakand Field Force*

11

IT HAPPENS SO FAST I HARDLY have time to think about it. One day I'm facing a summer fulfilling general education requirements at my community college; the next, I'm planning my trip to Kunar. My father has finally become the governor.

Something perplexing occurred just before his appointment. One afternoon my brother called me at home. "Hyder, check this out," he said. Then he read me a help-wanted ad from *Omaid Weekly,* a newspaper published in Alexandria, Virginia, that claims to be "the most widely read Afghan publication in the world."

The ad began with a sentence like, "Are you looking for a job in Afghanistan?" It then described the qualifications and application procedure for my father's position, presidential spokesman.

Like Fox News, *Omaid Weekly* has a clear bias—in its case, against Pashtuns. Omar and I wondered if this might be some sort of swipe at my dad. He was with Karzai in Washington, D.C., and I mentioned the ad when he called. "I've heard about it," my father said. "I don't know what it is. I think it's some kind of joke."

But it wasn't. "We're not trying to replace you," Karzai told my father on the way back to Kabul. They were waiting for a flight in Frankfurt. "We're just trying to find somebody who can help you." Karzai had been told there was a need to hire someone who could enhance the technology of the press office.

My father was angry about the process. "You could have gone over it with me beforehand," he said to Karzai. "What are you thinking? Any foreign agent could come in and he could be"—my father quoted from the ad—" 'fluent in English, Pashto, and Dari,' and you could have an informant right in the middle of your government. It's not just that I'm offended, but you're making a joke of this government by putting a help-wanted ad in the newspaper."

I had to agree with him. Did the Bush administration take out a notice in the *Washington Post* to find Ari Fleischer's replacement? Karzai hadn't been consulted about the ad; it had been placed by one of his staff members, a former Bay Area attorney. I saw the act as a telling sign of how professionally trained exiles were, in their own ways, as ill suited to governance as the warlords. They operated by the rules of their previous world—filling a presidential spokesman position through the classifieds, as if they were looking for a new paralegal.

In Frankfurt, all of the officials along on the trip observed the argument between Karzai and my father. "The real fight's left in Kabul," my father said, before they stepped onto the plane.

"That's fine, we will do that in Kabul," Karzai said.

But back in Kabul there was no need to take up the matter again. The new interior minister, Ali Ahmed Jalali, had resolved to tighten control of the countryside, and he wanted my father to go to Kunar. My father was excited about his new position, and glad to be relieved of his old one. As the government's public face, he was assumed to wield greater influence than he actually did. He was beginning to feel as if he were being blamed for problems over which he had no control.

He moved into the governor's house in Asadabad, the provincial capital, on April 28, 2003, and soon after he called my mother and said, "Summer's coming up. Do you think Hyder would want to come back?" Within ten minutes my plans had totally changed. So I'd have a fuller load in school next semester; big deal. I'd never again have a chance to witness the first months of my father trying to impose order in the Afghan countryside.

* * *

For months I've been typing "Kunar" into the Yahoo! News search box about fifty times a day. Now that my father is there, I actually get a hit every now and then. One story tells of a U.S. Special Forces raid on a home of a Taliban official. Three Afghans, including two women, were injured in the resulting gun battle. The Taliban commander "jumped into the river, leaving his pistol on the bank," and his body was later found downstream. I feel guilty, but I have to be honest with myself. This is the kind of Billy the Kid stuff I dream of seeing in Kunar—shootouts, action sequences, a notorious outlaw's last stand.

One day my Kunar search yields a link to an AP story that opens with a description of the central government's recent effort to collect revenue from the provinces: "Afghan President Hamid Karzai has made his boldest bid yet to assert authority beyond the capital," the article says, "wresting governors and warlords into a deal to hand over millions of dollars in customs duties to Kabul's near-empty treasury."

I scroll down to find the part about Kunar, and when I do, I see that the AP reporter has written that my father was the target of a rocket attack upon arriving in Kunar. The information is completely false.

When my father calls, I bolt upstairs to my bedroom, lean into the computer screen, and read the story aloud to him in English:

> The eastern province of Kunar was the first to come through with any significant contribution, handing over $400,000. The cash allowed the Finance Ministry to start paying civil servants Wednesday for the first time in two months.
>
> The money came from Kunar only after Karzai appointed his former spokesman, Said Fazel Akbar, as governor in April.
>
> His predecessor, however, was reluctant to give up the post. Akbar was forced back to Kabul after his vehicle came under rocket attack. He returned only after U.S. pressure eased out former Gov. Said Shajan, a diplomat said. It's unclear whether force was used.

"Eased," I repeat to my father, "E-a-s-e-d, like *sust*."

My father takes notes and calls the AP bureau. He confronts the story's author about his incorrect account and invites him to visit Kunar to check out a province that is actually coming together. The reporter apologizes and promises to run a correction. (But when the "correction" appears, it is tacked onto the end of another story, and presented as my father's claim rather than as a fact: "Meanwhile, Akbar denied recent reports by Western diplomats and Iranian radio that his vehicle was fired upon as he arrived in Asadabad to take up the governor's post.")

My father isn't concerned about the part of the article that diminishes the significance of his financial contribution to the central government. We may not like the reporter's spin—Karzai's buddy gets to the governor's house, opens up the vault, and sends back some cash—but it isn't inaccurate. Of course, my father would have sent the money whether or not Karzai was president. One of his goals is to strengthen the central government; one of Karzai's is to extend its reach.

Throughout Afghanistan's history, periods of dependency on foreign aid have alternated with attempts to strengthen domestic tax-collection systems. But complaints about the parsimonious provinces appear as far back as the sixteenth century. Babur, a titan of empire who conquered Kabul, wrote distastefully of Kunar, "The revenue is small because the area is remote and the people do not pay." Karzai's government has been promised a cash infusion from international donors. But the money is arriving slowly, and there is little to show for it in the way of reconstruction. It's no wonder Karzai has turned to the provinces to try to fill the gap—even if it means swimming against the current of centuries' worth of history.

I have a computer game I've been playing called Civilization. The premise is that you start a civilization from scratch in 4000 B.C. and see it through all the way to A.D. 2050. (It isn't a task you finish in one sitting.) I'm not a video game fanatic, but a friend recommended this one—it's actually pretty popular—and I bought it the next day. I even sprang for the expansion pack.

Right before I leave for Kunar, I'm in the middle of a game in which I'm playing the role of the Germans. (You pick your "character" from a list of sixteen civilizations that includes the Americans, the Greeks, and the Persians.) I started out with a single city of two people, but I built a strong military, and my civilization just grew and grew and grew. The Romans were on my continent, but I killed them all off. Now I'm at war with an unlikely coalition of the willing: Babylon, China, King Alexander of Greece, Queen Cleopatra of Egypt, and President Lincoln of America. I direct cannon fire and sink ships, and then, in the guise of Chancellor Bismarck, I receive a message: *Ancient and wise Egypt grants you an audience, Bismarck. Do you seek peace, or do you wish foolish war to continue?* It's a pretty addictive game.

Of course when I'm playing I sometimes think of Afghanistan. One of my cities may erupt in civil disorder, or my population may stop producing goods because they've been at war too long. The game is straightforward, and set to music, and lives only in the narrow world of my new flat-screen monitor. But I like to think that it's practice of a sort, for when I actually do take my own stab at nation-building.

I've been redefining my ambitions. Engineering, I've decided, is out. I'm more interested in the big picture: in creating order in which society can flourish. To that end, I've been reading a whole bunch of building-block books: among them, Plato's *Republic,* Sun-tzu's *Art of War,* Machiavelli's *The Prince,* Henry Kissinger's *Diplomacy.* I worry that parts of my syllabus give the impression that I'm sliding over to the dark side. But I just want to have some theoretical grounding for my practical experience in Afghanistan. I imagine a possible ten-year plan: I'll transfer out of community college, get my bachelor's degree, then my master's, then work for a couple years at someplace like the World Bank, because it'll be important to understand the politics of development assistance. All the while I'll be spending time in Kunar, building my base, and by my late twenties I'll be an Afghan parliament member, or even the governor, if my father has stepped down by then.

Of course, pretty much any long-range planning is ludicrous. Afghanistan is not exactly a rock on which to build a stable future.

Soon enough I'm racing to get ready to go. My room is a mess, the floor covered with a semester's worth of papers. There are sociology Xeroxes I'll never refer to again, like "Origins and Problems of Gang Research in the United States," and foreign policy articles I want to save, like "Our Way: The Trouble with Being the World's Only Superpower." Last year I had months to conjure up images of Afghanistan, but now all I have time to do is pack. I'm going to make another radio documentary, and I have new equipment, a minidisc recorder and a tiny mic that's so powerful, you can hear your eyeballs. I'm bringing gifts for commanders (a polite way of saying warlords) and supplies for my dad—batteries, mini DV tapes, and coats.

The coats are my mother's idea. She doesn't want my father to get cold during Kunar's frigid winters. His absence is getting harder on her; sometimes she says, "I should have never let him leave." I'm roughly the same size as my dad, and my mother and my sister Zulikha stand in the living room as I try the coats on. Zulikha picked out two for him, but my mother doesn't care for either; they're too short, and the long kameez partoog shirt will look weird sticking out underneath. While they debate the finer points of rural Afghan style, I race back up to my room to finish cleaning.

I still like U2, but lately I've also been listening to a lot of R.E.M. Picking up papers, I mumble along with the lyrics to "Stand":

> Stand in the place where you live
> Now face North
> Think about direction
> Wonder why you haven't
> Now stand in the place where you work
> Now face West
> Think about the place where you live
> Wonder why you haven't before

Think about direction. Okay. There's a TV commercial that shows a hole being dug, and then, at the bottom, a Chinese family eating dinner. A tunnel I started in Concord might shoot me straight through to Kunar; California and Afghanistan are on opposite sides of the planet. That much is obvious, even without the new atlas I ordered from Amazon.com. It's *The Oxford Atlas of the World*, a humongous book—I'm a big guy and I have trouble lifting it with one hand. One map color-codes the world by GNP growth. Two countries are gray, signifying that their growth rates are unknown: Somalia and Afghanistan. *These two are so poor that they can't even calculate how poor they are.* It's one of those moments when it really hits me. *For twenty-five years the world just passed Afghanistan by.*

Sometimes I worry it's happening again. The war with Iraq now dominates the political conversation and the news. CNN recently closed down its operation in Afghanistan, and to me that's as clear a sign as any that the world is moving on. But Afghanistan is still unstable. It seems to have been abandoned half-finished.

Though I'm less idealistic than I was on the eve of my first departure, I still have a lot of hope that Afghanistan will get better. Maybe because I'm shifting my whole life to this, and I can't afford to have it fail.

12

IT'S ONE HUNDRED DEGREES IN the middle of the night. I'm in a taxi, riding down Dubai's palm-tree-lined roads, taking in this twinkling city on the shore of the Persian Gulf. I've traveled halfway around the planet since yesterday, but the funny thing is, I don't feel far away at all. The world hasn't changed. Apart from the fact that the Domino's worker who rings up my pizza is wearing a head scarf, I could be in Southern California. Dubai is a new city, its skyscrapers and luxury shopping malls having risen from these dunes in tandem with the oil from its offshore depths, discovered there less than forty years ago.

The taxi driver takes me past the big landmarks, including a famous hotel called the Burj Al Arab, a sail-shaped building atop a man-made island. It seems like it's just floating in the gulf. The driver says that the hotel has seven stars—the only one in the world with the two extra.

Around one in the morning we go back to the airport and I enter Terminal 2, from which I'll depart for Kabul. Terminal 1, where I landed, was a sky-high-ceilinged, duty-free palace. You could enter to win a luxury car, or pull up to the bar at an Irish pub for a beer. Terminal 2 is small and dim. I see maybe one place to eat, selling ready-made sandwiches. Then I look up at the departure board. Nobody in this terminal is on their way to a financial center, like Frankfurt or Tokyo; and except for Tehran, the destinations include none of the major cities in the East. The board is crowded with names of locations in the Central Asian states. (Some of the Cyrillic letters look so weird side by side that you can hardly believe a system exists that encourages their placement next to each other.)

I sit down and wonder what I'm supposed to do now. Though the flight to Kabul leaves in just a few hours, I don't have a ticket. Ariana Afghan Airlines sells its seats at the airport. But I don't see an Ariana check-in podium, and I get a little paranoid: that this won't work out, that I'll be stuck here. The earlier hours—commandeering a taxi to drive me around town, the gemlike night rushing past the windows, the break for pizza before plunging back into the middle of the desert—suddenly seem like a mirage, now dissolved to reveal me, alone in a chair in an airport. Sometimes I still feel young to be in the middle of the world all by myself.

It's too complicated to figure out how much time has elapsed since I left San Francisco. Hours, maybe a whole day's worth, got lost as I flew west to Hong Kong; the jets sucked some of the time back up on the way to Dubai. If you stapled this itinerary to last year's, when I flew east, via London, I'd have the documentation for having circumnavigated the globe.

I went through Hong Kong because the travel agent said the ticket was cheaper. It only hit me later: SARS. I emerged from the flight bridge to a quiet airport dotted by people wearing white surgical masks. I had a nine-hour layover on the heels of what had been a fifteen-hour flight. I bought a Coke. I bought another Coke. I followed signs for a Burger King—or maybe a McDonald's—like a trail of sesame-seed-bun crumbs, only to arrive at a COMING SOON poster. I went to another restaurant and pointed to a picture of the most normal-looking combo plate. I ate what was possibly chicken and chow mein. I bought *Newsweek*. I got out my recording equipment and put the tiny microphone in my mouth and taped the inside of my body.

The *Newsweek*, at least, was diverting. An article about Karzai argued—correctly, I thought—that he wasn't entirely to blame for the country's continuing turmoil. But boredom soon advanced to exhaustion. The night before I left, I awoke at three with a pain in my back. I went to get the Tylenol, and when I couldn't find it, I got so mad I punched the wall. The outburst was totally unlike me, and I started to feel queasy. In bed, I lay awake, realizing as if for the first time: *I am going to Kunar*. Kabul, at least, is a semimodern city. Kunar is a barren, tribal area that's seen a lot of chaos. Imagining myself in the midst of it is intimidating.

In Dubai I strike up a conversation with an American sitting beside me. He's from Nebraska—I'm guessing from one of the universities there. "It's literally three hours until the flight leaves, and I still don't have a ticket," I tell him. "Is somebody just going to start selling tickets from the snack bar?" I joke.

"Actually," the Nebraskan says, "that's exactly what's going to happen. My wife just came through here last week."

Sure enough, around five in the morning, a man sits down at a nearby table. He doesn't make an announcement or prop up a sign; he isn't even wearing a uniform, just a regular suit. A few people approach, and I join the line that forms. It's almost like a drug deal: a quick series of handovers in cash.

Then it's my turn. "What do you want?" he says. He's a small-boned, dark-complexioned guy, Indian or Pakistani. He punches the buttons on his little calculator, pockets my money—about $380—writes out my ticket, and I'm all set. I think to myself, *This must be the only airline in the world that operates out of a snack bar*.

Then I have to recheck my bags. I'm hauling around two of them, plus my carry-on, altogether about 140 pounds of stuff. There are some Afghans in this line, speaking Pashto and wearing traditional clothes. Their things are wrapped in sheets or dumped inside huge plastic garbage bags, which they casually drop on the scale, like it's the most normal luggage in the world. We start talking, and they immediately know who my father is. Then they move on, and I stand at the front of a line, paying extra for my overage, still processing that I am now in a part of the world where people recognize my dad.

Again I wait. I see an American who keeps leaving and coming back, leaving and coming back, and finally I ask him, "Is there something going on?"

"Oh no," he says. "I drank a lot of Red Bull and water, so I have to go to the bathroom a lot."

"Oh, okay," I say, and we start talking. He's a civilian contractor who has been hired to work as part of President Karzai's security detail. American bodyguards have been protecting Karzai since soon after Haji Qadir's assassination. At first the U.S. Special Forces did the job; after a few months they were replaced with private contractors, who are an increasingly visible presence in both Afghanistan and in Iraq. To Afghans, the arrangement is shameful: are none of the president's countrymen good enough to protect him? Last summer my father protested the Americans' installment. "Sure, security is bad," he said to Karzai at a meeting. "We don't have enough trained people. But think of the price you'll pay for this, the legitimacy you'll lose." To a reporter, my father explained that this was a temporary measure while Afghan guards got trained. But now it seems as though the arrangement is becoming more permanent.

The guy I'm talking to looks small to be a security guard, skinny. But he's an ex-soldier who's been to disaster areas all over the world, and I ask him how Afghanistan stacks up. "Somalia was pretty bad," he says. "That place just smelled like shit all the time. Garbage was all over the place. Yup, Somalia, but other than that, I can't think of a place I've been to that's as bad as Afghanistan."

It occurs to me that just as the world's great cities have some special defining imprint, the war-torn places have their own unique styles of destruction.

I tell Karzai's security guy that after we land, I have an eight-hour drive to Kunar ahead of me. "Really?" he says, taken aback. "I've heard you shouldn't drive there. Be safe," he warns. "It's pretty scary outside of Kabul."

Soon we're gliding over Afghanistan. As we near the Kabul airport, with its field of destroyed aircraft, a baby cries, and we hear the same announcement three times, in Dari, Pashto, then English: "Ladies and gentlemen, in a few minutes we will be landing at Kabul International Airport. Please fasten your seatbelts and observe the no smoking sign. . . . Thank you and goodbye."

On the ground I unbuckle my seatbelt. Theme music trills, then slows, playing at warped low-battery speed. A guy who can't find his carry-on bag backs up traffic through the aisle, and then suddenly I'm out of the plane, taking my first breath of Kabul air. Before I'm even across the tarmac, I see a friend of my uncle's waiting to greet me. Airport workers are tossing all the bags into a huge pile, and he hurries to grab mine. Another friend speeds me through the passport check; yet another appears and says I'm to spend the night at his house. I'm incredibly grateful that they're all here.

But Sartor is supposed to be meeting me, too, and the whole time I'm looking for him, and finally I see his dark black head. "Sartor!" I yell. "Sartor!" Even from a distance, I can tell he's exactly the same as last summer: the same easygoing bearing, the same mirthful furrows around his mouth. I make my way to him through the crowd. "Let's go get some *shami* kabob," I say.

13

SARTOR AND I ARE RIDING in a pickup on the edge of a mountain. We've just crossed the southern border of Kunar. The pickup shudders, jolting us out of our seats even at our top speed of fifteen miles per hour. We stir up so much dust that it's like riding through a smoke machine. But when the air clears, there is nothing to obscure our view. Ahead of us, there's another mountain, and way down below, a vast open plain. The plain is breathtaking, a green and blue dreamscape scored with a silver river. Where we are is brown and rugged, creating a contrast so sharp that you wonder if this is something out of a different part of the country that got put here by mistake. I gaze at it in silent admiration.

"Man, what the hell is wrong with you?" Sartor suddenly turns to me. "That's Khas Kunar. Look at how beautiful it is. When your uncle came to visit, he was absolutely amazed. He made me stop the car, and he videotaped it. You didn't even say anything. What the hell is wrong with you?" he says again.

I protest, explain my quiet awe. Then the plain recedes, and we're kicking back up barrelfuls of dust. "Body-slam" would be the most accurate way to describe my interaction with my seat.

"How much longer?" I ask Sartor.

"Oh, um, another hour," he hedges.

* * *

We've been traveling for about five hours already; we started from Kabul at dawn. I spent only two days there, but even from what little of the city I did see, it's clear that the mood has changed tremendously. Last year I rarely observed a woman without a burka. Now, the balance has shifted, with perhaps only one out of four still covering themselves completely. Driving along Chicken Street, we passed two girls whose loose chadors flapped open, revealing jeans underneath.

Chicken Street, a bustling commercial area, was a hub for 1960s-era backpackers on the route known as the Hippie Trail. Now shopkeepers here are again attempting to lure foreigners. One afternoon Sartor and I stumbled across a restaurant called Park Milano Pizza and Burger. Inside there were several grimy booths. One of the signature pies was Rambo pizza, topped with beef and mushrooms. We ordered a large pizza and two burgers. The burgers, stacked double-decker like Big Macs, came out first. Sartor looked perplexed. "Open your mouth really wide like this," I demonstrated. We got so full that we could hardly eat the pizza, and a young Afghan kid handed us our leftover slices in a regular cardboard pizza box emblazoned with the restaurant's name. That blew me away, that they had not only the food but the accessories, too. Later we stopped at a store to buy a can of Barbecue Pringles, Sartor's favorite kind.

My father called us to check in. "Did it rain in Kabul?" he said.

"No," I told him.

"Oh, okay," he said. "It rained in Kunar, so I was wondering. Actually, it rained not just water, but rockets, too." The missiles had landed less than four hundred yards from the governor's compound. I hung up the phone knowing that the next day I would be there, right in the thick of it. But later, munching potato chips and watching satellite TV with Sartor, the Taliban hideouts in the border region seemed almost as far away as the tract houses in California.

In the morning we left the city. Sartor rode in the pickup by himself; I was in a Land Cruiser with a friend of the family. The sun rose higher in the sky as the city receded behind us. We stopped briefly at the Pul-i-Charki checkpoint, beyond which lies the notorious prison of the same name. Beat-up trucks lined the left side of the road, waiting for permission to pass, their sides painted with colorful designs and off-kilter greetings in English: *Good trip have!*

We drove through the Mahipur mountains. The road here snaked through a spectacular gorge; as we swept around each graceful curve, we glimpsed below us a demon drop. The rocks were arranged in crazy formations that seemed like they should be falling down. Tips of massive peaks lined up above us like skyscrapers.

Soon things flattened out, and we approached Sarobi. For years people passing through here were tyrannized by a commander named Zardad. Zardad and his men would allegedly beat, shoot, and kill travelers; they would loot their possessions. Zardad kept an insane man as, literally, a pet. The man, who was unusually hairy, was known as Zardad's dog; he was kept in a hole and would bite and attack his master's prisoners. Hearing stories like this, you can understand why people initially welcomed the stricture of the Taliban. When they took over, Zardad sought asylum in England, where he settled in London and ran a pizza parlor. (In the fall of 2004 Zardad will be tried in a British court for the crimes he allegedly committed in Afghanistan. His trial will come only months after the man rumored to be Zardad's dog is shot to death at Pul-i-Charki in the first execution since the fall of the Taliban.)

We continued along. Villages rose here and there along the Kabul River. As the altitude got lower and lower, the weather got hotter and hotter, and finally we reached Jalalabad, where we stopped for a kabob.

The family friend beside me in the Land Cruiser had been talking a lot, and trying to keep up the conversation was exhausting. "I think I better go with Sartor," I said, "because he's going to get upset if he has to drive alone the entire time."

But when I told Sartor, he said, "Trust me, you do not want to get into the pickup with me. It's so uncomfortable."

"Trust me," I replied, "I do."

So I switched cars, and we took a left out of the marketplace and headed for Kunar.

* * *

Crossing over a bridge, we look out at a park and at a picture of Abdul Haq. This was one of the first places Abdul Haq wanted to restore, and the foundation set up in his name after his death is working to carry out his wish.

During Afghanistan's mid-twentieth century, Jalalabad was a winter resort. Everyone from King Zahir Shah to middle-class Kabul families escaped their snowy city for this warmer climate. In those days, this bridge—called Lovers' Bridge—was a hangout for young people, who would cross back and forth along it, checking each other out. Even if the bridge gets restored, it will probably be years before anything but the ghosts of those carefree teenagers return to lean across the railing and whistle into the balmy night.

We continued, and near a village called Shewa, Sartor told me about a locally famous *khan*, or landowner. This eccentric man welcomes poor travelers to his home. He serves them a feast, and when they've finished eating, he orders them to lift up their shirts. Then he gets out a slingshot and pings rocks against their drumlike bellies.

Therein lies the absurdity of Afghanistan: that the story of the slingshot man takes place in contemporary times, and the one about the teenagers is the fable.

How did normal behavior become the stuff of myth? Afghanistan's social fabric collapsed alongside its infrastructure. Think of a time-lapse film that allows you to watch the long process of construction: a building rising jerkily in thirty seconds. Now play it backwards, and watch as it is disassembled. This is what happened in Afghanistan: a rapid, complete undoing.

"Do you see that?" Sartor said, pointing to a break in the mountain up ahead. "That's Kunar." The notch in the landscape marked the border crossing; there was no sign. Then we went around a bend, and suddenly we were gazing down into the verdant basin, and Sartor was chiding me for not having remarked upon Khas Kunar.

Now the road is really bad. We swerve right and left, looking for traction on what is basically a trail. We've lost the Land Cruiser, which is better equipped for the terrain and has zoomed ahead at twenty-five miles an hour. ("So, you still want to stay in this pickup?" Sartor teases.) Road reconstruction, at present, is extremely limited. The most high-profile effort is taking place along a highway linking Kabul to the southern city of Kandahar. Nothing is taking place in Kunar.

Since the fall of the Taliban, Kunar has been among the most volatile provinces in Afghanistan. The tumult is due in part to its position along the Pakistani border. As for the rest of it, you could almost say that "it's in the water." People in Kunar will tell you that theirs was the first province to rise up against the Communists, as well as the first place to which the Arabs came during the Soviet war; during that period, Kunar was especially chaotic. Last summer Gulbiddin Hekmatyar (recently deemed a "Specially Designated Global Terrorist" by his former patron, the U.S. government) was rumored to have set up shop here; at one point some agents working for my father actually had a position on him.

Whomp! My head hits the ceiling. We're carrying a TV and satellite dish in the bed of the pickup, and I hope they don't break before we have a chance to try them out. Sartor says that you can't get a sense of the road unless you come and drive on it yourself, and he's right. For instance, when you picture the worst road you can, you might imagine something gouged by potholes; but in Afghanistan potholes are actually a good sign, the remnants of a paved surface. We haven't come across any potholes for miles. Even before the war this was just a dirt pathway. Most of the Afghan countryside has always been cut off from the capital. The physical separation begets a cultural one. I traveled halfway around the planet on an airplane, and when I got off, everything seemed the same. But in Afghanistan you drive a hundred miles outside Kabul, and you're in a completely different world.

"Damn, is there someplace we could get a Coke or anything?" I say to Sartor. It's been at least three hours since Jalalabad. I'm hot and my mouth is filling with dust.

"*Murla,* there is no Coke here," Sartor says. *Murla* is, literally, "dead person"; in this context, it means something slangier, like, "Fool!"

We're approaching a village called Narang, and I see a small market with several stalls. "Let's try anyway," I say. "You never know."

"*Murla,*" Sartor says again. "I'm telling you, there's no Coke here."

"Just stop the car," I say. "We'll check."

Sartor's right; there isn't any Coke, or even any drink at all, just some biscuits from Pakistan.

If we had found a Coke, Sartor would have given me a hard time about littering. Or I should say, about *not* littering. The first few times I saw him throw a plastic water bottle out the driver's side window, I admonished him: "Hey, don't throw stuff out." But he harassed me about my habit of leaving my refuse rolling around under the seats: "Oh, so it's okay to make the car dirty but not the outside?"

Eventually I embraced Sartor's twisted environmentalism; it got to the point that back in California, I'd have to restrain myself from throwing a glass juice bottle out the window as I sped down Willow Pass Road.

We continue toward Asadabad, the pickup convulsing. Sartor gestures out the window. "You see all this destruction here?"

"Yeah," I say. It looks like an excavation site, something ancient.

"Well, you can thank your uncle for that," he jokes, referring to Rauf Mama's activities during the resistance. I scan the roofless houses, the jagged pieces of wall. We're nearing Sirkanay, a district in which, according to the UN, seventy percent of the houses were destroyed during the Soviet war; ninety percent of Sirkanay village has been destroyed "in general." Now people don't like to come here: Sirkanay is dangerous, a place through which troublemakers slip across the Pakistani border.

The mountains that separate the two countries are perhaps ten miles off the road to our right. We follow this chain of forbidding peaks. Yet the range is not like a bulwark, more like a screen. The people here have always clambered back and forth across these mountains. The border is an artificial invention of British imperialism; it divided Pashtun families spread across both sides of what they had always considered a single territory. During the Soviet war mujahedeen commuted along the trails, doing a shift of fighting in Kunar, then returning for a spell to their temporary refuge in Pakistan. Now insurgents sneak in and out under the cover of night to launch rockets.

"How much longer?" I say for the gazillionth time to Sartor.

"You see that bump right there?" He's pointing ahead of us. "Right when we get off that bump, it's going to be Asadabad."

"Oh!" I exclaim. "We're practically there."

"Um, yeah, it's right there," he says noncommittally.

The bump is like a sight gag. We go and go, but we don't get anywhere. I realize my perception of distance needs to be recalibrated down from a seventy-miles-per-hour scale. Almost ninety minutes later we crawl over the bump and onto a stretch of road that seems slightly improved, perhaps recently graded.

"We're right outside Asadabad," Sartor says, for real this time. "The Americans started working on this road, flattened it out a little bit." Apparently it lasted for only three or four days before cars started messing it up again. "There," Sartor says, pointing out the window. "There's your countrymen's base, right there."

I try to get a look at the local U.S. military base, and then a few minutes go by and we're passing a little market. Raggedy stalls line the road. I see a pool table on the roof of a shack, some kids standing around with cues. "They saw pool tables in Pakistan," Sartor says, "so they play here now, too." There are no women in the market, only men, and every single one has come to a full stop in the middle of whatever he was doing before; they all recognize the white pickup as belonging to my father. Some of the men are squatting, in a way that looks uncomfortable, their knees deeply bent and their bottoms dangling, not touching the ground.

Then we reach the gates of the governor's house, and the pickup noses inside. Eight hours and 150 miles later, we're finally here. As I step out of the car, I am almost immediately embraced by a security guard. I see a whole line of them stretched out to greet me. "Salaam alaikum," I say to each. The security guards are wearing blue uniforms and have AKs slung over their shoulders. They are also carrying huge necklaces. Necklace isn't really the right word: these are almost as big as wearable billboards. They're like huge medallions made of party favors. They're studded with flowers in lime-green, white, and neon-pink; fringed with purple tinsel, shimmery yellow cellophane. Each guy leans forward, slipping a necklace over my head, and then we hug, the object bumping between us. Eventually

I'm wearing so many of the necklaces that I can hardly move. Then instead of putting more on, the security guards rush over and start taking them off.

At the end of the line, I reach my father. I remember my mother's instructions: *Don't forget to kiss your father's hand! He's the governor, and you can't just go up there and hug him. People will be watching, so don't go and lift him up or anything. Just give him a kiss on the hand as a sign of respect, and then when you go inside you guys can talk.* Obediently, I bend my head forward, but even as I do, my father is pulling his hand away, a modest gesture signaling, *Please—there's no need for that.* Now he gives me a quick hug and puts his hand to my cheek.

Then we stand there for a while, people milling around. We're in a court-yard, among plain white buildings. My father and I are standing under a canopy, in the shade. He's wearing a baby-blue kameez partoog. It's been seven months since I've seen him. He looks older, a little heavier, and his face is reddened, as if from sun. Everybody's watching us—it's this formal thing—and I feel awkward beside him.

When I was little, my father would come visit me in America, and I'd lead the way: *No, Dad, don't do this. No, Dad, not like that.* Now we're finally in Kunar, his place, where he grew up, where everybody knows him. The security guards disperse, and my father and I step inside the doorway, into the remote and daunting territory where he knows the rules and I don't.

14

THEY'VE HAD A MEETING," the man tells my father. "We have recordings. They've sworn allegiance to undermine you. They've pledged to work against you, to try to get you out." It's the same afternoon, only minutes later, and I'm inside the house with my father and two other men. I've shaken their hands, but I'm not exactly sure who they are. One is catlike, with a whiskery mustache. The other man is bearded and barely audible. As it is, I don't really understand what they're talking about, and I'm grateful when they leave and someone offers me a Coke. I sit down on a thin cushion.

"So, how'd you like the road," my father teases me. We chat for a bit, then decide to take a nap. Though it's been a long day, I can't sleep. The pillow I've chosen is too big, too hard, and too red. I try to squeeze the pillow down; next I nudge underneath it and hope the weight of it on my head will knock me out; finally I decide that it can only be used as something to hug, like a big teddy bear. I stare at the ceiling and wait for my father to wake up. When he does, he tells me that the men who visited were intelligence agents, and that today they infiltrated a meeting of ex-Communists.

I thought I had a pretty good sense of the array (or disarray) of problems my father would be facing this summer—opium, the Taliban, Al Qaeda, warlords, Hekmatyar, Pakistan. It hadn't occurred to me to include ex-Communists—Afghans who fought on the Soviet side during the resistance—on the list. Their ascendance has reopened deep wounds all over Afghanistan. The problem is especially acute in Kunar, where, on an April morning in 1979, Communists massacred more than one thousand local men.

That morning nearly all of the men in a nearby village called Kerala gathered for a jirga. When they arrived, they were slaughtered. The massacre—which took place eight months before the Soviet invasion—was intended to quell growing dissent. Instead, it served as a rallying cry for the resistance. An overwhelming proportion—ninety percent or more—of Kunar's population ultimately allied themselves with the mujahedeen.

The story is a startling introduction to Kunar, and a hint that this time around, there will be no easing into the place. The massacre site is so close that we can practically see it out the window, and my father tells me that we'll go there tomorrow.

The next day I stand with my father and his security guards before a mud wall, waiting to be let inside. The door is locked, and a search is on for the man who has the key. A crowd gathers, and while we wait, we're offered tea more than a dozen times. My father declines each offer politely, explaining we're just trying to see the mass grave; kids stand on nearby rooftops, trying to see the new governor. One guy offers to break the lock, saying, "It's all right, we can get a new one!"

"No, that's not all right," my father replies. "If you have the key, that's great. If not, we'll come back another time."

Finally a docile old man shows up. I don't know why he's the one with the key; perhaps it's because, as he tells us, he is one of only a handful of the survivors. We step through a wooden door into a place the size of an average backyard.

Three long bumps rise from the ground like waves. Each bump is about four feet high, and there are troughs in between. My father advances, but I'm having a hard time going forward. *What if I step on a body?* Then I see that the old man just avoids the lumps, and I do the same. One of my father's security guards veers onto the raised area, and the old man yells, "Stop stepping on the bodies!"

He tells us that most of the corpses were too ravaged to identify. You could recognize a friend only by the slippers he wore, or the length of his kameez partoog, or the kind of cuffs on his pants. At the very moment he's explaining about the clothes, an ex-Communist walks in.

Like several of his peers, this man is a director in the local division of the army. Now he changes the subject to the recent rocket attacks, seemingly oblivious to his surroundings. His audacity baffles me. How can he even show his face here? I think of a line of Nietzsche—"He who fights against monsters should see to it that he does not become a monster in the process"—that has been haunting me as I contemplate my future in Afghanistan.

I suppose I should look to my father, who's even-tempered and polite with the ex-Communist, betraying nothing. Soon we leave the mass grave, turning down tea one last time. Outside the mud wall there is no indication of the horror bound inside. We start back to the governor's compound. The situation with the ex-Communists is a challenge, my father tells me. They've been appointed to their positions by others, and he can't just push them aside. He's going through official channels to try to get some of the men removed, but until then it's better just to ignore them.

One day I go back to Kerala with Rauf Mama's nephew Shohab. (Rauf Mama and Shohab are both living with us at the compound this summer.) We stop in at a shop where one of his friends works as a carpenter. Carpentry is one of the very few ways to eke out a living here; my father recently bought an armoire from a local craftsman. Today I have my recording equipment with me, and I explain to the carpenter that I want to interview the old man with the key. Somebody goes to get him, and the carpenter takes us to the back and brings us some juice while we wait. An Indian movie is playing on satellite TV. When the old man arrives, we head toward the mass grave, trailed by a few interested villagers.

When we reach the mounds, the old man starts crying. I feel awkward, especially because I'm taping. I don't want to get in too close with the mic, so I stop and stare at an old pakol hat on the ground. Leaves crunch under my feet.

I give the old man a couple seconds, then ask if he could talk about what happened. "Whatever way is easiest for you," I say. "Whatever you remember, start with that."

He begins his story on the morning of the massacre, when he was arrested by Communist soldiers and held with thirty-four other prisoners. Soon a man arrived and announced, "Those of you that need to be killed will be killed. Those of you that should be released will be released. And those of you that should be in jail will be kept here." The old man was released.

Meanwhile the rest of the villagers had begun to gather for a jirga at which they'd been told they would receive weapons to fight the mujahedeen. Most of the villagers actually supported the mujahedeen; many even sheltered them. They showed up for the meeting only because they feared the consequences of absence. As is customary, they arrived at the jirga unarmed.

"Everybody came," the old man says. "All of the people came and sat down right here. And there was a youngster—his name was Amir Salaam. Such a capable youngster," he says. "So strong. And he got up immediately and said, 'People, people, I'm telling you! Grab the weapons of the soldiers! Grab the weapons, I'm telling you, because they're going to kill us all. They're going to kill us all.'

"I came by this bridge," the old man continues, pointing up at a wide stone arch perhaps thirty yards away. "All of a sudden I heard firing. It was so much firing at once that it wasn't firing." He struggles to describe the intensity of the sound. "A maaaassss"—he draws out the word—"of bullets."

The old man wasn't sure what was going on; at first all he could see was blood "jumping in the air." The effect was hideous. "So much red that it was like sunlight," the old man says. "Like the day coming up."

The firing continued for about fifteen minutes. When it stopped, everything became eerily quiet. Some of the living played dead. They lay still, perhaps thinking that the gunmen would just walk away. Then bulldozers came into the foreground and, the old man says, "started crushing the people." What he describes is gruesome—stomachs torn open, clothes soaked with blood. "They would go over the people's legs, not killing them, but injuring them badly," he remembers.

"They would purposely bury those that were trying to beg for their lives," the carpenter interjects. "They would push them down into the ground." Dirt was piled upon the injured, and they were buried alive. Many did not immediately succumb. The ground shook with the motion of people trapped underneath, trying to get out.

Those who did manage to escape soon met another cruel fate. Desperately wounded, they tried to crawl away, only to be shot by soldiers standing guard at the bridge. Their bodies began to fill the river before us. "It was flowing with red blood," the old man says.

A soldier on the bridge spied the old man and told him, "Get back! We've already killed enough people here today. I don't want to have to kill any more. Why did you have to pop up?" The enormity of his deeds must have been setting in, for the solider showed the old man mercy. He directed him to an escape route, along which the old man fled. He soon discovered that both of his brothers were dead.

As the old man speaks, he gestures up at the bridge. The action there is normal, people walking, cars crossing back and forth.

"Those that didn't see it had a hard time believing it," the carpenter tells me, as we gaze over the lumpy ground. "Nobody could believe such cruelty could ever happen."

The morning after the massacre, the old man came into town and saw a crowd of widows and their children on the other side of the river. A soldier was blocking them. Without crossing, they would be unable to leave Kerala.

The old man said to the soldier, "Look at the women and children, crying. Please, let them come to this side."

"Who are you trying to get me killed by?" the soldier said dismissively. Then he told the old man to go away and return after his evening prayers.

"When I came back, the soldier looked at me and said, 'Did you do your evening prayers?'

"I said, 'Yes.'

"Then he said, 'Here, take my Kalashnikov.'

"I said, 'What for?'

"And he said, 'Just kill me with it.'

"I said, 'Are you that much of a coward?' I started walking away from him.

"I took a couple steps, and he said, 'Turn around.' I turned around, and he said, 'Come over here.' I went over there, and he said, 'Why don't you start moving them in little groups.' "

The old man went over to the crowd. "All of a sudden they were like ants!" he exclaims. "Like little ants! Long lines of women and children, all coming out like ants next to the river."

The group walked "in little distances"; the next morning they reached a district called Shigal. In Pashto, when we want to indicate an exceptionally large amount, we say *de khudai*—God's. "There were God's Muslims there for us," the old man remembers now. "Some gave us food, some gave us money, some gave us shelter." The group stayed in Shigal for eight days, after which they became refugees in Pakistan. Except for the dead, there was almost no one left in Kerala.

"This village started being abandoned," the carpenter explains. "Before this there were mujahedeen in certain valleys, but after this everybody rose up in arms against the government. It was because of these martyrs that the jihad started en masse."

Perhaps eight or nine hundred bodies are buried beneath us. The graves of two or three hundred others lie nearby. And the old man points in another direction as well: "You see that area there? About sixty-five people were killed in that area. Weren't you part of that family?" He turns to a shy young man who's been listening quietly. The young man does not answer.

"Yeah, that's him," confirms the carpenter. "It's his father that was killed there. His family had the unfortunate luck of having their grandmother die the night before, so all of the male relatives were at their house. His whole family was killed in front of him."

"Do you remember the incident yourself?" I ask the young man.

"Yes, I do. I was little at the time," he affirms.

"Do you remember your age?" I ask.

"I was in fifth grade," he says.

Then the carpenter breaks in with another story, and it's only later, when we all leave the mass grave and return to the back of the shop, that the young man talks about what happened.

He begins with his grandmother's death, to which he refers in the Afghan way: "She reached her right on Thursday," he says. All of his family members were there on Friday when the Communist soldiers came and, outside his house, began to separate the men from the women and children. "They took my father," the young man says. "I didn't know why they were grabbing my father. So I ran after him, I grabbed my father's hand. But the soldier pulled me away and threw me back in front of the house." The soldiers lined the men up, "and then they just started shooting at them with

Kalashnikovs. They killed sixty-three people, sixty-three men in my house." In unison—in a kind of keening wave of grief—the women and children fell to the ground, faced Mecca, and began to pray.

"I remember it like it was right now," the young man says. "Because it all happened in front of my eyes."

This is the story that gets to me. Was it Stalin who said that the death of one million people is a statistic and the death of one person is a tragedy? The scene at the bridge—the red sky, the bulldozers—is hard to picture. But here is a situation I can imagine myself within—a big family gathering, reaching for my father as he's pulled across the lawn, watching him shot and killed in front of the familiar house. The young man is soft-spoken and describes these events calmly. In his early thirties, he is the oldest man left in his family.

Now another young man approaches me. Any initial hesitation has disappeared; now everyone seems eager to get his story out. As the men speak, workers hammer elsewhere in the shop. There's a tiny *thump, thump,* the tumbling of a tool to the floor. The men seem unaffected by one another's stories; this is their common experience. For me it's different. The microphone helps perpetuate the illusion that I'm just doing an interview. But I'm unsettled to the point of physical exhaustion. I've never heard anything like this.

The tragedy of Kerala is compounded by its invisibility. Though there are lines dedicated to the massacre here and there in certain books—"In response to rural uprisings the government also engaged in such collective reprisals as the killing of an estimated 1,170 unarmed villagers in Kerala, Kunar, on April 20, 1979"—there is none of the accounting you would expect had this happened in almost any other part of the world. A report compiled by the UN in the early 1980s, and a single chapter in an out-of-print book by a former *Christian Science Monitor* reporter—these two works comprise basically the entire historical record of the event.

The *Monitor* reporter, Edward Girardet, was one of the first Western journalists to write about the massacre; he unearthed the story almost a year after it occurred. Until the Soviets invaded, the world had not been watching closely. Kerala was one of a number of sickening atrocities that had been hidden from view.

One of the masterminds of the slaughter at Kerala was once the governor of Kunar. His name was Nizamuddin, to which he added *eh Beh Khudah*—Nizamuddin the Godless. The moniker would have angered and alienated the devout people in Kunar. But framing it that way—in terms of the contrast between the believers and the non—is somehow less chilling. The name places its beholder outside the sphere of any moral or spiritual influence. It's like the name of a comic book villain, a superhero's evil foe.

One day several months after the massacre, Nizamuddin received word that some mujahedeen being held at a Communist garrison were ready to surrender. The message was a ruse, part of a plan by the mujahedeen (my uncle Rauf Mama among them) to capture the governor. At the garrison they hid in wait behind some bushes. But when Nizamuddin arrived, one of the men couldn't control himself; he jumped out and shot him.

The mujahedeen dragged his corpse—and those of his bodyguards—all through the town. Along the way, villagers beat the bodies with rocks. At the hands of these men, they had endured not only the horror of the Kerala massacre but months of rage and frustration as their way of life was upended and their religion attacked. Now they lived in what was basically a war zone, their province having become a battlefield between those brutally trying to impose their new, godless system and those fighting to stop them.

The villagers threw Nizamuddin into the river. Downstream some others pulled him out and set fire to his body, then tossed the charred corpse into the water again.

It will come as no surprise that the local people have been conditioned to view the occupant of the governor's compound with deep distrust. My father is determined to prove that he is different. One of the first things he did when he arrived here was visit the mass grave and pay his respects. The villagers told him it was the first time in ages anyone had asked them about it. The villain had been vanquished, but the memory of his terrible deeds had been buried, too.

15

MY FATHER LIKES TO SAY THAT he's the only governor in Afghanistan without a beard. He's always been clean-shaven and strict about it—even with me. When I was younger, I'd go two or three days, accumulate some stubble. Then I'd be lying around on the couch, watching TV, and suddenly my father would be looming above. "Shave," he'd say.

If my uncle was around, he'd say, "If he wants to leave a beard, let him leave a beard."

My father would laugh. "He's not leaving a beard for the reasons you think he's leaving a beard. He's just lazy."

My father believes that the beard is a symbol of what's gone wrong with Islam. It's a superficial preoccupation. By itself, it tells you nothing about a person's faith except that he has learned it by rote.

But in Afghanistan, the beard means a lot. Many people said the traditional, religious people in Kunar would not accept a governor without a beard. Defense Minister Fahim was among those who told my father he would not succeed in Kunar with a shaved face.

But plenty of others didn't care one way or another about my father's facial hair; at least one man even advocated for him remaining clean-shaven. In Pashto we refer to something called *ghraiwan,* which is kind of like your conscience; it's located just below your Adam's apple. This man joked, "It's a good thing Fazel Akbar doesn't have a beard. He can look inside himself." Others' beards obscured their *ghraiwan*: "They can't look inside, so they can do whatever they want."

He was teasing, but it's true that the beard lets you get away with a lot here. Obviously, it gives you a kind of spiritual standing—a convenient cover for your misdeeds. But it's also sort of like the sweatshirt emblazoned with the name of the state college football team: when you wear it on fall Saturdays, neighbors wave and nod approvingly, *yes, he's one of us.* Then they glance warily at the guy in the plain old sweater. My father gets just as excited about heading over to the stadium as anyone; he just doesn't feel the need to wear a sweatshirt while he cheers.

One time during the resistance Jallaluddin Haqqani—the mujahedeen commander who once offered my brother the chance to kill a Communist—sat down with my father. "Fazel Akbar, you're such a good jihadi," Haqqani complimented him. "You've done so much for us in the jihad. You've spent rough nights with us, and you also go and talk to those foreigners. But you'd be such a great jihadi if you just left a beard. It would look so good if you left a beard. Please," he implored, "leave a beard."

There's something slightly suspect about refusing to embrace the convention of the masses. But when it came to Kunar, my father insisted there was no need to worry. He was completely confident that the masses would embrace him.

As it happens, my father is uniquely qualified for the governor's position. He has legitimacy from the resistance, yet he is an educated moderate, not a warlord or a fundamentalist. He did not ruin his reputation by participating in the civil war that followed the mujahedeen's takeover in 1992. And he has no tribal affiliation, which is an asset in Kunar, where sons inherit the feuds of their forefathers. We are a family of *Saids*, a title that means we are descended from the Prophet Muhammad. On a practical level, this means that my father is Said Fazel, I am Said Hyder, and my brother is Said Omar. More important, Saids are afforded great respect in Afghanistan. Karzai—half-jokingly, half-respectfully—likes to call my father *pacha*, which means "king."

Still, you can easily imagine the nightly news anchor's intro: *Afghan ex-*

iles are returning to their country to take up positions in the new govern-ment. But have the years they spent living peacefully in the West alienated them from their countrymen? From Kabul, So-and-So reports.

The question is valid but applies primarily to those who fled during the Soviet invasion. My father stepped out of the ring only when the Taliban came. Even some of the most hardened commanders spent those years in exile. Some people went to Pakistan, some to Iran, some to Dubai; my fa-ther was among those who happened to go to the United States. He under-stands Western culture just enough not to fear it. But it would be quite a stretch to call him Americanized.

Here's a story. Several months before assuming his position as governor, my father accompanied Karzai to an International Rescue Committee cere-mony in New York City. Karzai was presented with the organization's Free-dom Award in the Waldorf Astoria's Grand Ballroom. Among the guests was Robert DeNiro, who told Karzai that he'd once scouted filming loca-tions in Kunar. "Really?" said Karzai. "We have someone with us from Kunar. He could probably help you if you want to go back." They made their way through the crowd to my father, and Karzai made the introduc-tion. My father showed no recognition.

"Do you know who this is?" Karzai said.

"No," my father said.

"How could you not know who Robert DeNiro is? Have you seen *Taxi Driver? Goodfellas? Casino?*" Karzai prodded.

My father had not seen a single one of them. Karzai, who has never lived in the West, was incredulous. "Wow," he said. "You really are from Kunar, aren't you?"

My father was born north of Asadabad, in a tiny village called Shal, in 1945. Because of his father's early death, he was raised by the members of an older generation: his great-uncle, the former justice minister Said Sham-suddin Majrooh (Baba, whose funeral I attended last summer), and Shal Pacha, his grandfather, a locally mythologized spiritual leader.

Baba was the intellectual brother, immersed in books and ideas. Shal Pacha was his intuitive counterpart, a man of the people. But such facts are unnecessary—you can read their biographies in their names. Like other

Afghan writers and scholars, Baba adopted a new name; he chose *Majrooh,* which means "wounded." Just as that name indicates an identity apart from one's point of origin, Shal Pacha's is inextricable from it. *Shal* is for Shal, his home village, and *Pacha,* of course, is an honorific meaning "king." That was my great-grandfather: King of Shal.

I've tried to get my mother's older sister, who knew Shal Pacha and remembers him well, to narrow it down for me: "Come on, what was the most special thing about him?" I'll say. (Afghanistan is a close-knit society, and even before my mother and father met, their families were linked by marriage.)

But his essence seems difficult to define. "Oh, he was something else," she'll say. "He was something else."

So I piece my great-grandfather together from little bits of his legend. Shal Pacha is remembered as a fair arbitrator—one word from him could resolve a century-old blood feud. His religious knowledge was so complete that he taught a class in Islam to *jinns—jinns* being invisible spirits who inhabit our world. His moral purity had physical manifestations: people say that when he peed, his urine turned to milk. And on his deathbed, when he remembered that, as a child, he'd slapped another little boy, he called that man to him and, as one of his last deeds, asked his forgiveness.

These may sound like stories from a premodern era, but Shal Pacha died in the 1950s, and his legend is still well within reach. "Oh, I wish he were here now," people in Kunar say.

Shal Pacha died when my father was about seven, and soon afterward he was sent to live with Baba in Kabul. It wasn't an easy childhood, growing up without a father in a completely male-dominated society. But I think that the experience gave my father the psychological muscle to cope with everything that came later. A lot of the old elites had lived more protected lives, in greater ease and comfort. When the Soviets invaded, they chose to leave rather than adapt to the turmoil. But my father had always had to struggle a little; he had the tools to stay on and be effective.

In the 1960s my father entered Kabul University. Like most college students, he changed his major a couple times, finally settling on law and politics. He toyed with the idea of getting a diplomatic post outside the country, but when he graduated he instead accepted an offer from Kabul

Radio. During these years my mother was also in Kabul, studying to be a teacher. My father met her through her older brother, and my parents married in 1970.

Rauf Mama was present at the wedding festivities. Rauf Mama's father and Shal Pacha were close friends, and Rauf Mama and my father have known each other since they could crawl. To Rauf Mama, Shal Pacha was a hometown hero; his legacy was one of the reasons Rauf Mama really wanted my father to come back to lead Kunar. Now here he is, carrying on that family tradition and another: Baba was always clean-shaven, too.

When my father's convoy reached the Kunar border in late April, two hundred cars waited there to greet him. Two hundred cars is a lot of cars for a rural province. After my father crossed—on foot, as a ceremonial gesture—the convoy continued along the dusty roads, and somewhere south of Asadabad it stopped for lunch. On the videotape of these events you see a nice meal laid out on plastic sheets that protect a big red carpet. My father reaches for a piece of flatbread and dips it into a pool of yogurt; others scrape spoons against the bottoms of their bowls. Later in the tape my father walks past a line of saluting soldiers with a white-bearded man by his side. The white-bearded man is Shah Jan, the outgoing governor. (Jahan Dad, the warlord who occupied the governor's house during my first summer, is nowhere in sight.) Shah Jan was complacent about the news that my father would replace him; he knew that he would be unable to resist.

The video is like a highlights reel of my father's first weeks as governor: a feast under light-dappled trees, Rauf Mama leaning back and indulgently smoking. (He didn't know he was on camera; usually he sneaks into the bathroom when he wants a cigarette.) There are schoolchildren waiting to greet my father, and soldiers patrolling with guns the length of some of the kids in line. Necklaces are hung, confetti is strewn. My father sits on a raised platform, preparing to speak, an Afghan flag before him.

When the festivities ended, my father settled into the governor's compound, and got to work.

Some of his earliest tasks involved the compound itself. The compound consists of several soulless buildings that may have been constructed during the Communist era. Over the years the place has deteriorated; when my father arrived, there was no functioning toilet. Thus one of his first projects was renovating the bathroom in the main residence. Now it's tiled with peach-colored stone; shelves hold a bottle of mouthwash, a razor in a cup.

The entire place is under construction—you weave through piles of bricks and men with shovels and workmen painting walls. In the courtyard holes gape around the skinny trees that will grow to form a small garden's border. Nearby sits what we call "the container," which is literally a big container used as a vault. The bank stores its money here in little plastic bags; the compound has better security.

If security is good, electricity is less so. The supply is extremely weak and unpredictable, and we rely on a generator. It's always rumbling in the background when I stand in the courtyard, trying to aim the antenna on the satellite phone the right way so that my mother can hear me on the line. The generator powers our fans (the temperature here regularly climbs over one hundred degrees), our satellite TV (the only American channel we get is Fox News), and our refrigerator (a horizontal model).

The refrigerator is always breaking. Sartor tries to fix it, and then Shohab takes a stab at it, and then we get a guy from the market to come over—his qualification for being a repairman is that he sells batteries—and maybe he kicks it into gear, but inevitably it goes out again in a couple of days. Food is always getting spoiled. There's a cook, but not a good one. We eat plain meals. During my father's early weeks here, he consumed enough meat to last him months. He is still watching his blood pressure, as well as his gout, which makes his foot swell. So we dine on boiled chicken with potatoes, tomatoes, and no salt.

My father, Rauf Mama, and I all sleep outside on a second-floor balcony. It's too hot to rest anywhere else. The balcony is the size of a room, furnished with white plastic patio chairs and our *charpoys,* or rope beds, basic wood frames crisscrossed with strong strings. It gets so dark here that everyone is in bed by nine. Mosquito nets, like something you'd see on a Travel Channel show about Malaysia, protect us from the bugs. The Kunar River runs behind the house; we hear it rushing beneath us as we fall asleep.

We're often awakened by rocket fire. At first this was weird; now it's just annoying. *It's really rude of Al Qaeda to launch these missiles at night,* I think to myself, eyes wide open. *It would be much more convenient if they could launch them at twelve noon.* But one reward for being jolted awake is the stars. The sky has the fine-grained detail of a planetarium. I lie there under the brilliant canopy, thinking that in spite of everything, Kunar has to be one of the most beautiful places I've ever seen.

I spend my early days in Kunar following my father around, getting a sense of his work. Some of his obstacles, like lack of funding, are daunting; but at moments it seems that already he's making real change.

One afternoon we visit a local jail in response to a letter from the prisoners about their living conditions. The jail—just a little house set yards away from the governor's compound—is disgusting. The bathroom smells horrible, and the bedsheets are vile. Outside in the garden—dirt broken by tufts of grass—we sit with the prisoners on plastic tarps. At my father's request, someone brings out fruit, and we all share some mangoes. Flies buzz all around us. I'm recording, and they even land on the mic.

My father takes down each of the thirteen prisoners' names. Allegedly they are Al Qaeda members who entered the province to fight, but it's clear that they are really just impoverished Pashtun day laborers who crossed the border looking for work. They were thrown in jail simply because they carry Pakistani identification cards. Some of them have been imprisoned for a long time. One guy says he's been here three months. "And I have three wives, so for me it's like nine months," he jokes. "Because I'm missing three times the action."

My father talks to the prisoners about border relations with Pakistan. The situation is critical—we need to find a way to facilitate legitimate travel into Afghanistan while at the same time keeping insurgents out. The prisoners seem shocked to have been engaged in such an important discussion; my father is treating them with dignity, not scorn.

At the end of the visit, my father signs a form releasing the prisoners. Before they go home, they will enjoy a feast—my father will send over a goat that they can behead and barbecue. "We're so happy with your father!" they exclaim. Their glee is contagious: I am happy with him too.

Of course, it's easy to bask in the glow of that kind of progress. Other advances come with risks. Before I got here, I read an article in which some-one joked that officials in the Afghan government wouldn't be good life in-surance candidates. It's true. Armed guards accompany us even out to the back of the house for a walk by the river. My father and I speak over the strong current, the guards trudging alongside.

My father is in danger because he is cracking down on people who are not used to being caught. A couple weeks before I arrived, he confiscated nearly four hundred pounds of opium being transported by an Afghan mil-itary lieutenant and three associates. My father took me to see the smug-glers' car. It was a fancy Land Cruiser with tinted windows—a music-video drug lord's ride. Some of the opium had been hidden in the gas tank; I sniffed, and you could still smell something unusual inside. My father said that additional bales had been packed in boxes printed "Donations from the American people to the Afghan people." It was an unintentionally ironic touch—opium production, which fell to its lowest level in years un-der the Taliban, has flourished since the arrival of the U.S. forces. In 2002 it brought in an estimated $1.2 billion—a figure about equal to the amount of foreign aid Afghanistan received during that same time.

My father had made a bold, if hazardous, move. "This is a danger for me," he tells the *Christian Science Monitor*. "If they come to know that this man is an obstacle, it is easy for them to kill one man and get rid of the problem." By "this man," my father means himself.

It was all enough to make you wonder if my father should grow a beard: if protection from his own conscience would be, in the end, the only good life insurance policy.

16

IN KABUL I RARELY CAME into contact with U.S. soldiers. In Kunar they are a regular presence in our lives. Perhaps a couple hundred of the nine thousand troops in Afghanistan are stationed at the local base, which sits just outside Asadabad. (I have to guess at both their numbers and their composition, which seems to range from reserves to special forces. Secrecy abides, and they won't tell me on their own.) Everyone in Kunar calls the base Toopchi, which is Pashto for "artillery man." Since the late 1970s, this small complex, in one of the most remote regions of one of the most remote countries on earth, has housed a series of artillery men whose fusillade has had worldwide reverberations. First came the Afghan Communists, who were followed by their backers, the Soviets. The Soviets were succeeded by the mujahedeen, who eventually gave the base to local Arabs. The Arabs used it as a terrorist training camp before ceding it to their new hosts, the Taliban—who, of course, lost it to the Americans. Whenever I'm at Toopchi, I can't help but wonder how long the Americans are going to last, and who will replace them.

One morning we pile into the pickup and head down to the base. Fifteen minutes later we pull in, navigating a maze of barbed wire that resembles a massive, glinting version of the zigzag processionals at airport check-ins. I'm here with my father and his aide Yossef, who's carrying a digital video camera. He points it up to the overcast sky, zooming in tight on a helicop-ter as it crosses against the mountains. "Don't record," an American tells him. "You're going to get us in trouble." Yossef is just taping for fun, but the troops are on edge—Major General John Vines, the top U.S. com-mander in Afghanistan, is coming for a visit. Long-bodied helicopters with thin propellers patrol in anticipation of his arrival. Nobody was supposed to know of Vines's visit, but I accidentally told Sartor he was coming. But I can't be the only one worried about slipping up. At the base everyone is on their best behavior. The soldiers have even shaved their beards. The younger ones look especially different—suddenly as vulnerable as their newly exposed skin.

Walking through the base, you get the feeling that if these walls could talk, they would tell you to get out while you can. The rattling fans seem to beat out echoes of the conversations that must have taken place in these rooms: Afghan Communists laughing menacingly to themselves as they plan ex-actly how they're going to "redistribute" a local khan's landholdings (among themselves, of course); Soviet Spetsnaz discussing—in that cold way you picture Russian soldiers to be talking—how to subdue the unruly rebels; mujahedeen taking over the base and immediately beginning to ar-gue loudly and simultaneously—the way only a bunch of Pashtun tribes-men can—over the spoils; Arab terrorists planning to infiltrate the mountains of Kashmir or the concrete jungles of New York; turbaned Tal-iban striding the halls with their whips in hand. If you stand out back and look across the fierce Kunar River, you can almost hear the galloping horses of Alexander the Great, who scurried away for safety after being hit by an arrow in this very valley.

It's easy to get caught up in the history of this place. For the Americans who sleep here, the atmosphere must on occasion resemble a summer camp at which boys whisper ghost stories about the dead counselor whose spirit still haunts the lake. One time an American asked me if Rauf Mama might be able to tell them "about the Russians who were beheaded here." The sol-diers were anxious to hear details of how the mujahedeen seized Toopchi and decapitated Soviet troops. But Rauf Mama told them, "No, no, most of them had fled." When the mujahedeen entered the base, it was empty but for four or five dead Russian bodies.

Now there is no trace of the Soviets (at least in the areas I see). Nothing of anyone adheres; there seems to be a tacit understanding that soon enough, somebody else will inhabit this blank space.

General Vines is visiting today to clear up some recent confusion. Not long ago my father received reports of a Pakistani incursion near Khas Kunar. Military forces were said to have crossed the Afghan border and clashed with members of a local tribe. We went down to see what was going on.

Khas Kunar is the place that from the road had seemed like a silvery paradise. But once inside we found ourselves skittering past unremarkable dirt houses. ("Is this the same Khas Kunar?" Sartor joked.) There we met with a group of tribal elders, security officials, and government workers. They were going berserk. They had seen Pakistani forces in their area, and they were now banding together to go up to the mountains and stop the "invasion." It took some time to sort things out, but eventually my father determined that Khas Kunar had not been invaded. We came to understand that the villagers had observed a U.S.-troop-led operation—part of the continuing campaign to rid the border areas of insurgents. At the same time, Pakistani forces had conducted their own offensive; they denied that they had crossed the border, and also denied that the exercise was a "joint operation." But now the tribal elders were not the only ones who were upset. In interviews with the local-language radio services, my father complained about the lack of coordination: why hadn't the American forces relayed their intentions? As governor, he'd had no idea what was going on.

Lapses in communication are becoming a nuisance. At night it's difficult to discern who is firing the missiles—is it the enemy, or is it our ally, conducting rocket practice in the dark? When three A.M. hits, the explosions start, and from our beds Rauf Mama and I begin the guessing game: "Okay, what's that?" one of us says. "Is this an attack, or are the Americans just getting some training in?" Local Afghans like to joke about the soldiers' nighttime drills: *I hope they had some practice before they got here.*

* * *

In a small room we wait for the general to arrive. Several wood-framed chairs with cushions are arranged around a coffee table. From the window behind my chair, I see a line of Humvees rumbling in.

My father and I are talking with a new major named Chris. Chris has buzzed dark hair and a slightly glum demeanor, perhaps because he's still getting used to this place. Earlier, when he was introduced to my father, he greeted him with a regular "Pleased to meet you." Once he's been here awhile, he'll probably adopt the habit of the other soldiers, who toss out friendly "Salaam alaikums!" in their flat American accents.

Chris asks my father if murders or rapes—"or any of the kind of stuff we have in the United States"—are a problem here.

"Murders?" considers my father. "Not yet, but—there are enemies."

"Tribal feuds," I say.

"Blood feuds," my father specifies.

"Random murders, like you said would happen in the United States, or people getting mugged, they're not usually like that," I explain to Chris.

"And that's fair game?" Chris wonders. "I mean if I did something to your family, and you killed me, it's over?"

"Then it's your turn," my father says, and I laugh.

"Oh, like the Mafia," Chris suggests.

"Yeah, kind of like the Mafia," I agree.

The Mafia is an apt point of reference; it evokes a more contemporary image than "blood feud." These anachronistic conflicts are often settled with twenty-first-century flair. Some of these stories would put Scarface to shame. Take, for instance, a feud involving a friend of my father's whom I'll call Abdullah. In the 1970s Abdullah learned that his nephews were interested in his niece. (Marriages between cousins are customary in Afghanistan.) The niece did not share their feelings, and Abdullah told his brother that his sons had to back off. But they continued their pursuit. In accordance with tribal tradition, one of the nephews stood before the niece's house and shot a gun into the sky, laying claim to the girl. In retaliation, Abdullah killed his brother. To protect themselves from their uncle's wrath, the nephews fled to Pakistan.

Years later Abdullah's nephews returned to Afghanistan, and as a peace-making gesture, they invited Abdullah's son to their home. When Abdullah's son arrived for dinner, the nephews welcomed him, then asked his driver to run out and buy a watermelon. As soon as the driver left, the nephews butchered Abdullah's son with kitchen knives. When the driver returned with the watermelon, the nephews slaughtered him, too. They set off to bury the bodies but were thwarted by a Taliban convoy. Rushing to escape the soldiers, they abandoned their car with the corpses inside.

When Abdullah, who was in exile in the West, learned of his son's murder, he was delirious with anger. He flipped through what amounted to a Rolodex of hit men, and offered a guy $50,000 to murder his nephews. When, sometime later, Abdullah received the videotape he'd requested of their deaths, the family celebrated the culmination of the feud.

Five months later Abdullah opened a letter from Pakistan. Inside were photographs of one nephew's wedding. "Thanks for sending the money for us," read the accompanying note. "It helped pay for the wedding. We appreciate you looking out for us, especially since our father's gone."

It turned out that the hit man had liked the nephews. "Look, I'm supposed to kill you guys," he'd told them. "But I'll make you a deal. I'll find some druggies or homeless guys about your size and kill them instead. I'll record the video in the dark, from a distance. You won't say anything about it, and we'll split the money." The parties agreed and struck up a friendship.

And that's where the feud stands—one of hundreds of old scores that spin on and on and on and remain as unsettled as Afghanistan itself.

"He's coming, he's coming!" someone says now, and then soldiers are standing and saluting as General Vines walks in. He's tall and lean and appears to be about sixty years old.

"This'll be your seat," Chris says, showing General Vines to the place beside my father. Soldiers have filled the small room. One guy flips open a spiral notepad; another, his black sunglasses pushed atop his head, sips bottled water. Earlier my father and I were told that "space is at a premium," and it certainly seems as if a lot of soldiers were vying to be here. (I have to admit that I'm probably just as excited as they are. I try to work out the chain of command: Vines to Tommy Franks to Donald Rumsfeld?)

"An operation we conducted recently created some friction for you," General Vines says to my father. "If I could share with you something," he continues, touching his fingers to the arm of his chair. "It is our intention, when we have any knowledge of Pakistan conducting operations on the other side of the border, we would like to coordinate with you, or with the appropriate governor, and place U.S. forces in proximity to the border." This will "minimize the possibility that the citizens of Afghanistan would be interacting with the Pakistani army."

It seems like a good solution—placing U.S. soldiers as a kind of fence between hot-tempered neighbors. Of course, it's not as simple as it sounds. "We do not always know when they're going to do this," General Vines acknowledges of the Pakistani military's operations.

The United States has made Pakistan an ally in the war on terror. But from where we sit, it seems as though Pakistan is more interested in harboring the insurgency than in tamping it down. (To take a singular but vivid example: Within months *Time* magazine will report that the United States has photographs that show Pakistani army vehicles picking up militants who'd just raced across the border after an attack.) America needs to choose: either keep Pakistan happy, or build a stable Afghanistan. It will be impossible to do both.

"The dilemma is this." General Vines cups both hands in front of him. "The dilemma is that both the government of Afghanistan and the government of the United States have been pressing Pakistan to stop these attacks from across in the tribal regions," Vines says, referring to the nighttime rocket attacks by insurgents.

"The point I would make, sir," he continues, then suddenly halts. "Am I speaking—can you understand me okay?" he asks my father. My father nods that everything is fine.

"If something happens, I can help," I offer.

Vines continues, looking at my father: "As you know, I don't speak English, I speak American."

There's some obligatory laughter. "I understand American," I say.

The conversation continues. We learn that Afghanistan's central government had been charged with the responsibility of passing the information about the border operation along to my father. The mistake was theirs, not the U.S. military's. Coca-Colas are served straight from the can, and at the end of the meeting, we exchange gifts. My father gives General Vines a *patou*—a kind of all-purpose blanket, used as everything from a shawl to a prayer rug—and a pakol. Then General Vines presents my father with a special gold coin. "Operation Enduring Freedom," General Vines reads from its face.

Vines's aide slips me one of the coins, too. (He places it in my palm with a sly move approximating a secret handshake.) The face shows a dragon and the outline of Afghanistan; the flip side reads, FOR EXCELLENCE PRESENTED BY THE COMMANDING GENERAL. It's kind of cool when a commanding general gives you something that says "For excellence."

General Vines says it would be fine if I asked him a question for my radio documentary. "Sir, the U.S. forces have been here in Afghanistan over a year now," I say. "What do you think their biggest successes have been?"

"Let me think about that," General Vines says. He pauses, and I hold the little microphone up toward his mouth. There's an American flag patch sewn on the brown sleeve of his uniform.

"I think that the average citizen has access to a level of peace and stability, access to goods and services and things from the outside world, that they previously were denied," General Vines begins. "I believe there's a level of freedom here to do good—and not good, if they choose—that was not here under the previous regime." He goes on to say: "But our goal is to provide a government that is elected through its own institutions, by its own constitution. That election is scheduled to take place next summer and, Allah willing, it will happen." I thank General Vines and turn off the recorder.

Earlier General Vines told me, "Good luck with Berkeley." *How did he know that I want to transfer there?* I wonder. I decide that some soldier must have mentioned it to him. It's strange to think that you've been the subject of even a hastily whispered briefing. I slide into the backseat of the pickup, and we leave the base. I look up at the mountains, where insurgents lurk inside shadowy folds. If only it were as easy for the Americans to collect intelligence on them as it is on me.

17

"Van Halen," the U.S. soldier says. "Def Leppard, Styx, Foreigner, Journey." We're driving west in Kunar, and Doug from Indiana is telling me about his favorite bands. "A lot of the old eighties stuff," he sums up.

Doug is behind the wheel of our armored Humvee; I'm sitting shotgun, an M-16 rolling around at my feet. We're on our way to a remote village called Kurangal. The people there are suspected of running a lucrative timber-smuggling operation. In densely forested Kunar, the black market in timber is on par with the drug trade. Thirty percent of the trees here are already gone; the scarcity ratchets up the value of those that remain.

An Afghan security official named Shah Wali who works with the Americans recently went up to Kurangal to investigate. When he returned, he complained that the villagers were not cooperating; they had flouted his authority. But the villagers themselves told a different story. Some say he tried to extort their money. Complicating the matter is the fact that Shah Wali is an ex-Communist. The people of Kurangal see Shah Wali as a despised traitor aided by a new foreign power; the Americans see him as a partner in the war on terror. In an attempt to sort things out, the Americans have decided to bring Shah Wali up to Kurangal to face his accusers. This morning he's riding in another of the vehicles in our convoy.

The other reason for the trip is that the Americans just want to see Kurangal, introduce themselves to the tribesmen in Kunar's wooded interior, and let them know that they're around. And as for me, I'm here because I'm curious to see how the Americans work, how they talk with people.

"The Beach Boys," Doug tells me, as we rattle up the road. "I like the Beach Boys. All sorts of stuff."

Sartor and the security guards tease me when they see the Americans. "Oh, there's your tribe," they joke. This morning Rauf Mama and I met my "tribesmen" down at their base a little before six. We were greeted by Brian, to whom people refer as "Chief." Brian has a skinny neck and a prominent jaw; among Afghans, his physique inspires a certain curiosity: *What is wrong with the Americans? Don't they feed their soldiers?* To me it just looks like he's in really good shape, but to people in Kunar, if somebody has a six-pack, it means he doesn't get enough to eat.

The rides the Americans take through Kunar are carefully determined in advance, and my presence threw things out of whack. Brian scurried to adjust. He wondered if Rauf Mama and I might be willing to ride in separate cars. Rauf Mama said no, he wanted to tell me about all the places I'd be seeing today. I knew that he also wanted me as his translator. The Americans employ their own interpreters, but you can never be sure who they are or, more dangerously, who they know.

Rauf Mama is a respected and oft-requested mediator. Whenever there's a jirga or conflict in which the government should be involved—like this one in Kurangal—my father almost always sends him. (He is basically my father's unofficial deputy.) Rauf Mama sat out the internal conflicts that followed the Soviet war, making him an unusually agreeable figure. During the resistance itself, Rauf Mama was a prominent commander of the Wahhabi party, which evolved into Al Qaeda. Though he never held extremist beliefs, his partnerships with men who did enhance his credibility. When Rauf Mama sits with a group of tribesmen, blinking weirdly because of his false eye, bullets bulging from beneath the skin of his hand, and says, *This is not a jihad. I am not fighting this war against the Americans and the new government.*

Why are you?—it becomes difficult for the holdouts to legitimize their resistance.

These Humvees are the real thing, definitely not the kind you see rap stars or soccer moms driving. The inside of our car is austere and metallic. In the place where you'd see a cup holder, we have tracers and grenades. We pick up speed, reaching almost thirty-five miles per hour—lightning-fast by Kunar standards. The ride is noisy, like a bin of aluminum cans, but compared to our pickup, the Humvee is incredibly comfortable.

Doug tells me he got here a month and a half ago, then says, "When it's all said and done, I will have been here nine months and four days. Not that I'm keeping track."

"What do you guys get to do for your free time in Kunar?" I ask.

"Get shot at," Doug says. He takes out a snack of dried banana chips and offers them around. Rauf Mama chews one thoughtfully and announces that it's "definitely something different."

Rauf Mama is sitting in the back next to Brian. A fifth passenger, John, stands in the middle of the vehicle. His head pokes out through a kind of supersize sunroof, and he mans a gun on the top of the car.

Doug and I talk sports. "Are you a Pacers fan?" I ask, naming his home state's pro basketball team. We discuss the San Antonio Spurs' six-game championship triumph; the Giants and the 49ers; Sammy Sosa and his corked bat. ("Why would you even use it for practice?" I wonder.) The conversation is strangely normal. *Soldiers are just regular people, from places like Indiana,* I consider.

We barrel through some water, which splashes up around our tires. There are six cars in the convoy, one carrying several Afghan Military Force (AMF) soldiers who are along for the trip. (The AMF is basically a national collection of unrelated private militias filling in the gap while the new army is being trained.) As we move along, everyone is in constant radio contact. Whenever someone falls behind by even a couple hundred yards, the others pull over and wait for him to catch up; when the lead car gets ahead, it slows down until the chain rejoins. After about two hours we reach a bridge passable only on foot, so we get out of our Humvees. Then we do a head count. All of this meticulous planning seems familiar to me—it reminds me of elementary-school field trips—but is very strange to Rauf Mama.

We walk toward the bridge, a wood-and-rope contraption that looks like something out of an Indiana Jones movie. I step on, start swaying, and feel like I'm going to fall off; I steady myself and slow down. One of the Afghan soldiers yells, "Be careful! These bridges are tricky! You don't want to get hurt." His warning makes me defiant, and I cross in a quick jog.

On the other side villagers await us with pickups, and we pile in and begin a steep climb. Rauf Mama came up to Kurangal to take his own look around with a group of his young tribesmen who work as security guards at the governor's compound. They did the trip on foot, which must have been grueling; one of the young men couldn't walk for the next five days, and even the tireless Rauf Mama admitted that the journey was "a bit long."

During that trip Rauf Mama warned the group, "Be polite. They don't have much, so if they offer you something to drink, don't be greedy." But when they arrived in Kurangal, the villagers immediately offered them Coke. "Be polite, it's going to be warm," Rauf Mama whispered. The Cokes came out ice cold. "Wow," Rauf Mama said. "How do you get these Cokes so cold? Do you hide them in caves or something?"

"No, we have a fridge," one of the guys from Kurangal said.

"How did you get the fridge up here?" Rauf Mama asked, thinking back over the punishing climb.

"Oh, we have cars," the villager said.

"How is the refrigerator running?" Rauf Mama asked.

"Well, we have a generator," the man explained. "Everyone has a generator here."

That clinched it; these tribesmen were living in luxury worthy of an Afghan version of *Cribs*. Clearly somebody was profiting from the illegal timber trade. The trees in this area were about three feet around and jutted at weird angles from the sloping ground. Rauf Mama said the tribesmen used a special tool to fell them, "this thing called a *chunsha*."

"A *chunsha*?" I said. "What's a *chunsha*?"

"It's a really weird equipment that can cut down trees really fast," he said. "I heard a motor in the background, and I thought someone was on a motorcycle somewhere off in the distance, but a soldier told me, 'Oh no, that's a *chunsha.*'" (Or, of course, a *chainsaw;* somebody probably smuggled the tool down from China, in through Pakistan, and by the time it reached Kurangal, the international game of telephone had turned it into a *chunsha.*) When Rauf Mama and the guards found a man with a *chunsha,* they told him to stay still. Instead he ran, and as he fled, one of the guards fired his Kalashnikov. Luckily no one was hurt, but Rauf Mama slapped the guard on the head for being so careless. He was upset that the guard had taken the chance of injuring someone; later he told me he was sad that he'd had to become angry at one of his men like that.

The road beneath us is one of the worst I've seen. It's basically just loose rocks piled on top of one another. The whole thing seems as though it might collapse if one slips out of place, shooting us down to the bottom. One curve is so treacherous that we have to get out of the cars, perhaps so that they won't tip over.

Finally we make it to the village. It's taken us close to four hours to cover perhaps thirty miles—a distance I'd drive in California for an In-N-Out burger. A few Americans remain outside, for security purposes, and the rest of us proceed into a one-room structure—sort of a town hall. There are carpets and mats on the floor, some chairs, and a couple of sofas. We meet the members of the local shura. Some of them have dyed their beards red, and some are wearing eyeliner. The shura's speaker announces that they're still waiting for a few members to show up.

"Chief, they are still waiting for the other 'olders' to come," the Americans' translator says. The translator is an Afghan. His English is awkward and accented. He's dressed in a baggy T-shirt and is unshaven, with a three- or four-day shadow.

"There's more elders coming," someone clarifies.

"How long is that going to be?" Brian asks. "Guesstimation?"

"How long is this going to take?" the translator demands in Pashto. "Hurry it up! What's going on? These people are sitting here waiting. They don't have all day!" he exclaims rudely.

"It was really hard for me to round up all the tribal elders and the people of the shura," the shura's designated speaker apologizes. "Ever since five o'clock in the morning, I've sent out cars to get each person here. They're coming."

I jump in. "They're curious, they have a schedule they're trying to maintain," I say to the speaker. "Can you just give an approximate time, a half-hour—*nim sat*—an hour—*yo sat*—two hours—*dwa sat*?" The speaker estimates an hour.

"Is it possible to start now with the shura members we have," Brian wonders, "especially since we have the eldest and the speaker?"

I translate his question into Pashto as politely as I can, adding for good measure that "the Americans need to make it back before nightfall, they don't like to travel when it's dark, for security reasons."

Goodwill is easily lost in translation. Because their translator is himself disrespectful and condescending, the Americans come off as arrogant. Unfortunately, the pool of qualified interpreters is extremely limited. The explosion of interest in Arabic after 9/11 was not accompanied by a similar upsurge in attention to Afghan languages. Only a handful of universities in the United States offer courses in Pashto or Dari. The CIA is so desperate for Afghan-language speakers that a friend of my brother's found himself locked in a room for twenty-hour translating shifts; private contracting firms offer a cushier existence. I could easily make $100,000 a year if I offered myself up to such an outfit.

Now we're almost ready to begin. "Guys, we should have strategized," Brian says to the others. "You want me to lay it on the line, and we can spend an hour schmoozing it—or do you want to spend an hour schmoozing it, and have me lay it on the line at the end? Which one?" They choose option one, and Brian goes over the game plan: "Respect, reporting, and decent actions toward officials." They break the huddle, ready to go execute the play.

A soldier named Major Mark addresses the shura. He's a former football player with a huge build and a comb-over. "His father represents President Karzai," Mark says, indicating me. "President Karzai has imposed—it's a moratorium—anyway, he's preventing people from cutting down all the trees." At some length Mark discusses regulations, enforcement, and taxes; the translator relays the information in a drone. The shura's speaker gives a detailed, animated response. The translator offers Mark the barest summation: "He's saying that nobody ordered us before. He said we promise with this government that we're not going to cut it."

This translator is the one who isn't going to cut it. I look over to him and he tells me, in English, "Go ahead, man, go ahead," raising his hands in surrender. He's probably never been observed by someone who speaks both English and Pashto—someone who knows whether he's getting things right.

I start to tell Mark that there's more to the speaker's answer, but he stops me. "I have some English to translate to him," he says.

"It's something important," I insist. The speaker had noted that a lot of regimes have passed through Afghanistan in the last couple decades. During Rabbani's time, during the Taliban's time, during the time of Jahan Dad— the villagers did not stop smuggling, because the government was in on it. It was almost like a competition. "But we appreciate the appointment of this new governor," I translate, "and we respect him and will obey him, and we will listen to him."

As we speak, Shah Wali sits on the sofa, expressionless. His beard is so long it actually dangles and, as Rauf Mama says, "makes you think he might be a mullah instead of a godless Communist." Shah Wali is just one of a number of questionable characters who've gone over to the base and ingratiated themselves with its occupants. Rauf Mama would never go and kiss Major Mark's ass for a job—but the Communists will do that. They're opportunists; they've worked for foreigners before, and they'll do it again.

The people of Kurangal claim that when they refused to pay the bribes he demanded, Shah Wali beat them up; he arrested and imprisoned those who fought back. But the Americans seem blind to his possible misdeeds. The substance of the villagers' complaints about Shah Wali does not seem to reach them. For them, the only part of the story that matters is that the people of Kurangal responded inappropriately to a figure of authority.

"Just because people don't like other people?" Mark posits earnestly. "There's a personality conflict? Doesn't mean that you can't follow the duly appointed people in those positions." When I think of a personality conflict, I think of co-workers bad-mouthing each other beside the water cooler, not adversaries who fought a brutal war. That the Americans often fail to appreciate the intensity of the nation's past worries me. Their point of reference isn't Afghanistan's experience—it's their own.

"For instance, in the United States, if I get fined from a policeman for driving too fast," says Mark, "but I think I was driving the speed limit, I don't shoot the policeman. I don't run him over and say, 'I'm not going to listen to you because I was right and you were wrong.' I go through the official system."

I translate, substituting *jareyma,* or "fine," for "speeding ticket," but the words are more fundamentally flawed. This policeman analogy, if Mark really wanted to use it, would go something like this: Imagine that this policeman had come into your house and robbed you, raped your wife, and maybe killed a couple of your kids. Then the next time you see him, he's pulling you over for going 57 in a 55-miles-per-hour zone.

The exchange continues. I translate the speaker's words to Mark: "We understand that we have to obey the central government, the provincial government, and we do obey them. But if there's some guy coming here, like thuggery, or running it like a mafia, I can't be responsible for that."

Translation is like an extremely elongated satellite delay. The person on the other end has long been idle by the time the words come through. They seem to spend the interval thinking of the next thing they want to say, and inevitably they forge ahead with the statement they've planned out— making the conversation a series of declarations rather than reactions.

"He still gets the point I'm talking about?" Mark backtracks now. "When an official representative comes, if he has a problem with an official representative, if he thinks they're being corrupt or doing something, then it's his responsibility as a leader to take it to the next level." He continues: "Do you see what I'm saying? There's other ways to work around it versus armed revolt and getting in conflict with the government forces."

When Shah Wali finally joins the conversation, you can tell he's a little worried. He speaks superfast, his beard flopping over his belly, and soon the shura members are interrupting, and everyone's words overlap.

"He's saying I wasn't there at that time," the translator interjects, trying to sift through the din.

"Stop! Stop! Stop!" Mark yells.

"They are just pouring their hearts out," I try to explain. " 'Oh you did this, then you did that.' "

"It's like the Ahmed Springer show," Mark says. "Are you familiar with the Jerry Springer show?" he asks, making sure I get the joke. He attempts to restore order. "One person at a time," he declares. "In short paragraphs or short sentences."

When the commotion dwindles, Mark tries to wrap things up. He says that Shah Wali is going to get another government order to "make sure no illegal cutting is going on. That means he's going to be back here."

The reaction to this news isn't good; the fight is on the verge of breaking out again. "We might as well move on from it," I say, trying to stanch it. "Don't mention either him or—"

Mark interrupts. "I'm giving them a solution," he insists.

But Mark's solution does little to address the problem that the people of Kurangal are too afraid to say anything. The meeting has reinforced the perception that Shah Wali is backed by the U.S. troops, and nobody wants to risk upsetting them. Think of it this way: Shah Wali is like the neighborhood bully who derives his power by invoking the threat of his older brother. The older brother is unaware of the bluff, but when he shows up, everyone is cowed. *Oh my God, here comes the older brother.* Similarly, the ex-Communists' alliance with the Americans is an act of self-protection. These men—seen as the firestarters of Afghanistan's long inferno—are often so reviled that they can't go back to their own villages. They've alienated themselves from their countrymen; by befriending them, the Americans are in danger of doing the same.

Mark says, "Everybody's calm now?" There are murmurs of agreement. Next, he says, we'll talk about "the projects that we can do to bring peace and stability."

Everyone is eager to discuss the improvements the Americans might be able to facilitate—a school, a health clinic, a real bridge down at the bottom of the mountain. Doug, our Humvee driver, takes charge.

"I am going to tell you that I cannot promise you we're going to build you a clinic, a school, a road, or a bridge," Doug says plainly. "I will not promise you that, and if another soldier promised you that, I can't guarantee that those things are going to happen." He continues, "I can tell you that we have submitted the paperwork to try and build a school here, but I am waiting on approval from my generals to see if we can do that."

Sometimes it seems like nobody can make a decision except for President

Bush; everybody else has to wait around for their bosses' opinions. It doesn't make the Americans seem like the strongest of allies when they can't even promise to build a bridge. Here in Kurangal the infrastructure is nonexistent. Villagers don't even have plumbing; they collect their water in buckets. "We can get some pipe," Doug offers now, "if they can provide the labor to do their project."

I translate, then tell Doug, "Labor isn't a problem."

"I don't want them to take the pipe and just look at it," Doug warns. "Or I don't want the pipe to be sold again."

Then it becomes clear that the pipe is literally all the Americans are supplying; engineers and plans aren't part of the package.

"They don't have engineers capable of doing that," I report back to Doug. "They thought you meant hard labor."

The villagers want us to have lunch with them, but before we sit down to eat, there's one last thing. "I want to get a picture of him"—Mark indicates the shura's speaker—"shaking Shah Wali's hand." The Americans have been taking pictures all morning, posing before backdrops like the Indiana Jones bridge, holding up their guns. Now, next to a pile of wood, the speaker and Shah Wali smile and shake hands. A camera snaps, and the meeting is frozen on this congenial end.

Then we stand around outside while the villagers prepare the meal. I'm talking with Brian when a man comes up and says that Shah Wali robbed him of more than a thousand dollars. This might be three times a year's salary. Brian explains that taking such a complaint to the proper authorities—for example, to my father instead of to a U.S. soldier—is "the big picture that we're trying to stress." Still, he promises to discuss this particular incident with Shah Wali's boss.

As I translate, Shah Wali stands nearby, eyeing us menacingly.

"I think he's getting kind of worried because Shah Wali is right behind us," I tell Brian.

Brian looks over and confirms that Shah Wali is staring at us. He tells the man that he is always welcome to visit the base. The man seems disappointed, but there's nothing left to say. He nods and walks away.

Then I stand around by the pickups with a couple soldiers. "Everybody's just so tribal in this area," John says. "They're used to having their own way and shit."

John appears to be among the youngest of the troops. "I was amazed when I got here," he tells me. "I've been all over," he says. "But never to basically a fourth-world country."

"One of the few things that we have going for us is, they're pretty much just weary of war," observes Brian.

"Exactly," I say, getting excited. Sometimes the Americans read the mood just right. "That's why I think Afghanistan has a chance, especially compared to other areas."

"There's hope," John agrees. "There's hope."

I see a soldier with some flags. "What's he doing? Putting out the American flag?" I'm unable to mask my disapproval.

But the flag features a dove and represents Afghan-American cooperation. "It's kind of a neat product—you ought to grab one," Brian suggests.

"Yeah, that's pretty cool," I say.

"Some people tear them up and throw them away," another soldier says. "Some people are real assholes about it."

"Are you serious? Why?" I ask.

"'Cause there's some shitheads out there, I guess," the soldier ventures. "Some people honestly think we're the Russians."

We sit on the floor for lunch, at which we're served bread, Coke, and meat. There's also a big bowl of hard candy. One soldier scoops up fifteen or twenty pieces. I explain to a villager curious about the American diet that the soldier won't eat this himself; he's stockpiling it to throw to children along the road.

I notice that Shah Wali is pretty enthusiastic about the lunch. He's eating the meat down to the bone, then breaking the bone and sucking the marrow out of that. One of the Americans turns to his friend and says, "Holy shit. Did you see that? He chewed out the bone, man." His tone is deliberately casual, as if he's trying to conceal from the villagers his true shock. But it doesn't matter; English is gibberish to all of them.

In California my brother and I often switch into Pashto when we want to discuss something private. We could be among strangers in a crowded restaurant, or even in the presence of people we know. I've always thought of it as sort of our code language. Once you get used to it, it's hard to imagine existing without it. I do it here in Kunar, too, when I'm around the Americans, consulting with my father in Pashto in the midst of a conversation conducted in English.

The lunch continues, Shah Wali suctioning out marrow, the Afghans dipping their bread in pools of yogurt, the Americans shifting their cramped, muscular limbs as we're poured yet another cup of tea, everyone chattering, but both sides speaking in code.

18

WE DRIVE BACK FROM KURANGAL in the rain. It's like being in a Humvee commercial, the car bucking through a spectacular setting. We're on the floor of the Pech Valley. It's a real valley—you can see its outlines—not some gigantic metro area referred to by the term. Gold-colored mountains rise up on either side of us like walls. Trees are clustered here and there, but for the most part this place is open. It's a lush stripe of land, as green as a golf course fairway—with landmines in place of sandtraps.

No matter where you go in Kunar, the trip home takes longer than the trip out. The road you travel in on is almost always the one on which you return. Anyone who saw our convoy pass this morning has had plenty of time to plant a mine in our path, so the Americans are being extra-vigilant. A threat has already stopped us once.

After lunch we said our goodbyes and started back down the mountain, the villagers' pickups bumping over the lips of unevenly laid rock. Suddenly we stopped, and the Americans got out of the cars, stationed themselves in lookout positions, and started yelling commands at one another: *I want to make sure we're looking that way, all right? Mark, set 'em up. Concentrate. Maintain awareness over there.*

I slid out of my seat. "Is there something going on?" I asked John.

"Yeah, there's a wire across the road down there," he said.

"Hey John, send Hyder down here!" a soldier yelled, and I jogged to meet him. "There's a possible IED explosive in the road—that's why we stopped," he explained. (An IED is an "improvised explosive device.") The soldiers were "watching a ridgeline for the bad guys," and they wanted me to ask some of the Afghans to move out of the way.

The group shifted, and I asked, "Is that cool?"

"Yeah, yeah," the soldier said. "I just need some space here." The whole area felt tight. We were hemmed in by mountains, and the pickups crowded the narrow road.

An American wearing what looked like a very small metal detector approached. Then he flopped down on his belly and began slithering toward the wire. The Afghans broke into laughter, including Rauf Mama, who offered, "Just let me yank it. Trust me. We don't have to waste so much time."

"Can you please move away from the area? He's trying to concentrate," an American scolded. The Afghans quieted down once they realized the guy's feelings might be getting hurt. But the spectacle only confirmed their impression that the Americans are too cautious.

In Kunar the U.S. troops are viewed as tense—quick to raise alarm—which hurts their reputation. (I talk to Doug about Sammy Sosa and come to this conclusion: *Hey, these guys are so vulnerable—they're just like us!* The Afghans see a technician with an electronic box on his belly and arrive at the inverse: *Hey, these guys are so vulnerable—they're not at all like us!*) In a place where institutions are weak, people are going to align themselves with who's strong. You don't have to have the biggest guns or the best airplanes, but you must have courage. Mixed with the almost universal hatred of the Russians is a genuine measure of respect. The Soviet forces were tenacious; they confronted the mujahedeen in areas where the Americans strain to imagine doing battle. Earlier today in Kurangal Mark told me to ask the villagers if the Russians had really come up here.

"Yes, of course," one of the elders replied.

Mark shook his head in disbelief. "How the hell did they fight up here?" he wondered.

Now, as the American technician continued inchworming toward the mine, somebody mentioned an old couple we'd passed moments earlier. "Why don't you go ask that fucker if he's got a phone or a radio," a soldier suggested.

"We could hike up to 'em," someone offered. A guy cleared his throat and spit out a loogie. Then a group of us set off to talk to the pair. The suspicion was that the old man might be the signal guy, carrying a communications device over which he could issue the instruction to detonate the mine. Our feet crunched on the quiet road.

We found the old couple sitting together on the ground. The man's head was hunched down into his shoulders, and he hugged himself with a beat-up shawl. His wife was wearing a burka. Because a woman was present, Rauf Mama said we should stop. "Yeah, he's got his wife with him. I don't think—" I started. "Can we call him over here?"

"Sure, not gonna disturb his wife?" Brian said.

"Yeah," I said.

Rauf Mama began to question the old man, who trembled as he spoke. He and his wife were on their way to Asadabad; they were tired, so they'd stopped here to rest. They thought they might be able to hitch a ride along this road.

Brian still wanted to search him. "Gotta check," he said. "Can't be too careful when your life's on the line. I don't know what he's got in there"— Brian indicated the man's bundles—"as long as it ain't something that could kill me."

The man was carrying a plant, holy water, and a prayer rug.

Now Brian apologized for the encounter. "Please forgive us if we disturbed your rest," he began.

I translated, then relayed the old man's response: "No, we don't have a problem. This is our country. We want peace and security, so we don't mind you guys taking measures."

"I'm always glad when I hear a humble man express that," said Brian. He continued: "If you see something in the road that looks like an explosive, or a wire, don't do anything about it yourself. Contact an official." It was like a lecture from a forest ranger who thinks he sees a lighter in your hand, but you don't have a lighter in your hand, so to cover his blunder, he acts like what he intended to do all along was to remind you never to smoke.

"Another thing, for your own safety, don't get any closer to us than you are now," Brian warned, indicating the span of a couple hundred yards that separated us from the troops below. The man's wife sat off to the side like a ghost.

Then someone must have waved reassuringly to Brian, because he announced, "All right, we're heading back. They've either got it cleared, or realized it wasn't a danger. Have a good day, man," he said to the old peasant.

"*Tashakur,*" I told him. *Thank you.*

Brian shot down the road ahead of me and Rauf Mama. "Unusual stick," a soldier announced as we approached. He waved a little twig. "Just sticking straight out of the road. It was just good exercise," he joked.

"A dress rehearsal," offered John.

"Hey, Hyder," another soldier called. "Tell them everything's okay. We're going to head out." I yelled out in Pashto to the Afghans and climbed back into the car.

As we continued down the mountain, the wind picked up, and by the time we reached the Indiana Jones bridge, the gusts had stirred up so much dust that I could hardly see. I ducked my head and bore forward, stepping quickly, so that the person behind me wouldn't think I was—God forbid—being cautious. The Afghan soldier who'd told me to watch myself this morning now announced, "Damn, you're pretty fast!" On the other side, people coughed and cleared their throats. We got into the Humvees, the engines began to rumble, the rushing sound of the river faded, and we took a right into the valley.

Now the convoy is passing through villages that are quiet in the late afternoon. In our car, the Americans ask me to tell Rauf Mama that they've realized Shah Wali isn't a very good guy—that they understand this makes Rauf Mama happy. We're also talking about reconstruction. Brian tells Rauf Mama that America wants to bring peace and stability to Afghanistan—build roads, furnish electricity, fulfill the hopes of the people here. Doug brings up the theory of the social contract, and the idea appeals to Rauf Mama. "Hey, their driver's kind of smart," he tells me.

I realize that Rauf Mama thinks that driving the Humvee is Doug's only job. "No, no, he's not like a chauffeur," I correct him. I explain that I think Doug is an engineer in the civil affairs unit.

"Oh, he's an engineer! I thought he was just a driver. No wonder he's talking so smart," Rauf Mama says.

Then one of the cars in the convoy breaks down. "Six-seven-oh," someone says into the radio. "Roger, just west of the Watapur district."

Suddenly I really have to go to the bathroom. My stomach twists, and I turn to my uncle. "Mama, I gotta go. Where should I go?" I ask.

Rauf Mama and I get out of the car. Thankfully today I've followed my father's standard advice: *Don't forget toilet paper—you're going to need it.* Rauf Mama leads the way, and I walk behind him, pulling the wad out of my pocket. I'm in luck, because we're near the local district office—a mud hut—and they might actually have a bathroom. When we get there, it's occupied; the man inside is taking forever, and I try to distract myself, but it's not working. Meanwhile I'm trying to be polite to the people in the office, who know I'm the governor's son. They keep yelling, "Hurry the hell up! The governor's son is in line!" Then at last it's my turn, and I climb a ladder made of sticks. At the top are the facilities—a little hole.

When I emerge, we're offered tea, but because we have to get back to the convoy, we refuse. It's not long before we're off. We go only a couple hundred yards before there's a *bang!*

Flat tire, I think to myself. But then smoke rises, and I realize that this isn't a blow-out—it's an ambush.

I feel a rush of blood and I duck to the floor. I see John's brown pants and hear the din of the gun he mans up above. The fire is constant, like drums, occasionally punctuated by the *ping* of a shell falling to the floor, like a cymbal. Instinctively, I turn on my minidisc recorder.

Everybody's yelling at one another:
Check the fire, John, check the fire!
Watch those civilians!
Point of origin, point of origin, point of origin!
Reloading!
Where they at? I can't see shit!

I definitely hear it downrange, I just don't see it.

They're still shootin'!

Where is that?

"You guys just stay down over there, all right?" That's Doug, shouting to me and Rauf Mama. "Yeah, I'm trying to stay down as much as I can," I say anxiously. "How can I get down more than this?" I'm totally exposed; a bullet could easily strike me through the open windows out of which Brian and Doug point their M-16s. They're protected head to toe, encased in helmets and plated vests; my kameez partoog offers no defense.

"Like a cake almost," Brian advises. "Just stay low."

Urgently, I turn to Rauf Mama. But as I'm telling him to stay low, I realize he's acting as though there's nothing to fear. "I'm fine," he assures me. "I've been through this a lot of times. They're just trying to scare the Americans." He explains that there's almost no way the shots could hit us from this angle. His only suggestion is editorial: "Turn on your recorder. Those people might be interested in this." I tell him it's already going.

Fuckin' fire, I can't tell whether it was coming in or going out.

Line those up! Line those up!

Do you see anybody out in the open?

No, I don't.

There's firing out on the ridge.

That's ours.

I can't see anything.

In the mountains, but I don't see shit else.

Hey, you guys got anything?

If you don't have a target . . . QUIT SHOOTING!

"I'm not sure about your buddies here," Rauf Mama says. "I'm more worried about one of them shooting us than ambushers."

I notice that everybody seems to be looking in just one direction, off to our left. I try to make sure that they're aware of the unsecured area; John signals to a soldier named Terry, who whips around accordingly.

"Okay, John, check our three o'clock. Somebody's pointing to our three," Doug says.

"No, no, I was pointing to him," John says, "tellin' him, they're all lookin' this way."

"Terry was pointing to our three o'clock," Doug maintains. Now there's confusion; Brian jumps out of his seat and runs around to the right side of the car for a better view. *Oh man,* I think, *I should have kept quiet. Now they think they're getting ambushed from two sides.*

Then there's an urgent yell—*Get in! Get in!*—and the car door slams. John's shooting from up top—a deafening *poohpingpoohpingpoohping-poohping!* We start barreling through the valley. The heat from the guns makes it smell like something's burning. Shells have cascaded to the floor. They're busted scraps of metal with little circles the bullet broke through.

"Don't shoot wild, guys!" someone yells. "Stop! Stop!"

We brake and I crouch down again.

What ya got, Chief?

Nine o'clock!

Only shoot at targets, okay! Only shoot at targets!

Brian gets out of the car and addresses me. "You're going to have to relay commands from these guys, who are gonna be on the radio," he instructs. "You're gonna yell at me, I'm gonna be on that hilltop with those AMF guys, okay?"

"All right, do you want me to get down?" I say a little hopefully. Now, full of adrenaline, I wouldn't mind entering the fray.

"No, you just stay in here, you stay safe, but if he has something that comes over the radio, you yell it to me, I'll hear ya," Brian says.

"All right, all right, sure," I agree.

Major Mark, standing alongside, indicates Rauf Mama: "And tell him to pull up his glass so he doesn't get a bullet." I start to translate, but Mark breaks in before I finish: "We don't need him to lose the other eye." I laugh loudly at his joke.

I hear where they're coming from, but I don't see anybody.

Now they're just running wild.

This one right here to our nine o'clock, that's where I heard it coming out of.

Okay, where the tracers just hit?

Roger that, I can't get a good target.

Where at? Our nine o'clock? Nine o'clock high on the ridge? Where at? Mark the target!

Is it on the ridgeline or down below, John?

From where you're sitting, your nine.

Now, perhaps in place of fear, I feel outrage: *Who the fuck are these people? God, that pisses me off. I've never really been shot at before.* I'm seized with the desire to pick up the M-16 at my feet. It's a primal impulse: anger at another who dares to try to take your life. *Hell no, how dare you?*

I wish I had better eyes on.

The soldier's comment reminds me of the joke about Rauf Mama, and I turn back to him to go over it again. Then Doug tries to get my attention: "Hey! Hey! Yell to Chief, we're gonna move, get everybody back over here."

"Chief, we're gonna move, get everybody outta here, back in the cars!" I holler to Brian. There's no reaction. "I don't think he heard me—he's way down," I say to Doug. "Chief!" I try again.

Then there's a strange dull boom.

"What the fuck was that?" John says. "Was that a rocket?"

Shells rain down from John's gun. At times he pumps it furiously, like a guy in a movie. I call for Brian again. "Chief! Chief!" I try.

"Is he listenin'? Can he hear you?" Doug asks.

"Want me to go down and try and get him?" I offer.

"Get Chief back here, John," Doug orders.

"If you want, I can go down," I say again.

"One and four, one and four, this is five," Doug says over the radio.

I holler, "Chief!" and finally, Brian starts heading over. Major Mark is on his way, too. "Hold it up! Hold it up!" he booms from a distance.

"Here's what's happening," Mark says when he reaches the car. His words come out in urgent bursts. "We're going to bound through—our two vehicles—we'll take the lead—establish another support position—then we're gonna bound through and keep on going."

"Roger," someone affirms.

"Hey, sir?" Doug says.

"What?" Mark says brusquely.

Doug says something about the AMF soldiers, and Mark's response is almost delirious with impatience: "That's right—we need to—you give me your fucking thumbs-up, go, get 'em in the vehicle! Go!" he yells, running off. "Goddammit, let's go!"

The guns start pattering. Mark yells, "Move it, get ready to come follow on me!"

Something clinks as it tumbles to the floor of our Humvee, and Doug says, "I got it sir, I got it sir."

"Can you grab that next box of fifty?" John says.

Our Humvees peel out. The soldiers are still firing, and someone yells, "Watch the civilians, John!" I see a guy hiding behind a tree, a dog running away. Even after we've escaped the danger, our speed is breakneck, and nothing feels normal. I wave to some kids on the side of the road, conscious of myself waving to some kids on the side of the road, of a mundane activity following an extraordinary one.

It takes us only about twenty minutes to reach Asadabad. "Hey, are you guys still comfortable getting out at the traffic circle?" Brian asks.

"Yeah, yeah, we're fine," I say. We pull in near the rotary at the end of the marketplace, and Rauf Mama and I hop out of the car.

"Sure you don't want a ride?" Brian checks again. "They're yellin' and hollerin'. Something's goin' on."

Suddenly the people in the marketplace are running in different directions, and a soldier is shouting, "Go! Go! Go!" and making threatening motions with the machine gun on top of his car.

"Do you want us to get back in the car?" I ask Brian.

"I would be more comfortable," he says. "I would protect you with my life as long as I can."

Back at the governor's compound, I hop down out of the Humvee. "See you guys soon," I say. "Take care."

"All right, buddy," one of the soldiers says. "We'll play pool, watch movies, do something."

"Yeah, watch movies, all right, man," I say.

I walk through the gates, now officially on the other side of the experience. Almost as soon as I enter the courtyard, I see Sartor. I give him my headphones and watch as he listens to the recording of the ambush. Soon the security guards gather. *My turn!* they say, passing the headphones around. *Look, he's not scared! He's talking into his microphone!* I feel as if I've undergone the baptism for Kunar; the ambush was a kind of initiation rite. Proud that I've earned some legitimacy with the guards, I go to find my father.

He's sitting beside the river, talking to a couple of people. I make a beeline for the group and say, "I have to tell you something."

"All right, just wait until I'm done," he says.

"No, no, you have to get up for just a minute," I say firmly.

My father excuses himself, and we walk a little distance away. "I just got ambushed," I tell him. "It was a twenty-five-minute firefight." The story spills out of me.

"Did anybody get killed?" my father asks. His expression is impassive.

"No," I say.

"Did anybody get injured?"

"No," I say.

"You really interrupted my meeting for that, Hyder?" my father says sternly.

Inside I'm screaming: *But I got ambushed!* I attempt to interest my father in my minidisc recording. He listens briefly and gives the headphones back to me. Then, seeming to realize he might be ruining my moment, he alludes to my radio documentary—"It's a good thing they're American forces so that the conversation is in English"—and then he returns to the river's edge. I start back up to the house. One of the most electric experiences of my life has elicited a shrug—and a reprimand—from my father. But it isn't hard to figure out why. *Maybe it isn't such a big deal for my dad,* I reason, *who's seen a lot of that.*

My father acted as though his meeting were more serious than my ambush, and in a way he was right. It was easy to be brave just for a second; working day in and day out for the country was harder. My glory was fleeting. My father's setbacks—like the event that was about to follow—were not.

19

"PLEASE, PLEASE," THE MAN SAYS to me in shaky English. "Please save my brother."

I don't like the fact that the man, an Afghan in his twenties, is speaking English. Someone has probably told him that the governor's son is here from America and he thinks he knows how to ingratiate himself with me. The man's watery eyes are fixed on mine, awaiting my response, and I want to tell him to speak to me in Pashto, but I don't. Instead I give him a non-committal nod and take a seat against the wall.

It's a Wednesday afternoon, and I'm in my father's office. Here with us are several tribal elders from a valley near the border; the English speaker, who continues to look at me imploringly; and his brother, who has flowing hair and sits slightly apart from the rest of us, his special status deriving from his position on the U.S. forces' most-wanted list. His name is Abdul Wali, and he is a suspected insurgent.

It's quiet in the room; sun falls through the windows that look out over the garden. My father thanks the elders for coming, and attention turns to Abdul Wali. "Were you involved in the rocket attacks?" says my father.

The rockets continue to awaken us a couple of times a week. Launched from the border areas to the east, they spin out over the Kunar River, then land, miles or yards away, with a whistle and a boom. American journalists and politicians would blame the strikes on their bogeyman, Al Qaeda, but here in Kunar we blame the "opposition" or, in Pashto, the *mukhalafeen*. The mukhalafeen are too multifarious to categorize. These rocket attacks, for example, are not the work of a single group. The attacks are probably funded by Arabs who are sheltered by Pakistan; orchestrated by loyalists of Gulbiddin Hekmatyar or the Taliban; and carried out by deeply impoverished men who are paid for their efforts.

There's little reason to be frightened by the rockets. They're wildly inaccurate—they usually land in a random-ass field. They're launched willy-nilly by the mukhalafeen to scare away nongovernmental organizations (NGOs) and other foreign aid groups, and in this aim, at least, they hit their mark. One evening a rocket lands about a quarter-mile from the UN refugee aid office in Asadabad, and within a week the group (the UNHCR) has pulled out of Kunar. A subsequent UN press briefing says that "unless there will be some level of security guarantees by all concerned at the border area, it is difficult to foresee when we will be able to resume aid operations there." It's easy to see how each such departure creates a ripple effect that ultimately stalls development.

But the Americans and my father joke that the rockets are a good sign. Before my father arrived, the rockets landed down the road near the U.S. base. Now they're being directed at the governor's house, too, an indication that unlike his predecessors, my father represents a genuine threat to the mukhalafeen.

"Thank you for coming and turning him in," my father tells the tribal elders who've accompanied Abdul Wali. "We have to promote stability and ensure security by ourselves." *By ourselves*—meaning, *without the Americans*. The coalition forces are a temporary balm; any lasting peace will be up to us. We discuss issues like these for a while, and eventually the tribal elders file out of the room, leaving me and my father alone with Abdul Wali and his brother.

After a number of reports linked Abdul Wali to the rocket attacks, the U.S. troops decided to apprehend him. They wanted to capture him in a nighttime raid. But my father asked them to let him try to get in touch with

Abdul Wali himself, and soon it was arranged that he would come to the compound to discuss the situation.

Today in my father's office Abdul Wali tells us he is innocent. When he speaks, his voice cracks, and he strikes me as too fearful to be the kind of person who would trek into the border areas to launch rockets. There's a simplicity to him, and it's easier for me to picture him plowing a field than plotting a terror attack.

I don't know what to make of his brother. He stares at me with a look that seems almost ablaze. But then his light-colored eyes will dart away and he'll start crying, making him seem, if anything, more unsettled than the actual suspect, Abdul Wali. Together their agitation reaches such a pitch that occasionally it's difficult to understand their meaning: "Did you do it or not?" my father says at one point, in exasperation. *No, no, no, of course not,* they insist.

Abdul Wali believes he's been targeted by some adversaries in a tribal feud. After so many years of war, there are very few people in Kunar without enemies. Everybody has a side, but there aren't just two sides, like Taliban or anti-Taliban—there are dozens. I can't even name all the tribes in Kunar. There are Mashwanai, who come from the higher parts of the mountains; Salarzai, who straddle both sides of the border; and Safi, who are everywhere. (Their ubiquity is fodder for jokes: *The men went to the moon, and they ran into a guy from Safi who was already there.*) Of course the Americans are used as tools in these internal battles. Don't like a certain Ahmed or Mahmoud? Say that he has a Taliban hideout in his home. If you're lucky, the Americans will bomb it for you, wiping out your enemy and his male relatives in a single swoop.

The U.S. troops in Kunar are in an unenviable position—one American tells me that perhaps ninety percent of the information they get is completely false. The targets of these allegations are also backed into a corner. How can they trust newcomers who clearly don't understand the situation? You can see why even the innocent hole up in their houses, hoping that suspicion will just disappear, their silence all the while increasing the risk of a raid by the U.S. forces.

Today in the office Abdul Wali is scared. "Please, can't you make the

Americans come here?" he pleads with my father. Though he's a grown man in his twenties, his fear is almost childlike.

His brother explains that Abdul Wali might have a hard time answering the Americans' questions. I can see what he means; there's something a little off about Abdul Wali. Mentally, maybe he's slow; or perhaps he's just lived such a simple life that he's at a loss in any unfamiliar element. By comparison, his brother seems almost worldly, with his few phrases of English, his trimmed beard, and the way the tribal elders sometimes refer to him as "doctor." Still, he is clearly frightened of what awaits his brother at the American base.

There are pervasive rumors of torture. Abdul Wali and his brother have heard all kinds of stories. The Americans wake you in the middle of the night and beat you, they tell us; they strip you naked and make you lie on the floor. They even mention disembowelment.

"That's nonsense," my father says. Then he does something known in Afghanistan as *zamanat*. In Islamic law, *zamanat* refers to a financial transaction, to backing someone as a guarantor. But *zamanat* can also mean vouching for someone's aptitude or character—in this case, my father's personal avowal of the Americans' trustworthiness and virtue.

"I will send my son with you to the Americans," my father reassures Abdul Wali. "He will be there with you to translate and talk to them."

My father sees Abdul Wali's presence in the capital, however tremulous, as an encouraging sign. It ratifies the outcome of a case resolved several weeks ago involving a local man named Saleh Muhammad.

Like Abdul Wali, Saleh Muhammad was wanted by the Americans. They raided his home, an incident that brought such shame upon the family that Saleh Muhammad was ready to flee to the Punjab region deep inside Pakistan, as if the tribal areas just across the border wouldn't be far enough. The Americans were planning another raid when my father suggested, "Let me try it the Afghan way." My father dispatched his aide Yossef with a letter asking Saleh Muhammad to come to the capital. Saleh Muhammad was relieved to get the letter and agreed to accompany Yossef back to Asadabad the very next day. There he met with my father at the governor's compound, proclaimed his innocence, and was sent to see the Americans.

The Americans interrogated him and held him for three days. Then they brought him back to the governor's compound and said that they had been mistaken. "Do whatever you want to do with him," they said to my father. "He's not a threat to us."

It worked out well for everyone. The Americans were saved a search mission and the accompanying risks. My father was happy that the resolution was reached cooperatively. And as for Saleh Muhammad, he stayed at the compound for a couple weeks, palled around with the security guards, and eventually tried to find a position with the local government.

Abdul Wali and I climb into the pickup, and start for the American base. If you were making a relief map of our location, you'd papier-mâché two rows of really high mountains, then set them down on posterboard so close together that you could barely peer down to see what was in between. That's where we are, bouncing along the narrow bed of the valley, hugging the Kunar River as we head south along the one main road in the province. The scenery is basically unchanging during the short ride to the base.

We pull in, and I tell an Afghan soldier on guard that I need to speak to a translator. When the translator, a local Afghan employed by the U.S. military, appears, I say that I need to talk to Steve, an intelligence officer, and that it's important.

The translator escorts us to a plain room. Inside are several wooden chairs with cushions. It's more than a hundred degrees, and above us a fan whirs wildly. Soon Abdul Wali and I are joined by three men, all of whom I've met before: Steve, Dave, and Brian.

"This is Abdul Wali," I say. The three men look surprised. But despite the unexpected visit, they seem well prepared, launching almost immediately into an interrogation. The local translator sits with us in the room, but perhaps because the Americans already know me and are more comfortable with me culturally, they don't even look at their own guy.

"Ask him this," Brian says to me. "Are you in contact with anyone in Al Qaeda?" Abdul Wali says no, and Brian follows up with, "Have you been in contact with anyone in Al Qaeda?" *No.*

"Are you in contact with anyone in Hig?" Brian asks. *What the hell,* I think. Then I realize Brian is speaking an acronym, HIG, that the Americans use to refer to Hizb-i-Islami, Gulbiddin Hekmatyar's fundamentalist party.

In his friendly southern accent, Brian dispenses with the nuts and bolts—*Have you been in contact with Taliban? Were you Taliban?*—lingering when the subject turns to Pakistan.

"Have you been to Pakistan recently?" Brian asks Abdul Wali, and the answer is yes. "What were you doing in Pakistan?"

"I had to get some money from somebody who owed me a debt," Abdul Wali replies, "and then pay another person off."

"How long ago were you in Pakistan?"

Abdul Wali looks confused, and I doubt he'll be able to answer. People in Kunar don't have calendars; most of them don't even know how old they are. (If you ask someone his age, you're in line for an exchange like:

Hmm, let's see—well, my beard started growing just as I began fighting the Soviets.

And when was that?

Well, right around the time we got the Stingers.

So then you calculate: The Stingers arrived in 1986, at which time his beard was just coming in, making him, let's say, sixteen then, so thirty-three now.)

"You don't have to give us a specific date," Brian says. "Was it two, three days ago, two, three weeks ago, two, three months ago?"

"I don't know," Abdul Wali replies. "It's really hard for me to say."

The Americans exchange glances. "Can you at least say a week or two weeks, or a month or two months, or something?" I prod him. But he can't. For him, time unfolds forward—there is no way to go back later and try to fix it in a structure.

"I just, I go to sleep, I wake up, and there's a next day. I feed myself, I go to sleep, and there's a next day," he explains.

The Americans aren't buying it. Dave, who is built like an out-of-shape Sylvester Stallone, asks Abdul Wali where he was fourteen days ago, on a night when three rockets were fired in quick succession at the American base. "How could you not know where you were on the night three rockets were fired?" he scoffs.

"I don't know," Abdul Wali says. "Maybe they woke me up, and I just went back to sleep and didn't pay too much attention to it." Abdul Wali explains that his nights are often punctuated by explosions. Missiles are launched from nearby locations, including the American base. Feuding tribesmen exchange gunfire or grenades. And explosives are sometimes detonated in the construction of new roads.

When I finish translating the answer, Brian says that villagers with a legitimate use for explosives inform the Americans of their plans weeks in advance. It's not really the right moment to explain that local Afghans are known to plan explosions for no reason, just to have an excuse to go to the Americans and ingratiate themselves by appearing to do the right thing. (Another common trick is to bury a mine, then call on the Americans to "alert" them to the hazard. "See, this is the kind of cooperation we're talking about," an unsuspecting soldier will say, when reporting such an incident to my father.)

Dave doesn't believe Abdul Wali's story, either. "Oh no," he says to him nastily, "missiles have a very distinct sound." We are all sitting in the wooden chairs; rarely does anyone stand. But even seated, Dave seems enlarged by anger. His demeanor feels put on, as if he is acting the role of a fearsome interrogator (especially compared to Brian, whose southern hospitality softens even his grilling of this suspected terrorist). Dave fixes Abdul Wali with an unrelenting stare. Abdul Wali returns a nervous smile.

"Translate this to him!" Dave explodes. "This is not a joking matter. Don't smile!"

"I'm sorry, I didn't mean to offend him," Abdul Wali replies anxiously. "It's very hard for me, I can't understand anything he's saying. He was staring at me, and I didn't know what to do. What should I do?" he asks me.

I'm not sure what to tell him. Dave's behavior is unpredictable. Only days ago I had a friendly conversation with him about his little son, who can say his ABCs and count from one to twenty and back down again. But now he seems full of rage. "If you're lying, your whole family, your kids, they'll all get hurt from this," he threatens.

As I translate, I start to feel like Dave's words to Abdul Wali are my own, and all I want to do is stop saying these things to him. "Your situation's getting worse," Dave warns. How am I supposed to tell that to Abdul

Wali, when my father assured him that coming to the base would make everything better?

Nobody is behaving the way they would with a regular translator; both sides add comments meant only for me. In one ear I have Abdul Wali pleading, "I'm innocent, I'm innocent." In the other I have Brian dismissing his account: "That is impossible." What am I supposed to do, argue or agree?

"Could you tell the Americans about the tobacco thing?" Abdul Wali asks.

Earlier Abdul Wali mentioned that he is a habitual user of *naswar,* a potent chewing tobacco. He wants to know if the Americans will allow it if he is detained. "No, no, just forget about it," I dismiss him now.

"Are you sure?" he says.

"Yeah," I say. Dave is so worked up that I don't want to risk it.

At some point I announce that Abdul Wali is making personal, emotional appeals to me and that the other translator should step in so that the interrogation can be conducted in a more professional manner. "I think he's talking to me as the governor's son, not as the translator," I explain.

Then I quietly try to share my largest concern with Brian. "I'm not going to translate for this guy," I whisper. "Look how he's acting."

"What do you mean? I'm totally calm," Brian replies, perhaps misunderstanding.

"You're calm, but look at Dave," I say.

Brian tilts his head to the side—like *What can I say?*—and shrugs his shoulders.

As the interrogation continues, I'm relieved to be on the sidelines, but still it isn't easy to watch Dave browbeat Abdul Wali. I wasn't suspecting Abdul Wali to be coddled, but Dave is treating him with pure contempt. "We think you're lying," he tells him. He implies that an attack on his house was imminent. "Did you know that we were coming after you tonight?" Dave says.

Abdul Wali grows increasingly fidgety, the Americans grow increasingly frustrated, and finally the interrogation winds down. Here I feel like Abdul Wali: I can't say with any certainty how long it lasted. Maybe thirty minutes. Maybe two hours. It was agonizing enough for me that it felt endless.

Abdul Wali will have to stay at the base awhile longer. "It's just standard procedure," Dave says. Abdul Wali stands with his hands against the wall, and the Americans pat him down, gathering his materials—the tobacco, a watch, some papers—in preparation for detention. "Is there anything you want to give to your family?" Dave asks.

The question terrifies Abdul Wali. "No, no," he stutters.

"I have one last thing to say to him," I tell the Americans. I approach Abdul Wali and, to calm him, put my hand on his shoulder. "Just say the truth," I tell him, trying to sound normal. "Nothing is going to happen if you just say the truth." He is so petrified that he can barely whisper his answer.

That evening at the governor's house, one of the security guards tells me that Abdul Wali's brother is at the door. He has a message for me: "Tell the governor's son that I am going to hold him personally responsible. Hyder, he's the one who gave my brother to the Americans. I've trusted him, and nothing better happen to my brother."

I know that he is not trying to threaten me, that he simply means to guilt me into an investment in Abdul Wali's welfare. He is clearly distressed, and I don't want him to think I'm heartless, so I decide to go see if I can reassure him, but when I come outside, a guard tells me, "Oh, he's already gone." I stand there a second, the Kunar River rushing behind me, and then go back inside.

A translator from the American base visits two days later. Abdul Wali has been uncooperative, and they're wondering if we could ask his brother to come back to Asadabad.

The following evening we return to the compound around five. Almost immediately we learn of two visitors; one is Abdul Wali's brother, and the other is the translator. My father's presence at the base is urgently required. We get worried—the Americans always meet with us at the compound when they have something to discuss. Never before have they asked my father to come to them.

Abdul Wali's brother is standing by the pickups. "We're going to take you to the Americans," I tell him, and he starts crying. The brother is starting to bother me. *Stop being such a wuss,* I think. This is a strange way for any male to act, but especially one who is young and Pashtun. His behavior falls far outside the cultural norms.

"Just be honest," my father says to the brother, who continues sobbing as we drive down to the base. When we arrive, we ask if we should bring him with us inside. "No, hold on one sec," someone says.

My father and I are shown to a room across the hall from the one in which Abdul Wali's interrogation was performed. The two of us sit down on the floor with Steve, Dave, and, today, Major Mark instead of Brian. My father and I cross our legs and set our backs against the wall. You can tell the Americans get a little irritated with all of the floor-sitting required in Afghanistan. Sometimes it seems like every single American has a problem with his knees. You'll sit down to lunch and the Afghans will be all huddled up, and the Americans will groan and explain that they played football in high school, and instead of crossing their legs, they will extend them. That's how they do it today, and—I'll admit—my knee is a little messed up from football too, so when I see them adjust, I slowly stretch my legs forward.

"Unfortunately, we have some bad news," Mark begins.

Oh man, I think. *Is Abdul Wali not cooperating? Did he admit to having a part in the missile attacks? What happened?*

"Unfortunately," Mark continues, "Abdul Wali passed away."

"What?" my father says. And then he starts shaking his head. "That's no good," he says in English.

They tell us that around three-thirty or four in the afternoon, Abdul Wali collapsed. They tried to make him stand, and he did so for only a second before falling again. They attempted to revive him by performing CPR; they tell us they used "brand-new equipment," perhaps referring to a defibrillator. They say no expense was spared, and they reacted just as they would have had an American life been at stake.

Dave tells us about the circumstances of Abdul Wali's detention. He says that he was given adequate food—he mentions PowerBars. He says Abdul Wali was not beaten, but that he tried, with real force, to break the shackles binding his feet and hit his head against the wall a couple times in these efforts. They employed sleep deprivation, awakening him at odd hours. Sometimes they splashed water on him. He was also given a lot of water to drink. I am not sure if Dave is referring to proper hydration, or if this was a technique designed to make Abdul Wali more forthcoming. (It will later be revealed that American interrogators in the southern city of Gardez forced prisoners to drink copious amounts of water.)

Dave also says that Abdul Wali would put rocks in his mouth, perhaps because he was used to chewing tobacco. That gets to me. *Maybe I should have asked,* I think.

Abdul Wali behaved erratically, saying, "Okay, okay, get Dave in here, I'm ready to talk about the missiles," then, upon Dave's arrival, refusing to do so. Dave says that he and Abdul Wali (who, Dave reports, had a twelve-year-old son and a one-year-old baby) talked about their children.

Today Dave is calm; his arrogant swagger has disappeared. But his seemingly forthright manner is just as disquieting. He's like a kid who breaks a vase and then takes his hand away and freezes, his eyes darting around: *It wasn't me, I didn't touch anything.*

My father and the Americans wonder together if Abdul Wali might have had some sort of disease. We start talking about how to inform Abdul Wali's family of his death. We send for Rauf Mama, who, in addition to being my father's closest adviser, is a respected mullah. We decide he will travel to Abdul Wali's village—hopefully he will reach it before the news spreads. Arrangements will be made for Abdul Wali's relatives to come to the base and view the body.

Now the Americans want us to view the body, too, so that we can see for ourselves that nothing happened to it. "Oh, I'll take you for your word," my father assures them. "If there are no marks or bruises, we don't have to see it."

"I think they want you to see it for themselves, not for you," I say in Pashto. I can tell that the proposal has been made as much for their benefit as for his; it will be helpful if my father can report that he saw no signs of abuse.

We leave the room and walk outside until we reach a row of several small huts. We stop in front of the one marked number five. There are bloodstains on the two small steps before the door. Someone—I think Dave—explains that this is where Abdul Wali collapsed.

Inside, it is extremely hot and damp; the walls and floors are made of something hard, maybe cement, and there are no windows. Abdul Wali lies on a rope bed with his hands crossed. His head is covered with a cloth—it looks like a thinned-out napkin—that is tied at the end, perhaps to close his mouth before the onset of rigor mortis. My father steps forward and removes the cloth from his face; the rest of us, standing close together in the small, dim space, hover behind. One of Abdul Wali's eyes is open and the other is closed. Dave points to a mark, perhaps more than one, on his face and says this was where he hit himself against the wall. There are also bruises at his ankles, around which the shackles ringed. That surprises me. I wouldn't have expected shackles to be bound so tightly—I'd always pictured them dangling like bracelets. Covered by the baggy top of the kameez partoog, Abdul Wali's physique had been unremarkable, but I can now see the well-defined muscles of his upper body. We do not thoroughly scrutinize him; his middle section is obscured, and we do not turn him over and view his backside.

After my father examines the body, I step forward. I touch his face and his chest. There is none of the heady mixture of adrenaline and bewilderment that defined my viewing of Haji Qadir's corpse last summer. The feeling is blunt. It is just Abdul Wali, his body before me, and he is dead.

We leave the hut and, standing outside it in a small group, begin to talk about an autopsy. My father tells Mark that to people in Kunar, an autopsy will merely serve as proof that the Americans are torturers.

See—these cuts are what killed him.

Of course he died of a heart attack; they opened him up and pulled his heart out and then put it back in.

"We understand," says Mark, "but these orders are coming from Bagram." Bagram is the U.S. military's central command base in Afghanistan; it's located outside Kabul. "They want the body, and they want an autopsy done so that they can clear us of any wrongdoing."

They go back and forth like this for a while, but my father stands firm: "You keep explaining the situation to me, but there's just no way. Compromise cannot be made on this." In additional to fueling speculation about torture, there would be cultural and religious opposition to a non-Muslim handling the corpse. And it might be days before the body could be returned.

Mark decides to call Bagram. Still standing before the hut, he takes out a satellite phone and pulls up the antenna. When he hangs up, he tells us that his superiors won't budge.

"I don't care," says my father. "You'll have to call them back. You're not going to take this body. And if you do, I'm not accepting any responsibility for what happens afterward." American rules and regulations cannot be transported to Afghanistan and work seamlessly within Islamic and local traditions.

There is another call, maybe two, and finally, it is resolved: there will be no autopsy.

The whole time Abdul Wali's brother has been waiting outside in the pickup. He has no idea what's happened. When we leave, Rauf Mama gets in the car with him and tells him of his brother's death. "Drop me off here," Abdul Wali's brother says, seeming to spill over with grief as they drive north through the valley. "Drop me off here." Eventually he is taken home, and I never see him again.

That night, staring through a web of mosquito netting at the dark sky, I keep picturing Abdul Wali: my hand on his shoulder as I said goodbye, and how terrifying it must have been for him when I stepped out of the room, and there was nobody left whom he trusted.

The next day we receive word that Abdul Wali's family has suffered another tragedy: a small child, perhaps Abdul Wali's own, has drowned in the river. The search for the child's body has delayed them on their journey to Asadabad.

At one-ten in the afternoon Dave calls the governor's compound, and I speak to him. Now a deadline has been imposed. Dave says that if Abdul Wali's body is not picked up in the next fifty minutes, the U.S. military is going to get involved, and they want to do an autopsy. If his family can't make it before two, the Americans will give the body to us. We rush to the market, climb into the beat-up pickup truck that serves as a local ambulance, and head down to the base. As we pull in, I see another pickup leaving; it turns out to hold Abdul Wali's family. They've arrived on time and claimed the body. I'm told they receive approximately $2,000 from the U.S. military as compensation for his death.

Abdul Wali's family says that he had a history of heart problems, and we come to believe that he suffered a heart attack. Still, his death deals a blow to the U.S. forces—and by extension to my father. It benefits—as the Americans like to call them—"the bad guys." *Don't go to the Americans. Don't listen to Said Fazel Akbar. Remember Abdul Wali? You're going to die like him if you go to him.*

Later, when I ask my father to name the hardest day of his governorship so far, he cites the one on which Abdul Wali died. "The reason that was such a difficult day," he explains, "was that for all of the backup I have received—of all of the support I have received from the people of Kunar— this did leave a dent in it. This did push that back. Because people were more hesitant now to come to me."

A tragedy—an accident—costly to both us and our ally; a singular, outlying occurrence. That's how my father and I will view these events until almost one year later, when the world learns about a jail called Abu Ghraib, a prisoner abuse scandal that involves American soldiers in both Iraq and Afghanistan, and the *New York Times* runs a front-page story about the death of Abdul Wali and the arrest of a man named Dave.

20

I SPENT MY FIRST SUMMER in Kabul wishing I was in California; now in Kunar, I wish I were in the place I'd wanted to leave. *Ooh, the city!* I think to myself of Kabul, on yet another hot, dull day in Asadabad. Living here is like having moved back into medieval—or at least pre-electrified—times. At dark we go to bed. There is simply nothing else to do until the sun comes up again.

But one morning we rise before the first light, pile into the car, and in the blackness set off—finally—for a trip to the capital. Around eight we stop for breakfast in Jalalabad. We've been in the car about four hours by then. We're near the Darunta Camp, which just a couple years ago was one of the most hard-core Al Qaeda training camps: an elite, Arab-only zone. Now, sitting at a little stand beside a river, my father, Sartor, Rauf Mama, and I eat a meal of fresh fish.

Though my father came to Kunar with the aim of strengthening the province's ties to the capital, Kabul isn't reciprocating. By early fall his contributions to the treasury will total $2.3 million, but he has yet to receive from them a single cent for reconstruction.

Yet it isn't exactly the central government's fault. Though the international community has pledged billions of dollars to Afghanistan, the funds are arriving in a trickle. The slow pace is especially frustrating in the context of recent history. Throughout the 1980s money poured into Afghanistan and was used to throttle the country. Back then there was a willingness to destroy; now there is a reluctance to rebuild. It makes me think the world has more confidence in Afghans as fighters than as functioning members of society.

Meanwhile the mukhalafeen are well financed, often by international benefactors. Whole nations are jockeying for position on what is hardly a level playing field, and we, the home team, are in danger of losing the game.

So my father is going to Kabul to discuss the funding issue, among others, as well as simply to check in with Karzai, touch base with his old colleagues and friends.

Around one-thirty, we reach the outskirts of the city. The narrow approach road is a crowded snarl. (If two cars were to approach at full speed from opposite directions, they'd find themselves in a game of chicken, with one having to slow down and swerve to the shoulder to avoid impact.) We sit in traffic, the manure-stench of a nearby truckful of cows wafting into our car. *One of the problems trying to get into Kabul is that the road's just too small,* I say into my minidisc recorder. *It can't handle all the traffic coming in.* Rauf Mama yells at a driver trying to skirt around to the front; shamed or scared, the man abandons his attempt. "Did that get recorded?" Rauf Mama asks triumphantly.

Then we see a sign that features a multicolored array of grenades, mines, and dynamite. A hand reaching down for the weapons is crossed out with a red X. Here we are: this sign alerts us not only to danger but to our arrival in Kabul.

Sartor and I go to a restaurant for *shami* kabob. Indian music plays through speakers as we eat; outside, a neighborhood that would have been dead at night last summer is vibrant. Somehow Afghans have managed to renovate their psyches, even as the international community has failed to renovate their streets.

We're staying with my uncle Abdullah Ali, who is still the minister of public works. At his house we watch a locally produced TV game show. There's a studio audience, a host with a microphone, and on stage people competing in a Coke-drinking contest. The first to finish a half-liter bottle will receive such a prize as cooking oil (six containers) or soap (two cases). The audience cheers as the contestants gulp their soda; one guy gives up; and finally the winner is awarded a box of detergent and a pair of shoes. In Kabul the stuff of everyday life is still a luxury.

Then there is Karzai, who does not have the luxury of an everyday life. The security situation keeps him increasingly confined to the palace, and the next evening we go to meet him there for dinner. As we drive through Kabul, I realize that the city that seemed so daunting last summer no longer overwhelms me. It's hard to believe I once spent my days here cloistered away in my hotel room, staring out the window at my single fixed view.

Now, outside his house on the palace grounds, Karzai gives me a tight hug. We're surrounded by men in suits; Karzai, my father, and I are the only ones in traditional clothing. "You dress like a Kunari," Karzai says approvingly.

His house is a clean-lined, modern structure that was once the home of the king's son. In the 1960s my uncle Abdullah Ali played a role in its design. The walls are made of something like cement, giving the house the feel of a bunker. Inside we sit on a U of couches arranged in front of a TV, which plays in the background. Karzai is talking to my father and Interior Minister Jalali when the BBC shows an advertisement for itself. A series of "incredible moments" run across the screen, last summer's assassination attempt on Karzai among them. Jolted by the strangeness of it, I look up at my father, who meets my eye; all the while Karzai chatters away, seemingly unaffected by, or purposely oblivious to, the commercial.

As we dine on rice, chicken korma, salad, and Coke, I listen to the discussion. Here is the unscripted hashing out of the geopolitical issues of our day: among them, developing a friendly relationship with Pakistan. The discussion is inconclusive, and this, in its own way, is more eye-opening than a state secret. I've always assumed that top politicians must possess a trove of privileged knowledge, an enormous set of information inaccessible to the general public. But here behind the curtain, they are men making educated guesses, same as me.

* * *

Whether or not he and his advisers are omniscient, Karzai is still the president, and I'm still nervous when I go to interview him for my radio documentary. I test two different microphones, check the minidisc recorder's battery icon, and listen to the sound through my headphones. It's the scale of Karzai's importance that gets to me. If President Bush died tomorrow, the United States as a nation would remain intact; without Karzai, Afghanistan might slip into chaos again.

I meet with Karzai on an early morning at his office in the Gul Khana palace. The windows on the first floor are pitted by bullet holes. Some say these shots were fired by the mujahedeen who stormed the palace in 1992; but the damage may just as likely have been done four years later by the Taliban. With so many regimes and so many battles, nobody really keeps track of who's responsible for what. More than a year into Karzai's tenure, nobody seems to care whether or not the windows are replaced, either. Here's my rule of thumb for evaluating the pace of reconstruction: if the bullet-ridden windows in the palace have not been replaced, chances are things are lagging in the rest of the country.

Now I sit across from Karzai at his desk. It's made of dark wood, edged in gold gilt, and the surface shines, reflecting my hand holding the microphone. Long curtains frame the windows, and chairs are upholstered in a rich red—except Karzai's own. His is a regular swivel chair with black rubbery armrests, like the kind you might see on display at Staples.

I wait for Karzai to finish a phone call, and then I begin. "There has been a lot of criticism of the transitional government," I say. "Reconstruction is lagging, the national army is behind schedule, warlords control areas outside of Kabul." It's a bit of a negative beginning. "However, there are some success stories," I add. "I've seen some myself. I was wondering if you can tell me what you think are some of the major successes of the transitional government."

"A lot of successes," replies Karzai, laying into the *a lot*. "The most important success is that Afghanistan is back again the home of all Afghans." He continues: "More than two-point-five million refugees have returned to Afghanistan." Among the other successes he mentions are the reconstruction of the roads; the introduction of a new currency; and the spread of education. But he acknowledges that the "formation of the national army is lagging" and that "there are armed groups around still, there are warlords that are bothering people."

"What do you feel are the major challenges holding Afghanistan back?" I wonder.

"Resources," he says immediately, before I can even get the mic all the way to his mouth. It's the same answer as my father. On Karzai's end the problem is exacerbated by a lack of control over the little that is available. Until recently funds earmarked for reconstruction were largely managed by other groups—by the UN, or various NGOs. According to Karzai, the Afghan government now has "a bigger say" over these resources. Still, there is no guarantee that the increased authority will lead to progress. On our satellite TV in Kunar, I watched an interview with Francesc Vendrell, the European Union's special envoy to Afghanistan. The interviewer noted that some are now saying that the $4.5 billion pledged in 2002 is far from enough to rebuild Afghanistan; the country will require $20 billion to get back on its feet. But Vendrell pointed out that Afghanistan is not capable of absorbing $20 billion in a short time. You have only to look at the example of Kurangal to see what he meant. You can donate all the pipes you want, but unless there are engineers to design a plan to put them together, the gift is useless. It will take years to train people to rebuild the country.

The warlords are another long-term problem. "It will take time," says Karzai. "It is not a thing that you can cure in a day. Stability in Afghanistan, reconstruction of Afghanistan, and institution building in Afghanistan: The more you do this, the lesser you will have the impact of warlords and armed groups. So it's a process. It's not a sudden thing."

"One last question," I say. "I haven't seen you wear a suit yet. I was wondering if you have a reason for this?" This subject had been debated endlessly in California after the fall of the Taliban. Many people, including my mother, thought that Karzai should wear a suit; the Western uniform would be appropriate for the world stage. But then suddenly Karzai's traditional Afghan clothing became a selling point. Tom Ford of Gucci named him "the chicest man on the planet"; I watched a CNN fashion segment that broke down the elements of his style; a New York boutique began selling $250 *karakul* hats; and when I went to the mosque for holiday prayers, dozens of grown Afghan men sported Karzai's trademark green *chapon*. I'm still curious about his choice.

"No reason," Karzai says now. "No particular reason. It's just that I feel more comfortable in my national dress. If the time comes—I like to wear suits as well. I like suits. I like good neckties. I like all that. So maybe someday I'll wear it."

"Do you think on your next trip abroad—maybe to the UN General Assembly—that you might wear a suit?" I press.

"Well, I don't have a suit at this time," Karzai explains. "But if an Afghan tailor can make me a good suit, why not?"

"Thank you so much for your time," I say.

"Thank you," Karzai says with an official flourish, and the interview is over.

The solution is simple: Afghanistan must establish peace and security by moving from strong warlords to strong institutions. Karzai said as much. But there's a difference between knowing what needs to be done and knowing how to do it. I'm discovering that there's a gap between intent and implementation.

On bridging the two, the United States has staked its hopes on Zalmay Khalilzad, who serves as President Bush's "special envoy" to Afghanistan; his status will later be upgraded to ambassador. But neither word really describes his role. Some people call him *asli pacha*—"the real king." He is knowledgable about Afghanistan, close to Karzai, and influential in the Bush administration. Western journalists report speculation that he is the guiding force behind Karzai's decisions, and that via his person the United States wields undue influence over Afghanistan's affairs. But my father tells me that, to the contrary, he and many other Afghans consider Khalilzad to be one of their own.

I first met Khalilzad last summer. This year I go with my father to see him at the U.S. embassy. A group has assembled to discuss the situation in Kunar. The meeting begins when Khalilzad smacks his hands down on the table before my father, and says severely, "Where's Gulbiddin?" Then Khalilzad says, "Just kidding," and everyone starts laughing.

Khalilzad, Karzai, and my father share a propensity for jokes. Karzai once signed a budget proposal of my father's with his name and an unusual postscript: *Dega chitoor astee?* Meaning, approximately, "So, what's up, man?" or "How are you otherwise?" Khalilzad saw the proposal and now, when he runs into my father, greets him with "*Dega chitoor astee?*" and cracks up.

Khalilzad is a big man in a business suit with graying hair. Now, at the embassy, he acknowledges me and says to the rest of the room, "Oh, we have a celebrity here." On a visit to the United States several months ago, Khalilzad was in the car listening to NPR, when my radio documentary came on. As soon as the hour was over, he began receiving phone calls from people who were wondering if he'd heard it. "It was so moving," he says now. "I liked it so much. He's a big man over there," he tells the group.

Since he's a fan of the first documentary, I figure he won't mind being interviewed for the second. Of course, with the microphone on, Khalilzad doesn't make any jokes; as soon as I press record, he turns into a smooth diplomat. I ask him for a brief biography. He explains that he was raised in Kabul and spent a year during high school as a foreign exchange student in the United States. Later he received his Ph.D. from the University of Chicago and was working as a professor at Columbia University when he got a call from the Reagan administration, and he began his career in politics.

I take this in. Then I say, "So far—the last report I heard—one-point-three billion dollars have poured into Afghanistan." I continue: "I don't see any tangible reconstruction going on. Can you tell me where this money might have gone?" (Many people speculate that the money has been used to purchase Land Cruisers and houses in newly upscale Kabul neighborhoods for foreign aid workers.)

Khalilzad says that the money went first into projects "to keep people from dying." (The fall of the Taliban, combined with droughts and food shortages, created a humanitarian crisis.) Since then funds have been assigned to small-scale initiatives, like schools and clinics; as well as to bigger ones, like the Kabul-Kandahar highway. And a lot of the money has been devoted to the development of the national army.

"You mentioned that the biggest reconstruction project so far has been the national army. And you also mentioned that it's been going rather slowly," I say. "What are the obstacles—I want to say obstacles because I see certain things that are standing in front of the national army being built—what do you see these obstacles being?" I choose my words carefully; warlords and their minions are planting themselves in the way of forward progress like actual roadblocks. Though the five-year goal is seventy thousand troops, eighteen months into the plan only several thousand soldiers have been trained. Khalilzad explains that Afghanistan has been through hell during the past thirty years; the private militias that formed to cope with that horror are reluctant to cooperate. They need to be slowly integrated into the new army.

We wind up the interview, and I ask Khalilzad if I can take a quick picture with him.

"Good luck," he says when we're through. "It was a real pleasure meeting you. Say hello to your father."

Though the interview went well, I have a bad feeling about it, and when I get back to my uncle's, my suspicions are confirmed. My conversation with Khalilzad was recorded with a layer of static over it. It will be impossible to broadcast on the radio. You have to reach down through a layer of fuzz to get to the words. In a way, it's a metaphor for my own experience doing these interviews; though I asked the questions, the answers remain obscure. I can't figure it out; can't determine why the superheroes are always losing, and the bad guys always getting power, and winning in the end.

We leave Kabul at night. For security reasons we'll sleep somewhere discreet in Jalalabad and complete our trip to Kunar in the morning. We drive in the pickup along an itty-bitty road that winds through the mountains. My father and Rauf Mama tell stories, laughing uproariously. The windows are down, and an Ahmed Zahir tape plays in the background. Ahmed Zahir was the Afghan Elvis Presley; he died tragically in a car accident, an event that solidified his legend. To me, his haunting melodies and songs offer a glimpse into Kabul in the 1970s—a world my parents inhabited but that I never knew. Now, driving away from that city thirty years later, I sit in the backseat, the wind beating against my face. This is the first time I've driven through rural Afghanistan at night. The experience is different in the dark. Every now and then a truck will approach in the opposite lane— *zoom!*—and the world will shudder a little in its wake. Besides the trucks there are no other cars; the road seems populated only by us and the ghosts of empires that previously traversed this treacherous path. I sit back contentedly and think of a line from *Soldiers of God*, a book about Afghanistan by the journalist Robert D. Kaplan: "Was there ever such rich terrain for romantic self-delusion?"

The romance fades pretty quickly when we get to Jalalabad. We stay in the same guest house in which Sartor and I discussed escape strategies with his friends last year. The heat is stifling and none of us can sleep. Finally Rauf Mama gets up and, because there isn't anything else to do, starts praying, just for the hell of it.

When rockets are fired on our first night back in Asadabad, I joke with myself that the attack is a kind of welcome. I guess I've gotten Kabul out of my system. But it's more than that; here in Kunar, I feel like I am home.

21

I WANT TO LEARN HOW TO shoot. All summer Rauf Mama has been saying we'll go somewhere to practice, and finally there comes a day when
we are both free. Sartor is recruited, and the three of us meet by the
pickups—along with seven or eight security guards. I'd thought that Sartor
and Rauf Mama would be the only witnesses to my training session. "Man,
I wish it was just us," I say to Sartor. "I would be more comfortable."

"*Murla,* you want to go up into the mountains of Kunar without anybody?" he replies.

"I guess that makes sense," I admit.

We buck away from the Kunar River and up into the mouth of the Pech
Valley, stopping at an open patch of ground.

"What's around here?" I ask.

"Nothing, nothing," one of the guards replies. "Just a kids' school a
couple hundred yards away."

"Come on," Rauf Mama says. "Let the kids study or whatever they're
doing. They'll get disturbed if we start shooting," he reasons.

So we continue, and soon we get out of the cars and begin a search for a
target. One of the guards finds a white rock; he heads off across the field
and sets it on the ground. The rock now looks like a pebble. The guard
seems to have chosen the outer limit of the distance over which the gun can

be reliably aimed. "Whoa!" I yell. "It's my first time shooting. Maybe you could come back a little?" But the rock stays where it is.

Another man picks up the Kalashnikov first. The sound of his shot explodes into the still air around us. He misses the target; a second aims and fails as well. Then it's my turn.

"Maybe we should put the safety on," says one of the guards.

"Or maybe we should take the clip out and just leave one bullet in there," another says.

"Shut up, man," says Rauf Mama. "He's not retarded, he's just here from America."

I bend one knee to the ground. The gun feels lighter than I expected. Holding the weapon very still, I stare through the indent on the barrel, matching it up with the little hole in the front. Then I pull the trigger. "I hit it!" I cry.

"No," says one of the guards. "You hit right above it."

"Are you sure?" I ask. I get into position and, more confidently, fire again. Oddly, the gun sounds quieter when you're firing it yourself. I feel good; this is coming out right, I'm not embarrassing myself.

"No, no, no, not that one," I'm told, and a guard runs toward the correct pebble and points at it. Determined, I try again, and this third shot is successful.

"Oh my God!" exclaims one of the guards.

"I don't think I could have gotten that on my third try," says another.

Everyone is pretty impressed. "I knew he would get it," says Rauf Mama. Then he tells how my father, as a young man, had shot at targets behind his back with the aid of a mirror; and how my brother, as a teenager, had with a single bullet killed two birds, both of them thudding to the ground right here in Kunar. Now, regarding me approvingly, Rauf Mama concludes, "It's in his blood."

I blend in here. Most people in Kunar would not assume at the outset that I'm from America, and I am not necessarily presented as such. "When Mullah Omar captured Herat, his beard hadn't grown yet," my father says, explaining my age.

Sartor gives his own age this way: "I was in fourth grade when the

Daoud Khan coup happened." Daoud Khan was killed in 1978, so I take this to mean that Sartor was born around 1969. Sartor is light-skinned and laid back and can seem strikingly American. One time, packing a bag in my room, I toss him a shirt and a pair of jeans, and just for fun he puts them on. He looks like a bearded Matt Damon.

American pop culture mystifies Sartor and the others. One of our satellite channels shows music videos, and a hip-hop program plays every day at six P.M. Though I wouldn't go out of my way to watch such a show in California, here it is a novelty to which I am devoted. Sartor sits with me, learning the rappers. "That's Jay-Z," I say. "He has his own private jet." Sartor summons Rauf Mama's nephew Shohab. "Come in here, come in here!" he shouts, then indicates the TV. "Look at this goofy guy," he says. "Can you believe he has an airplane for himself?"

Sometimes people ask me about teenagers in Kunar. Do I ever see people my own age? What are they doing? These are impossible questions to answer. There is no distinct teenage world here, no separate youth culture; just simple village life. People my age are working fields, or getting married, or finding employment as security guards. Sartor, in his early thirties, is my closest peer.

Sartor's picture of America is the Las Vegas strip cross-hatched over the entire fifty states. I do what I can to dispel him of this notion, but the truth is that we talk about Afghanistan more than we talk about the West. Sartor spent some of the Taliban years as a driver for a French NGO called MADERA, and his descriptions of this period can make the regime sound more absurd than repressive. One early morning he was driving some of the NGO's female employees. When he reached the outskirts of Jalalabad, he slipped into the tape deck one of the cassettes he kept beneath his seat. Then, as luck would have it, he passed the Taliban with music wafting out his windows.

The Taliban stopped him. "Are you listening to tapes?" they said.

"No, what are you talking about?" said Sartor. "We weren't listening to anything."

"Get out of the car," they ordered, then looked around and found the tapes under his seat.

"I just picked this car up this morning from the NGO—it's not even my car," Sartor lied. "These must be somebody else's tapes. I have no idea where they came from." It was like a high school kid trying to explain away a Baggie of marijuana.

"Yeah, sure," the Taliban said. "All right. We're going to put this tape in and blast it really loudly, and you're going to have to dance for everyone here."

The prospect of dancing before his female passengers embarrassed Sartor. "Come on, man," he appealed.

So instead the Taliban ripped the strips of tape from their plastic casings, then attached them to Sartor's car like a tail. The tail is a serious insult in Afghan culture; when you say of someone, "All he's missing is a tail," you mean he is hardly better than a donkey. As ordered, Sartor drove along. Then he jammed on the brakes, bolted out, and ripped the tail off. He sped away and was too quick for the Taliban to catch him.

Tapes were always getting him into trouble, Sartor says, tapes and beards. Sartor's beard doesn't really grow out. It was never long enough to meet the Taliban's requirements—they liked a beard by which they could grab you with their fists—and they were always stopping Sartor, checking to see if the hair had the rough texture of a recent trim, or if this really was all that he could muster.

Westerners usually hear stories of the Taliban's depravity. Yet something is missed in this rendering. There is no doubt that the Taliban instituted a repressive and inordinately cruel regime. But in already conservative Pashtun areas, their impact was less acute. The men already had beards; the women already covered themselves up. During the Taliban era some American women pinned mesh fabric swatches to their clothes to symbolize their solidarity with their burka-clad counterparts in Afghanistan. But the targets of these good intentions may have had no desire to rip off their protective garments.

Now, though many people in Kunar are not sorry to see the Taliban gone, they do miss the safety of those years. Back then you could walk anywhere in the province at three A.M.; you could leave the door to your shop open and nobody would come in and steal your stuff. (Amputation is a powerful theft deterrent.) The major difference in Kunar since the fall of the regime is that there is no longer good security. When the bank, which is next door to the governor's compound, gets a satellite Internet connection, I tell my father that I'm going over to check it out. "Take the guards with you," he replies. I regard him querulously. "You have to leave the gate," he says. "Take the guards."

His order doesn't make me fearful, just baffled. It's too hard to imagine myself as a target; it just doesn't seem real. But it's all very clear to my father. "If they can't reach me, they will take a shot at you," he tells me. "They will not take a shot so easily if there are four or five people around you."

My father is matter-of-fact about the dangers; these are practicalities, no more, no less. But at times I suspect that his cool manner is just a pose he's adopted to prevent any anxiety on my part. When I ask him if he ever worries about my security, he tells me that whenever I leave the compound, he is "expecting something to happen." In his head he goes over how he would feel if he heard "the news—*Hyder was killed in an ambush*." But though his worries are "heightened" in Kunar, they are not confined to here. "Even when you are in America, in San Francisco, driving on the highways, I worry, *What if he gets in an accident?*" The feeling is more than just geographically universal: "Every time a son leaves his father, he worries what will happen."

But my father does not restrict my movement. He even agrees to let me go to Nuristan, an isolated province that until a generation ago was considered part of Kunar. Nuristan is one of the most extraordinary places in all of Afghanistan: a remote enclave of exceptional beauty. Legend has it that Nuristan is populated by blond-haired, blue-eyed tribesmen who are descendants of Alexander the Great. One of the more notable contemporary inhabitants is a man named Mullah Fakirullah.

Mullah Fakirullah—or as at least one American memorably pronounces his name, Mullah Fuckerula—is suspected of harboring Osama bin Laden after September 11. I'm not sure of the specifics of the evidence against Mullah Fakirullah, but the American describes him to me as "one of the guys that we're huntin'." This may be more of a theoretical hunt than a practical one. Some of Nuristan's jagged peaks seem like they would be hard to reach even by helicopter; and to set out on foot for Mullah Fakirullah would mean annihilation by a horde of easily mobilized villagers. So the

Americans are stymied—they know where their man is but are not agile enough to go seize him. Several times they ask my father for help; the commander of the local military division even sends a jirga to try to coax Mullah Fakirullah down to Asadabad. He refuses.

My mission in Nuristan is easier. One morning Sartor, Rauf Mama, and I leave for a sort of road trip through the province. We stop along the way in the Pech Valley at the home of a wealthy *khan*. Men in white kameez partoog lounge around his terrace. Over the railing extends a cord that stretches way, way down to the ground. A man at a pulley unspools the cord, and a blue bucket bobbles toward the river below, from which it scoops up water. It takes two men, grasping the dowels hand over hand, to wind the bucket back up. On the way, water sloshes over the edge, and the bucket arrives at the top two-thirds full. This plumbing system is an actual luxury.

We also go to visit a gemstone trader. Kunar and Nuristan hold some of Afghanistan's most significant gemstone deposits. Legend has it that during the Soviet war Afghans would pitch tents over promising outcroppings, then wait around for bombs to explode open their targets. (The Panjshir Valley is also lined with riches; Massoud partially financed the Northern Alliance through the emerald trade there.) After we look at the trader's stones, a group of us heads over to the mines. They are so dark that you have to hold a lantern right in front of your nose. A lot of people forgo the tour and wait outside. I don't think anything of it until later, when Rauf Mama tells me that the mines sometimes collapse. He hadn't mentioned it to me beforehand, just quietly accompanied me inside.

Finally we reach Nuristan. It is as spectacular a landscape as advertised. The sky is bright blue. Clouds wisp around the peaks. We see a mountain that looks like a mile-long rock, and we drive along a river on a rudimentary road. The narrowness of this space cannot be exaggerated. There is literally just this strand of river boring through two craggy walls.

I zoom my camera up the side of a mountain to get a closer look at a cluster of houses that look like shoeboxes on stilts. I saw a settlement like this in an old book about Afghanistan; in that photograph, ladders led from the roof of one dwelling to another. I've heard that people can get stranded here; that the inhabitants of these houses will pull the ladders away, leaving a soldier unable to continue after a person he's pursuing, not to mention extremely vulnerable himself.

I was falling-down sick right before we left for Nuristan, and as we return home, so too does my illness. I'm sicker than ever in my life, and I'm actually a little worried. *I hope this is nothing serious,* I think, the car heaving along with my stomach. The landscape is as relentless as my misery: mountain after mountain, with no clearing in sight. This seems like such a god-forsaken place, and I just want to get the hell out. *Whatever, man, I think. I'm not coming back to Kunar. Screw this.* Then I ask Sartor to stop at a cliff so that I can throw up. The absolute most disgusting thing comes up out of my mouth. It's a big green chunk, and for a moment I stare at it on the ground, wondering if I should poke it, see whether it's hard or soft. Then I lift my head and suddenly feel as well as if I'd never been sick. When I get back in the car, the late-day sun casts the world in a magical light, and the mountains become beautiful again, one after another.

When you're sick in Afghanistan, you despise the place; as soon as you feel good, you can't stop laughing and smiling. You swing from one emotional cliff to another in this land of extremes. One night I'll lie in bed, looking up at the sky, marveling that perhaps no other eighteen-year-old in the world is doing anything quite like this; moments later I'll wonder why I'm exhausting myself with these summers and consider whether youth is passing me by. Oddly, it's mostly the slack—the downtime—that I dislike. The prospect of another ambush doesn't terrify me; being cooped up in the compound does. Everyday life is the hardest thing here, especially after coming from America, where boredom is viewed as an actual injustice.

In America one of my hedges against boredom is politics. It's so easy to be into politics there: wake up, look at nytimes.com, read Thomas Friedman. Make my way downstairs, turn on the TV, get absorbed in something on CNN. *Oooh, that's so interesting. Oooh, hold on. Let me go grab a sandwich.* There politics are an intellectual exercise, something you can gnaw over along with your lunch. But here in Afghanistan politics are a matter of life and death.

So much is stacked against Afghanistan that I sometimes wonder if these summers here are useless. That sense of futility makes it hard to seriously commit to spending my life here. But at the same time the more daunting the tasks seem, the more motivated I become. The bigger the odds, the more monumental the weight of history, the greater is my chance of being remembered. I want to do something lasting—I can't pretend otherwise. This is part of why I am here rather than anyplace else. Here on the balcony, with my father sleeping soundly beside me, and the whistle of a rocket through the black sky. There's something so exciting about taming these mountains.

22

I'M WALKING UP A SCRUBBY MOUNTAIN path in sandals, stubbing my toe—*ow*—breathing a little quicker. It's a cool morning, kind of foggy, and Rauf Mama and I are hiking to Pakistan. We're traveling along a route used by fleeing, and returning, members of Al Qaeda and the Taliban. By local standards we have everything we need for our trip: six guards, six Kalashnikovs, no map, and no water. We're still in Afghanistan, but we'll soon see for ourselves just how porous this infamous border really is.

It's the end of the summer, and if there's one conclusion I've come to, it's that ninety percent of Kunar's troubles are caused by its proximity to Pakistan. The mukhalafeen duck in and out via these mountain paths. There's been so much hand-wringing about the impossibility of policing these areas that I wanted to get inside them and see for myself just how hard the border would be to seal.

I also wanted to see where Rauf Mama lives. Rauf Mama has walked this route, or a variation, hundreds of times, crossing between Kunar and his home in Bajaur, a Pashtun tribal area on Pakistan's side of the border. Bajaur—where Rauf Mama settled his family during the Soviet war—is only nominally beholden to the laws of Pakistan. I pictured Bajaur as a crazy, wild, wild, wild West; I imagined the organizing principle of life there to be revenge. My own myth of the place long predates my conscious interest in it. When my brother and sisters were little, our parents used to scare them into submission by saying, "You better behave, or we're going to take you to Bajaur and leave you there." My first summer in Afghanistan, I tried to get a sense of what Rauf Mama's life might be like in such a place.

"So, what's your house like in Bajaur?" I asked him one day when we were sitting around at Kabul Hotel.

"Um, well, it has about thirty-five rooms," he began.

"Thirty-five rooms!" I exclaimed. "That's huge!"

"Well, my five brothers and their families all live there, too," he said.

"So how many people live there altogether?" I asked.

He tried to figure it out—*there's me and my wife, and we have this many kids, then there's my one brother, and he has this many kids, and then his son has this many kids*—but once he got up around fifty, he lost count.

"That's not a house," I joked. "That's a military compound." And that's basically correct. In a place with little government control, thirty fighting men offer as good a guarantee as any that nobody's going to mess with you.

That first summer I'd hoped to travel with Rauf Mama to Bajaur—I told myself ominously, *You could get killed there, and no one would know*— but the trip never came together. This year I would finally cross the border on foot, the same way my father, my brother, Abdul Haq, and even dozens of reporters had.

But I was suffering from a problem that threatened to derail the expedition. It was slightly mortifying: I had an infected toe.

Your feet take a beating in Afghanistan. Last summer in Kabul my Kenneth Cole oxfords basically collapsed. This year I decided to buy something sturdier, and a couple days before I left Concord, my friend Matin came with me to Walnut Creek, where they have a bigger variety of stores. "We'll see if they have stuff for people looking to go to eastern Afghanistan," I said.

The first shop I visited told me everything they had was for "trail running" and that I should try a store called Any Mountain at the Broadway Plaza mall, about a half-mile away. It was a breezy day, and Matin and I walked.

"Afghan," he said in a low voice along the way, pointing at some girls.

"You think so?" I said, looking over.

"Yeah," he said.

"I think they're Persian," I decided. "They look Persian."

"You might be right," conceded Matin.

Nearby we saw an Audi sports car. "I don't like the Audi TTs," I told Matin. "They're, like, too round."

"They look like a Beetle," Matin said.

"Yeah," I agreed. "Like a Beetle stretched out a little bit. Like the front was just pulled or something."

Any Mountain was next to Macy's. Inside the store they had camping and backpacking gear. They were playing Bananarama. *Yeah, baby, she's got it,* the band trilled. I told the salesman I needed some tough shoes for eastern Afghanistan. "Don't worry about price," I said grandly. "It's really important. Where I'm going, I don't think I'll be able to buy another pair."

The salesman brought out two types of hiking boots. One I wasn't sure I'd be able to use later. "Could you wear that with normal clothes, do you think?" I asked Matin.

"Jeans," Matin replied.

"You think so?" I wondered.

"Jeans will go over them," he said.

The boots looked heavy and hot. "Socks play a huge part in it," the salesman told me. "Cotton socks are bad because they're going to hold on to moisture. Most of the CoolMax socks will tend to get that moisture away from your foot."

I slipped into one of the pairs. "You've got some more laces you can lace up top," the salesman urged.

The boots were size thirteen, and they were a little big. "You guys don't have these in twelves?" I checked.

"No," the salesman said. "How long are you going to be in Afghanistan?" he wanted to know.

"About two months," I replied.

"You gonna be doing a lot of walking?" he asked. "Or are you just going to"—he tried and failed to come up with another recreational activity one might plausibly pursue in Afghanistan—"be there?"

"I'm probably going to be going around a lot," I told him.

I laced the boots to the top and moved around a little. "I think I'm going to take these," I decided, and untied them. The salesman put them back in the box.

And the box is where they should have stayed. Thirteen is a big size to begin with, but in hiking boots it's huge. It took about five seconds for Sartor to start teasing me. "Hyder, when you go back to America, don't take those shoes with you," he'd say. "We could use them as a bomb shelter." He'd turn to the security guards, make sure they were in on the joke. "Who needs caves?" he'd shrug. "We can just use his shoes."

Of course, I stopped wearing them and started walking around in sandals, like everybody else. And then my big toe got infected—due to a hangnail—swelling to the point where it was difficult to walk. One day over at Toopchi I showed it to a soldier who shook his head and sent me over to the clinic. The clinic is basically just a room near the base's gates. It's the only functioning health care facility in the area, and there's usually a line of Afghans waiting for treatment. Today I heard a child shrieking—someone said the little boy had fallen into a fire.

The American medic examined my toe. "That's kind of tricky," he said. "I don't want to squeeze it out yet. It might get more infected." He gave me an antibiotic, and he asked, "Do you want pain-killers, too?"

It was really hurting, but I'm in Kunar—I can't say, *Yeah, I want pain-killers for my toe.* "No, thanks," I told him.

"Are you sure?" he said. "Something like that happened to me, and it hurt so much that I got back pain from walking on it the wrong way."

"No, no," I said, limping out the door. "I'm fine, I'm fine."

Back at the governor's compound, Shohab proposed his own solution: "Let me pop it for you."

"No, no, the Americans said just let it be," I told him. "It might get more infected. It's fine, they gave me antibiotics."

"Come on, let me pop it for you," he said again.

I couldn't refuse without looking like a wimp. "Okay," I agreed. "Sure, go ahead."

Shohab got a needle, bent over my right foot, poked, and my toe burst open. It must have taken ten or fifteen minutes for all the blood and pus to seep out of there. Shohab squeezed, helping it along. It hurt like heck, but I just nodded nonchalantly: "Yeah, yeah, it's coming out. Yeah, yeah, I see it." Afterward the only pain was from the sting of the air against the open wound. Still, when Rauf Mama saw my toe, he decided that we should travel to Pakistan by car instead. I was disappointed—I wanted to trek across the border, not roll over it in a Ford Ranger—but at least I would still see Bajaur. That night I packed a bag with a toothbrush, a couple pairs of kameez partoog, and my minidisc recorder, and in the morning we left as soon as we'd finished prayers.

Sartor drove us and several security guards north. We were heading toward the Marawarai district, so named for the people who settled there after losing their original homeland to another tribe. *Marawar* means to be sad or angry in a defiant or disappointed way; if Sartor's barbs about my boots had offended me to the point that I sulked and refused to talk to him anymore, people would say, "Oh, Hyder is *marawar.*"

Soon we reached the Marawarai bridge. Blocks at either end narrow its span, making it too tight a fit for trucks smuggling timber. Even in our pickup there was really no room to maneuver. Because our passenger weight might have pushed the bridge to the breaking point, we got out and Sartor drove the empty car over. As we crossed on foot, I saw the scrapes and chips left by drivers less skilled than him.

Back in the pickup we zigzagged up the mountains toward the border crossing at Ghakhai Kandao (Teeth Pass). The place was a mess of dirt and stones and little grasses; the border was marked by an ordinary chain hung between two thin stakes.

Sometime before we arrived, the Afghan guards had exchanged words with their Pakistani counterparts. They were sick of the Pakistanis' extracting bribes from the Afghans who wanted to cross. Now there was a retaliatory shutdown, and Afghan families squatted by the chain, waiting for the issue to be resolved.

The Afghan guards recognized my father's white pickup and served our group tea and biscuits. Then the haggling began. As the Afghans insisted to the Pakistanis that the governor's son should be allowed across, Rauf Mama and I sipped our tea. "I'm not going to sit here and wait to let the whims of those dumb Pakistanis decide where I go," he told me.

The cup of tea had refreshed me, and I felt invigorated by the cool morning air. "Yeah! Of course not," I agreed.

"We'll just take a walk around," Rauf Mama announced. There was a footpath leading away from the checkpoint. We'd begin on this, skirting the border guards as well as a couple of mountains, then cross over into Pakistan. This was one of the shorter but harder routes to Bajaur—a four- or five-hour trip, Rauf Mama said.

But our security guards were reluctant; they claimed the trail was too difficult. "I've seen much harder trails than this," Rauf Mama dismissed them. "This is like a short walk."

"No, no, no, not you!" one corrected, anxious not to offend Rauf Mama. "It's Hyder that we're worried about."

"Oh, aside from a little toe problem, he's good to go," Rauf Mama replied confidently. "He can do this trail with ease—trust me."

We said goodbye to Sartor and made arrangements for the delivery of our bags. Then we finished our tea and prepared to leave. I was exhilarated. I was actually going to see the trails on foot, the way I'd wanted to—the way the insurgents did. Turning my back on Teeth Pass, I followed Rauf Mama down the trail.

Now we're on our way and except for my toe, which is bleeding, this doesn't seem all that bad. I've got my microphone pinned to me, and my minidisc recorder in my pocket. We pass two donkeys carrying water; in the distance we hear the faint song of a shepherd.

Then I get tired. I start to sweat. Some of the uphill parts are so steep that I feel as if I might fall backward. We take a break when we reach a man serving tea from a little tent. I know that Rauf Mama wouldn't have stopped if I weren't here. Five minutes later he tells me that I should go along now with one of the slower guards, get a head start. I leave right away, grateful that I won't have to worry about keeping up with the others' quicker pace.

I'm out front for a while before I hear the group getting closer. One of the guards is yelling at me to come back; he tells me that we're not going on this trail anymore, that we're climbing up another way instead. The thing he's pointing to is basically the unimproved vertical wall of the mountain, so I assume he's just trying to pull my chain, and I keep walking. Then he yells again and says he's serious—it's time to go this way now.

We start up the side. You can see places a little flattened from where people have walked on them, but there is no designated trail. The pain in my toe is excruciating, and I try not to use my right foot at all. Finally, I resort to using my hands. I begin literally crawling up the mountain.

"Look, Hyder's on four-wheel drive!" one of the guards jokes. Everyone gets a good laugh out of this, including me. (The guard says *qoomak,* or "help," which is what four-wheel drive is called here.)

At last I manage to raise myself up, my clothes soaked with sweat, only to come face to face with two armed Pakistani soldiers.

Rauf Mama begins talking to the soldiers, trying to convince them to let us across. But they'd probably decided the case in our favor the moment they saw our six armed men. The soldiers don't even demand a bribe. Then, perhaps because they feel sort of degraded, they say that they have taken part in jihad, too, having fought in Kashmir. "Yes, of course," Rauf Mama says cordially. "I've been there, I've visited Kashmir and seen it myself."

Then we say goodbye to all but one of our bodyguards, Musa Kareem, who will continue along with us to Bajaur. I slip the others some money so that back in Asadabad they can get some Cokes.

Soon we're standing at the summit. I shiver a little as the cool air buffets my wet back. Birds chirp in the thin fog, and it feels as though we are up in the sky. Rauf Mama walks over to a cliff and squats at its very edge. His feet are centimeters from the brink; one small slip, and he'll fall off. But he doesn't seem to be in danger. Rather, Rauf Mama seems incredibly, buoyantly free. Perching at the rim of the cliff and gazing into the distance, he looks almost like an eagle. Right now it wouldn't shock me if he raised some wings out of his shoulder blades and just flew off over the range.

"Do you think you can walk out here?" he asks me. "I'm sure you can, but be careful, because of your toe."

I approach slowly, as much to prevent myself from stumbling as to preserve the stillness. At the edge, I crouch down next to Rauf Mama. Looking straight down from perhaps ten thousand feet, I feel calm. I'm certain I'm protected, that there's no chance of falling; and that even if I did begin to plummet, somehow my uncle would save me.

We start talking. Rauf Mama and I always click in conversations; people call us *yaran*, which means "close friends." "Rauf Mama, that was nice of you to try to be polite to the men about being in Kashmir," I say.

"Hmm?" he asks.

"You know," I say, "how you pretended for the guards that you'd gone over to Kashmir."

"Hyder, I really did go to Kashmir!" Rauf Mama exclaims.

Sometimes I feel like I could talk to Rauf Mama forever and still not know all his stories. "What was it like?" I ask. "Is it as beautiful as they say it is?"

"Yeah, it's an amazing place," Rauf Mama says. "They invited me over because of me fighting the jihad against the Soviets. They wanted me to see their resistance. I didn't want to be rude, so I said I'd go. Man, they really treated me with a lot of respect out there. They thought I was something special," he laughs.

I don't want to admit to Rauf Mama that I'm exhausted. So I say instead that before we continue, I need to record a little. I stay there at the edge with the mic, recording mostly the soft sound of the air at the top of the mountain. A goat darts around nearby; I can hear its rattly *baa*. Aside from that and the birds, the world up here is silent. I don't know how you could catch Taliban or Al Qaeda in these trails. It's no wonder that Afghanistan is called the graveyard of empires; there's no way anyone could conquer the areas I've seen today.

The break ends, and we go downhill. The downhill is frigging scary. My toe is turning black, which can't be good. I hobble down the steep slope, using a branch as a cane. We're stepping from rock to rock—*Ow! Fuck. I keep hitting my toe*—and occasionally our path seems to fall away from us completely, rocks slipping out from under our feet. Twice I fall. My thighs ache. I would trade this downhill for another five hours of uphill.

Finally we get to a trail, and I step on it with relief. Musa Kareem taps me on the shoulder. He gestures to the peak towering above us—*Look, we just did that!* High up we see a group of maybe fifteen people. "They look like they're coming down from the sky," says Rauf Mama. I'm pretty impressed with myself—until I see a kid, maybe twelve years old, skip-

224

ping along with a bureau drawer almost as big as he is strapped onto his back with a rope. He's carrying a piece of furniture, and I can barely carry myself.

From here the rest is easy. At the bottom of the mountain a couple of pickups wait to retrieve arriving travelers, like a cabs at an airport terminal. I don't think I've ever been so happy to see a pickup in my life. It's about a forty-five-minute ride from here to Rauf Mama's house, and on the way I evaluate my condition: scraped-up knees, a rash, a toe with a nail that's about to fall off. Anyone can climb mountains, I decide, but it's the way you do it in Afghanistan that makes it hard—in the backcountry, outfitted in basically slippers and pajamas.

My kameez partoog is filthy, and so am I. When we reach a marketplace, I pay a guy to use a public shower stall. I'm the only one who takes a shower because I'm the only one who looks like he needs to. I've sweated so much today that I wouldn't be surprised if I've lost ten pounds. The shower stall is slippery, and the water comes out in a strong stream. Afterward I buy an old-fashioned bottled Coke; the guy pops the cap off for me with an opener.

Now I'm feeling an exhausted satisfaction. Sometimes it seems like the mountains in Afghanistan were painted in the background just to make you romanticize the place even more. Each peak taunts you, daring you to come give it a try. I'm a little impressed with myself for having met the challenge. I think back to last summer, which now seems easy. *What am I going to do next year?* I wonder.

I get back in the pickup with Rauf Mama. He's not tired at all. Today he scrambled up and down the mountain, a man in his late fifties who could have outrun anyone of any age we'd have come across on the trails. To me the trip was an actual mission; to Rauf Mama it was a walk home.

And then we're at his house, slowing down along a wall that stretches toward endless green fields. Rauf Mama gets out of the car. This is just his life, and he proceeds through it without a trace of self-consciousness.

23

Sometimes Rauf Mama's head will just start shaking. The motion is barely perceptible, like that of a bobblehead doll right before it stops. Doctors say that it's the result of exposure to chemical weapons during the Soviet war. Remnants of two bullets are lodged in the back of his hand; you can press down on them, the same as veins. He also has tiny pieces of shrapnel—like crumbs—embedded in his skin. One time he called me over and asked me to help him work one of the bits loose from his forehead. I scratched at it, and out came a silver flake. On his forehead is a big black permanent bruise, which is not to be confused with a nearby mark that represents a lifetime of touching his head to a hard surface during five prayer sessions a day. Then there's his false eye, which takes some getting used to. In the night I'll turn over and see him snoring in a bed nearby; his left, functional eye will be pushed into his pillow, but the false right one will be wide awake even as he's asleep, staring straight ahead. (My father jokes that Rauf Mama's injury is a boon to our security.) When Rauf Mama wants to remove his eye, he just starts touching it—like some people do with soft contacts—and the next thing you know, it's in his hand. Then there is just a pocket of skin. One time Rauf Mama was chiding my father about having misplaced some papers, and my father returned, teasingly, "Who are you to talk? You lost your own eye"; which Rauf Mama had, on *hajj*, the pilgrimage Muslims undertake to Mecca.

As a young man, Rauf Mama was a *talib*, or religious student; back then the name did not connote radicalism. After he married, he started a couple of businesses: a timber venture, a taxi company with a fleet of three or four cars. In the late 1970s Rauf Mama began to wonder about the Communist government. His friends' opinions were divided. "I said that until your dad tells me what to do, I'm not going to make a decision," Rauf Mama explains. "I wasn't that knowledgeable about the government, and your dad had been in the middle of it all. So I decided to go to Kabul and talk to your dad about it."

On the day of Rauf Mama's visit, one of my father's cousins also came over. Rauf Mama didn't know that he was a Communist informant. "As soon as I opened my mouth, your dad started shaking his head in a signal to shut up about it," Rauf Mama says.

Eventually my father and Rauf Mama left for a walk. "This government is a Communist dictatorship and is basically opening the door for Russia to come in," my father told him. "Slowly, it's going to happen. Why don't you take refuge in Pakistan, and while you're at it, find a house for me, too?"

But instead of heading straight for Pakistan, Rauf Mama went back to Kunar and rounded up ten of his friends to join him in resisting the Communists. By the time of the Soviet invasion, his days had taken on a pattern. Each morning when the sun came up, Rauf Mama and the others would drop their wives and children off at caves near the river. They'd go out and fight and, at the end of the day, pick their families back up.

One day Soviet soldiers dropped out of their helicopters and the mujahedeen moved in. "I had a Kalashnikov with me that had forty bullets in it," Rauf Mama remembers. "I emptied all forty bullets into two guys, right in the middle of their chests. One of them, when he was hit, all he did was go, 'Aaaaahhh!' It wouldn't penetrate him at all."

Rauf Mama and the others had never heard of armored vests. They knew only this: *These new kind of Soviets are going to create problems for us. Not even bullets can penetrate them.*

"And that," Rauf Mama says, "is when we decided to become refugees in Pakistan."

* * *

Rauf Mama lives in a hilly section of Bajaur. He has many acres—the exact number I don't know—and one of his sons sometimes rides around the fields on a tractor. A road divides the large main house and the smaller *hujera*. When Rauf Mama talks about how his property value has more than quadrupled in the years since the purchase, he sounds like someone who bought in San Francisco before the dot-com boom, rather than in a rural tribal region before a refugee influx.

I spend most of my time in the *hujera*, sleeping in the small bedroom or sitting with guests in a newly painted room filled with cushions. But one day Rauf Mama meets me out front, and we head across to the main house for a tour. As soon as we enter, women scatter. Perhaps seventy people—twenty beyond where Rauf Mama loses count—live in the compound. Rauf Mama begins our tour with the room called the depot. The depot holds huge sacks of flour and wheat and rice and barley. Meals are cooked in extra-large pots and pans and served cafeteria style, with everyone carrying plates off to separate locations.

Next we enter an area in which kids dressed in tiny kameez partoog are running around a large water tank. I try to count the children. *One, two, three, four, five, six, seven, eight, nine, ten, eleven, twelve, thirteen, fourteen, fifteen, sixteen—popped out of that corner—seventeen. I just counted seventeen of them,* I say into my minidisc recorder, water burbling in the background. *Like little, little kids.* Rauf Mama's grandchildren greet their *baba* with a spirited "Talib Baba!"—a reference to his days as a religious student. (A brother who studied at Kabul University is "Kabul Baba.") For his part, Rauf Mama often identifies his grandchildren with a certain inexactitude. "Who's that kid?" I'll ask. "Oh. That looks like my older brother's middle son's eldest son," he'll conjecture.

Now we enter Rauf Mama's quarters. His own bedroom is medium-size, with mattresses atop carpets—but more striking than the decor is the presence of his wife, whom I've never met. "Salaam alaikum," I say softly.

Rauf Mama's wife is shy and very traditional; when a male news anchor appears on the TV screen, she will cover her face and look away. It is unusual for someone of Rauf Mama's tribal stature not to have taken additional wives; the fact that he has not done so can be attributed to the cosmopolitan influence of my father, as well as to the depth of his own tenderness. He feels bad about what his wife has had to go through, just by dint of being married to him; he dreams of taking her on a special trip to Mecca.

Now, in a corner, Rauf Mama's wife huddles over something on which she appears to be working. *This is Rauf Mama's own personal room,* I say into my recorder. *This is where he sleeps.*

When Rauf Mama talks about his friends, he always adds an unconscious parenthetical—"he's still alive" or often "he's dead"—before continuing on with the story. He's had the kind of life where mortality is more a matter of course than of note; survival isn't taken for granted. One evening in Bajaur, Rauf Mama receives a visit from a man who is scared to go home to Kunar because somebody there wants him dead. I sit there listening to them talk, trying to take notes. This is the second man in a single day who's come to discuss such a problem with my uncle. It's straight out of my philosophy reading, a real-life Hobbesian spectacle: *Fear of a violent death* is *a driving force here,* I write.

Bajaur is one of seven semi-autonomous tribal agencies that run along the Afghan-Pakistani border. The dominant inhabitants of this region are Pashtun tribes. These are not the "Pakistani versions"; Pashtuns existed in a contiguous territory until the British empire came along and, literally, drew a dividing line. The Durand Line—so named for its main negotiator, Sir Mortimer Durand—was imposed in 1893. To Pashtuns, the line has never been more than somebody else's abstraction. The feeling extends all the way to Kabul. No government of Afghanistan, not even the Taliban, has ever recognized the Durand Line as a valid international boundary.

The Pashtun presence here spills over into Pakistan's neighboring North-West Frontier Province (NWFP). This region has long been romanticized. It inspired the writing of Rudyard Kipling; and of Winston Churchill, whose first book, *The Story of the Malakand Field Force,* was an account of his military years in the NWFP. And now, more than a hundred years later, Western reporters write breathless stories about the tribal territory widely believed to house the world's most wanted fugitive, Osama bin Laden.

Efforts to find bin Laden are impaired by the American troops' inability to conduct operations in Pakistan, as well as by the unfamiliarity of Pakistan's own military with the region (until the hunt began, they'd basically stayed out of the tribal areas throughout Pakistan's entire half-century of existence). Of the seven tribal districts, Bajaur is an unlikely pick for bin Laden; the central government has managed to make some inroads here. Still, outside the market, most people walk around armed. And of course, everyone has a beard. Just as you'll never see my father with a beard, you'll never see Rauf Mama without one. His whole entire life, he has literally never shaved. Trimmed, yes, but shaved, no. Legend has it that he's the only soldier of his day to have skirted the Afghan military's facial hair policy; he paid a large bribe to keep his beard during his service.

One night during my visit a group gathers for dinner outside the *hujera*. Lanterns cast a spooky glow on the bearded faces, a fire pops and crackles, and I'm completely caught up in the moment, eating meat with these warriors. Then someone brings up George Tenet, the U.S. Senate intelligence committee hearings, and Iraq's missing weapons of mass destruction. A political discussion ensues, ranging from America's loss of credibility in the world to China's rising power, and I sit there, abashed at the romantic conception of these fierce tribesmen with which I entertained myself only moments before. They have a deeper knowledge of world affairs than most Americans.

In 1980, after moving his family to Bajaur, Rauf Mama continued his role in the war that largely contributed to the Soviet Union's collapse as a superpower and dissolution as a nation. To the surprise of a world that seemed not to have looked very hard at history, the mujahedeen proved extremely difficult to defeat. They knew where they had the advantage. Rauf Mama would attack the Russians on routes familiar to him from his travels in and out of Pakistan. One time Rauf Mama and his troops decided to insert themselves between two enemy convoys planning to rendezvous in northern Kunar. Nineteen men traveled across a river on trees, and on the way one fell in. "We tried to get him back, but it was the middle of the night," says Rauf Mama. "So we went by and he died."

The troops—on their third night without sleep and their second day without food—collapsed in a field when they completed their journey. The next thing Rauf Mama knew, one of his soldiers was whispering, "They're here, they're here. They're going to capture us." The Communists were so close that the mujahedeen could hear them talking. (Rauf Mama uses "Russians" and "Communists" interchangeably; the story here most likely involves Afghan Communist troops rather than Soviet soldiers.) Rauf Mama was momentarily stymied. "It was nighttime and in the middle of bushes and I couldn't really see," he remembers. "I didn't know what to do. They had come so close to us. It had to be within a couple of feet."

Rauf Mama was carrying three RPGs. Now he aimed one at a nearby rock. The rock shattered. "We killed two people right there," he says. A fight ensued; all in all nineteen Communists were killed and sixteen were captured. The rest fled.

Now the second convoy approached. Rauf Mama launched one of his two remaining RPGs at a tank. But the grenade exploded inside the river, and in response to the sound, the tank's driver swiveled around and headed straight for Rauf Mama. Rauf Mama hurled forth his last grenade, toppling the tank. Mujahedeen with machine guns moved in. The Communist troops, suspecting their manpower must be inferior, yelled, "We surrender! We surrender!"

They got a clearer picture of the enemy when they turned in their weapons. "Is this all of you?" they wondered. "Where's the rest of you guys?"

Rauf Mama's eighteen men had defeated a force of hundreds. He says it was the kind of thing that happened all the time: "The Russians would spend millions of dollars to bombard the place, and after all it would only be ten mujahedeen that had created the problem."

Not all battles ended so neatly for Rauf Mama. One day he and sixty of his soldiers set out to attack a Communist fort. Three men advanced forward, discovering too late the area had been mined. One man ("he's still alive") received shrapnel to his head. A second man ("he's dead") broke a foot. The third man was Rauf Mama. He says the mines "started jumping up" at him; one of them flew into his eye. There was a leaking sensation. Then he felt his eye dangling; he reached up and ripped it out. Meanwhile his abdomen had been perforated. Out of Saran Wrap (or something like it), Rauf Mama fashioned a tourniquet for his eye. Then he tied around his stomach a larger belt to contain his guts. "Didn't it hurt?" I ask him. "Not really," he says. "There was so much going on."

Now two Afghan Communists appeared before him and emptied their guns into his thigh. This, Rauf Mama admits, was "really painful." Knocked to the ground by their fire, he aimed back as best he could, and when he heard screams, he figured he had killed them both. He stood and ran and eventually collapsed. Some mujahedeen carried him over the mountains. He was in and out of consciousness and remembers little of this journey, except for "people crying."

He came to again three days later in a hospital in Peshawar, with my father at his side. Rauf Mama's oblivion had been fitful. While coming out from under surgical anesthesia, he'd issued commands, as if still on the battlefield: *Militia! Militia! Shoot that!* And he'd ranted about Gulbiddin Hekmatyar: *He's a traitor. He killed these Afghans here, and these Afghans here. I need to call Said Fazel Akbar and get him over here and tell him to tell the world that this guy's not a good guy.* (My father recorded Rauf Mama's tirades onto a cassette tape that I would love to unearth.) The doctors told Rauf Mama that his recovery would take two years. But only three months later Rauf Mama was back on the front lines. When, early on, he found himself in a minefield, his leg began shaking uncontrollably; perhaps it was the one place his body authorized to show fear.

For several of these years Rauf Mama was affiliated with Kunar's Wahhabi party. Wahhabism is a fundamentalist strain of Islam now associated with Al Qaeda. The party received Arab support, and its ranks included many Arab fighters. In Kunar it was stronger than the seven official parties. Rauf Mama was its *khat-e-awal,* or front-line commander. He didn't buy into the Wahhabi creed; he joined simply because they had the most money and the most weapons to offer.

Oddly, the party that would later affiliate itself with Osama bin Laden initially dismissed the Saudi benefactor. Rauf Mama's peers cautioned him against involvement with bin Laden and his followers. *Don't go to him,* they said. *They are not really that interested in the jihad and they are not really that interested in the faith; they're just interested in power.* The

Arabs who backed Rauf Mama's party were from established families who had no interest in overthrowing their government, whereas bin Laden was pedigreed but discontent. *Don't deal with those people,* Rauf Mama was warned. *They're not good people.*

So Rauf Mama didn't. Of course, the people who ran his own party turned out not to be such good people either.

One afternoon in Bajaur we take a five-minute drive down the street from Rauf Mama's house to have lunch with Ruhullah's father. Ruhullah is the adversary who attempted to undermine my father during my first summer in Afghanistan. He's the one who is said to have smuggled Al Qaeda operatives out of Tora Bora—the one who managed to ingratiate himself with the Americans before they wised up and whisked him off to Guantánamo. He is also the nephew of Jamil Rahman, who founded Kunar's Wahhabi party. Our lunch takes place at the very compound at which Jamil Rahman was shot to death.

We are welcomed to the compound by Ruhullah's father, who walks with some trouble on a twisted right foot—an injury that has earned him the moniker Mullah Gohd (Lame Mullah). One time during the 1980s Ruhullah attempted to arrange to have Rauf Mama killed. Rauf Mama confronted Mullah Gohd, who was so enraged by his son's behavior—"If I could disown him, I would"—that Rauf Mama actually felt sorry for the family.

Now he is much less sympathetic. Last summer Ruhullah was instrumental in fingering Rauf Mama as a member of Al Qaeda. As a result, several of Rauf Mama's men—including his nephew Shohab—were imprisoned at Bagram. I'd come across the news of Rauf Mama's "misdeeds" in a government newspaper in Karzai's office. The story said that Rauf Mama was a known member of Al Qaeda and had attacked American forces in Kunar. But at the time of the "attack," Rauf Mama had been hanging out with me in Kabul Hotel, standing before the bathroom mirror, holding hair dye and a toothbrush, coloring his graying beard.

Today Ruhullah's father is asking for our help in getting his son out of Guantánamo. Rauf Mama does most of the talking. I silently chuckle, hearing him explain how difficult it is to win from the Americans a prisoner's release. Rauf Mama lies that my father has done this and that and talked to everybody he knows, but that's just not how America works— personal connections won't get you anywhere. As the resident expert on the country, I confirm his assessment with a straight face. (*Maybe I have what it takes to make it in tribal politics after all*, I consider.)

For some reason Ruhullah's father keeps wondering if I want to take a nap. He literally asks me about it every fifteen minutes. Finally I head off to a *charpoy* outside, just to get him off my back. Then I lie there on the rope bed, waiting for the meeting to finish. Eventually our bodyguard joins me, and the two of us sit there and talk with a guy who identifies himself as Ruhullah's nephew. He's on summer vacation—he goes to school in Saudi Arabia. He asks me what I'm studying.

"I think I'm going to go with an economics major," I tell him. "What are you studying?"

"Islamic law," he replies.

Somehow I get the feeling that even though the nephew seems nice, he will be back to make big trouble for me.

When the mujahedeen took Kabul in 1992, Rauf Mama accepted a position as a representative to the Defense Ministry. But he soon found that he could not conscionably work with the new government, and he returned home to Bajaur.

A few years later Rauf Mama called my father and asked what he should do about this new group called the Taliban. Fresh off the meeting at which Abdul Haq had urged my father to give the movement a chance, he advised Rauf Mama to do the same. When an enemy with whom Rauf Mama was embroiled in a land feud took an anti-Taliban stance, it became unfeasible for Rauf Mama to do the same. As a result, Rauf Mama never actively fought the Taliban.

After 9/11, when the American military began its air campaign in Afghanistan, Rauf Mama called my father in California and once again asked his advice. My father told him to sit tight; he would be in Afghanistan soon, and they could discuss things then. "How's the bombing going?" he asked.

"The U.S. bombing is like a fireworks show," Rauf Mama reported.

"People go up to their rooftops and watch it. When the Russians came, they'd put down their helicopters, start shooting, and we would run from them. So compared to that," Rauf Mama said, "this is not that bad."

By the time we return from Bajaur, the summer is almost over. The day before I leave Afghanistan, I sit down with Rauf Mama to do an interview and nail down some of the details of his life. (We get off to a comical start; when I tell him, "You can start off with, 'I was born on this date,'" he just laughs. "Oh man, I can't do that," he says.) The fan above us powers on and off; periodically I take breaks to record the changed ambient sound of the room, or to translate into English a story Rauf Mama has just told me in Pashto.

At one point Rauf Mama begins to write something, hunching over his paper like a little kid. "What are you writing?" I ask him when I finish translating.

"Oh, I have a hard time writing five and four in English," he tells me.

I look at his paper, which is covered with fives. *These fives seem fine,* I say into my recorder. *I think I'm gonna keep this.* I fold the sheet and slip it into my pocket.

Then I ask Rauf Mama to tell me, out of everything he's been through, what was the hardest moment of his life. He answers with two stories, both from the Soviet war. In the first, Rauf Mama cuts ligament and bone off an injured soldier's leg, then carries the man on a long journey to safety. In the second story, Rauf Mama carries another man; but this man is dead. It's the middle of winter, hailing and bitterly cold, and Rauf Mama is alone with the dead man in the mountains. Miraculously, he happens upon a small mosque. He rests the dead body on a narrow bed inside, then lies on the floor and closes his eyes. Then there's an enormous *crack!* Hail pierces the roof of the mosque, which begins to fill with water. The water rises so high that Rauf Mama can no longer remain on the floor. He climbs into the bed with the dead body and hugs it toward him as he tries to sleep. The hail pelts down upon them.

"It was very hard for me to lie down next to him," he tells me. "But I had no choice—it was my third night without sleep. My clothes got blood-ied, and I started to smell. He was a good friend of mine—the same age—and just hours ago he was with me."

The story is grim. But it's the sum of Rauf Mama's life that gets to me. A fraction of his experience would be enough to make anyone rough, but Rauf Mama hasn't been hardened at all. I'm always trying to reconcile how one man can be both so tough and so tender.

Down by the river the other day, Rauf Mama said, "Ooooh, look at that kitten." The cat was small and gray. "It must have run away from home or something," he guessed, approaching it. "Oh, it's scared," he discovered. "I think we should get it some milk."

The security guards started to snicker, and Rauf Mama whipped around. "What are you laughing at?" he said to them. "Go get some milk, man! Hurry up!"

A guard ran up to the compound and returned with some milk and a little bowl. Rauf Mama poured the milk himself, then crouched down and began to murmur. The image was incongruous: here was a guy with a big beard, one eye, and metal bulging out of his forehead, easing a bowl of milk toward a lost kitten.

The contradictions get you at every turn; the man who's probably responsible for hundreds of deaths has a son whose name means peace. *Salaam.*

The first time I remember meeting Rauf Mama was when I was a child in India. At a hotel pool he taught me how to swim. I thought he was one of the friendliest people I had ever met, and he thought I was one of the smartest. In those days my father would give me little quizzes—ask me to locate a certain story in the newspaper. Rauf Mama would sit and watch. I was fluent in Hindi, and Rauf Mama, who couldn't speak it, would come find me when he needed to go to the market. He called me his "little translator." Who would have thought that ten years later Rauf Mama would be teaching me to sneak across an international border instead of stroke across a pool, and I would be translating for him with U.S. Special Forces instead of Indian shopkeepers.

One of my dreams is to get Rauf Mama a visa and take him on a trip to America. We'd drive from San Francisco to Los Angeles down Highway 101; maybe we'd fly to Vegas. If anyone deserves to lose themselves for a weekend in Vegas, it's Rauf Mama.

But most of my dreams for Rauf Mama take place in this country. I want him to see Afghanistan moving forward; I don't want everything he's gone through to have been in vain.

Then I have less than twenty-four hours to go. My bags are packed; I'm leaving for California in the morning. *This is probably going to be my last recording,* I whisper into my microphone. It's past midnight, but I can't sleep. I keep picturing Rauf Mama trembling with cold in the little mosque, his arms around his dead friend. *Just in case I ever get soft,* I say. *Like, "Maybe I should just stay in America . . ." That image of him having to do that will at least keep me going for another five years.*

He still can't walk past a kitten, I marvel. *He has that big of a heart.*

I lie there, fierce with resolve. *Despite everything, I'm gonna be pulled back here, I know it,* I whisper sharply. *I just can't do it any other way. I can't let my uncle down.*

24

I'VE BEEN BACK IN CALIFORNIA FOR about three months when I get the call. The only thing that surprises me is that it hasn't happened sooner: there's been an assassination attempt on my dad. Two bombs exploded at the compound, one near the bathroom, another behind a surrounding wall. Fortunately my father was out at the time of the blast, and my mother, who has finally returned with him to Afghanistan, was on the other side of the property. Sartor and Shohab received minor injuries—headaches and cuts from shards of glass. Dust blinded people for about five hundred yards. One of the bombs would have caused far more serious damage had not a huge cooking oven my mother purchased in Kabul absorbed the brunt of the impact.

The attack is thought to be retaliation for a recent seizure of opium. In early November my father's security forces stopped a car for a routine check and found it to contain more than five hundred pounds of the drug. The men in the car claimed that they were going to turn in the load to the Interior Ministry. My father called Interior Minister Jalali to check their story, and the next day officials arrived in Asadabad, confiscated the opium, and took the smugglers into custody. (One of the smugglers was actually an Interior Ministry official himself; the other, a military officer from Jalalabad.) Now, less than three weeks later, someone was getting revenge.

My mother sounded calm on the satellite phone; I wish I felt the same. It's harder to hear about this kind of thing in California. Life in Afghanistan doesn't seem as dangerous when you're actually inside it as it does when you're far away.

With my mother in Afghanistan, I spend a lot of nights at my brother's. It's hard to get used to being alone. During Ramadan I come home in the dark from school and break the fast by myself with reheated chili. After the holiday I buy some meat and chicken and salmon and make plans to cook for myself, to marinate it—but that never quite works out. Then there's housework. I'm used to keeping my room tidy but not to fluffing the pillows on the couch every time I walk in the door. One day I complain to my mother that I don't know how to iron. Maybe my aunt could come over and do my shirts for me? My father overhears my mother's end of the conversation and grabs the phone. "How do you say it in English?" he scolds me. "You need to stand on your own feet."

Earlier this fall—before my mother returned with him to Afghanistan—my father came to California for a visit. Again his trip followed the UN General Assembly. This year, I had a laugh over his name tag. Some organizer had managed to misspell Fazel as Fakar. The reaction was hilarious; my father said people would hesitate before saying his name, or just try to avoid addressing him entirely. It reminded me of the scene in *Meet the Parents* where Ben Stiller's future mother-in-law asks how to pronounce his "very unique" last name. "Oh, just like it's spelled," he replies. "F-o-c-k-e-r."

One day during my father's visit, we sat down with the microphone and I asked him if he'd observed any changes in me since I started making my trips to Afghanistan. "Yes," he answered immediately. "I do see a difference. A lot of people in America do not have real goals in life. I wasn't sure if you had any goals you wanted to achieve. But now I see your major goal is to bring change to Afghanistan. I see you working hard, making difficult trips to remote areas. I see you reading books, educating yourself. All this makes me happy.

"Most Afghan kids in America are not passionate about Afghanistan," he said, "and if they are, they haven't seen the country. Most who go are not as enthusiastic about returning—which is understandable, because there is nothing in Afghanistan for them to be enthusiastic about. But you've been there twice now and both times come back more passionate than you were before. This is a very good sign for me. Hopefully if you keep going on this path—keep working hard like you are now—I believe you will play a very big role in Afghanistan's future." I was glad that my passion for Afghanistan now had more legitimacy in my father's eyes.

"What do you think the greatest difficulty of living there will be for me?" I asked him. "When I move there permanently."

"I think the greatest difficulty for you will be the language," he replied. (Though I speak both Pashto and Dari fluently, I am still basically unable to read or write in them.) "That's one thing you'll have to work on," my father advised.

I would have devoted myself to the task immediately, but unfortunately I had a previous commitment to French. Because the languages I can speak aren't in my community college's curriculum, they don't count. It's annoying; what about their usefulness in the world? In all the recent talk about the U.S. intelligence forces' miserable language capabilities, has there ever been a moment in which we bemoaned a shortage of speakers of French? But I can't fulfill my general education requirements without a foreign language, so I slog along.

It's hard enough to focus on school as it is—especially when the call comes again. The news is assuming an air of inevitability: there's been another assassination attempt on my father. This time they'd gotten closer. My father had visited a school in a district called Naray and was returning to Asadabad in a convoy of several pickup trucks. Then there was a bang under my father's car and some smoke. *Maybe it was something with the engine,* the others figured. *Let's just keep going.* But my father identified the source of the problem immediately. He said, "It's a mine."

In the road a mine was found in an oil container. Apparently someone had attempted to trigger the device by remote control. Thankfully, their technology was flawed. With a mine like this, there was about a one-in-a-hundred chance of malfunction.

My father's survival was miraculous, and the people of Kunar responded accordingly. The next day everyone prayed and performed charities out of gratitude that he'd been spared. *This is a sign of your pure heart,* people told him. I think that even someone who wasn't religious might agree that my father had been protected by something.

That something certainly wasn't the reconstruction effort. A simple paved road would have prevented the incident. But as long as the routes remain unimproved, anyone who observes my father's convoy pass can easily bury a mine to strike him on his way back.

My mother seems more shaken up this time around; I even detect a solemnity in my father. Though objectively he is probably no less safe now than he was before, the stakes seem to have been raised. I was working on a book now. One publisher, conjuring up father-son morning show appearances, wondered if my father might be willing to participate in the publicity effort. *Sure,* I said. *If he's in the States, absolutely.* Now I prepare myself for the possibility that he might not be around at all.

My worlds are starting to overlap; the pull Afghanistan exerts on my "regular" year is increasing. Most of the time the effect is, if pronounced, mainly psychological; but in the early spring it becomes a reality, when my grandmother dies, and I have to go back. This was my father's mother, and she passed away in the Bay Area nursing home in which she'd lived for several years. My brother and I will transport her body to Kunar. It will be a short trip, just a couple weeks. It's strange to think that such an itinerary is possible. It's easy to go to Vegas, even Paris, for a quick jaunt, sure. But this is something entirely different; this is like a short hop through some kind of wrinkle in time. It makes me think of the trailer for a recent Michael Crichton movie: "Your father is in the fourteenth century," a scientist-type urgently informs a young man my age. "We need you to help us get him back!"

I'm excited that I'll be accompanied on this mission by my brother. Before we leave, there are various supplies we have to procure: weight gain powder, for example. Last summer in Bajaur I was talking with one of Rauf Mama's nephews about working out. He wanted to bulk up, and he'd tried everything, from protein to carbs. "Well, we have these weight gainers in America," I began. Word spread, and soon there was practically a waiting list for the bodybuilding supplement. I didn't have the heart to explain that the powder came in a huge jar that would be really hard to pack.

Instead Omar and I purchase other gifts at a sporting goods chain called Big 5. We select a bunch of digital watches, all the same kind, and we try to find something special for Rauf Mama. A young guy in a blue vest helps us out. "What's the most durable kind of knife?" we ask him. He shows us a $200 model.

But then we see the night-vision goggles. A flashlight is pretty much useless in Kunar—like a thin beam through a black hole. The goggles seem worth a shot. We look them over—they're made in Russia, which gives them a kind of sinister cred.

The salesman, who knows we're leaving for a trip, asks, "Where are you going?"

My brother and I kind of look at each other. "Afghanistan," I say.

The salesman, a white guy in his twenties, pauses before he asks us—two slightly darker-skinned guys of terrorist age—"Why are you going to Afghanistan?"

"Because our grandmother passed away," says Omar.

"We have family there to visit," I say, at exactly the same time.

It must seem like the classic *gotcha!* stumble. "Actually my grandmother passed away, and we're going to take her back, and the family's going to be there to visit," I explain. But we've already raised the salesman's suspicions. You know that as soon as we leave, he'll be telling his co-workers about how we bought night-vision goggles and matching digital watches to outfit our very own Al Qaeda cell.

In Afghanistan I notice small changes immediately, like a FedEx billboard rising alongside the airport road. And then there is the season; snow-covered mountains surround Kabul.

The experience is a million times more dramatic for my brother, who is aligning the new world with his childhood memory of it. Both he and the country have changed significantly. He was younger than I when he made his trips inside Afghanistan; his experiences here during the Soviet war overwhelmed him. At an age when most kids are standing in line at amusement parks, Omar visited the mass grave at Kerala. "Everyone told me the story of what happened," he says. "And I went around behind the place and cried for two hours."

In Kabul, Omar and I drive around, videotaping places he remembers from his childhood. Here is his apartment; over there, the neighborhood with all the mean kids. We walk around Chicken Street, stopping at various vendors. Omar puts his bags down on the ground and leans in to look at the wares. "What are you doing?" I say. "This isn't Nordstrom's, you know. You can't just put your bags down while you start looking through the racks or whatever. People are ready to pick up your stuff as soon as you turn your back."

"Oh, I'm sorry," he says.

We finish shopping and get back in the car. "Hey, wait," Omar says. "Where's the camera?"

The camera is gone; luckily we'd already removed the tape containing all his memories.

When we get to Kunar, Omar and I head down to Toopchi together. The last time he was here, the base was occupied by Arabs. "There were all these people going around Kunar that didn't look Afghan, that didn't act Afghan," he remembers. "They were so mean to everybody." Afghans were pious but laid back; the Arabs were dogmatic and severe. One day at the base Omar tried to mess with them. "Why are you here?" he ribbed them.

The Arabs bristled and gave Omar a talking-to about the length of his pants. Their doctrine dictated that a man's ankles should remain visible. "Your pants aren't supposed to drag on the floor like that," they told him.

My brother started laughing. "What's it to you if I want to put my pants like this?" he challenged. Then he pulled them down even farther. The quarrel escalated, and finally one of my father's guards warned Omar, "Calm down. These people are crazy."

"No, man," my brother said. "They're here in our country, and they keep messing things up."

Now, years later, when Omar shows up at the base, it's occupied by Americans; and he's come to talk not about hemlines but about new roads. Kunar is one of several provinces in which the Americans have recently installed a Provincial Reconstruction Team (PRT), a division of the military dedicated to rebuilding rather than fighting. The PRT guys get excited when we tell them that we have our own NGO. NGOs play an outsize role in a country like Afghanistan. When a government is unable to execute its basic responsibilities, NGOs step in to help.

Rauf Mama and I registered our family's NGO during my first summer in Kabul. We called it Wadan Afghanistan, which translates inadequately as Developed Afghanistan; the meaning is more poetic in Pashto. One day he and I went over to the Ministry of Planning for our paperwork. A couple minutes turned into an hour; finally the department chair showed up. "I'm sorry, but we seem to have misplaced your papers," he said. He stood on a chair to check a high shelf; I looked underneath the couches. Finally Rauf Mama told me what was going on. "Hyder, your papers aren't really lost," he said. "They are asking for a bribe." Feeling embarrassed, I offered the department chair all the money I had on me—$50—as a show of my appreciation for all the trouble he'd gone to on my behalf. He refused—this was just his duty—then accepted; five minutes later the Wadan Afghanistan paperwork was found.

Now there is the fortuitous convergence of our NGO and the Americans' PRT. We can team up for reconstruction projects. From the Americans' perspective, an alliance with our family is advantageous; my brother and I can navigate both worlds. And for our part, we're pleased that the PRT is around to give our NGO a jump start.

For some time my brother has been grappling with the idea of taking a sort of sabbatical in Afghanistan, and this decides it. Omar will remain in Kunar after my grandmother's funeral and get some projects off the ground.

But first he has some adjusting to do. We'll be sitting there at the compound with guests—a steady stream of mourners come to pay their respects—and Omar will reveal some inappropriate piece of information, and I'll tap his foot. "Why'd you tap my foot?" he'll say. "I didn't tap your foot," I'll reply. "No, you did," he'll maintain.

For years Omar has been in Walnut Creek mortgage-broker mode. He is accustomed to conducting his dealings with openness and honesty. But if you deploy these qualities incautiously in Kunar, you could wind up dead.

One night when we share a meal with Kunar's director of religious affairs and several others, Omar launches into a story about how earlier in the day I'd scolded him for going to the marketplace without any guards. (I've effortlessly shifted into the knowing role previously occupied by my father: *If they see you have five people with you, they won't shoot,* I tell Omar. *But they will if you're out there by yourself.*) Now, as he relays the tale to our dinner companions, I know I'll have to reprimand him again, this time for needlessly revealing just how green he is.

After the meal Omar turns to me and says, correctly, "Hey, you're going to Kabul on Sunday, right?"

"No, I'm not going to Kabul on Sunday," I reply.

Omar will not be deterred. "No, remember, your flight's on Monday, and Dad said you were going to go on Sunday."

"No, no," I brush him off. "I think you got it confused."

Now Rauf Mama's brother Ghousoudin Mama, who earlier lectured Omar about security, jokes, "I think Hyder's got you again."

"Huh?" says Omar. "I don't get it."

"Be quiet, Omar," I say. "I'll tell you about it later."

Soon enough Omar seems to have absorbed the lesson. He takes out his daily planner and writes on the top of each page: *Don't mention dates. Don't mention dates.* Now his education is almost complete. "Make sure you're careful about what you say on the phone," I caution him. "You don't even know how many people listen in, who try to."

"Okay," he says. "Got it."

The night before we leave for Kabul, I see him just after he hangs up with his wife, Sofia. "You told Sofia you're going to Kabul in the morning, huh," I say.

"Oh shit, yes I did," he realizes.

"If you say it on the phone, you might as well just announce it in the middle of the mosque!" I exclaim.

These days, my father is getting needled about security precautions, too. Rauf Mama teases him all the time: "What, are you getting money on your own death or something?" It seems that even the close shaves have not significantly changed his habits.

My father's unguardedness grows out of a lifetime of assessing risk; my brother's, out of enthusiasm. Omar gets right into the swing of things, traveling with Rauf Mama to a jirga in a remote valley home to an ethnic group called the Gujar. Rauf Mama mediates a land feud, and he and Omar spend the night in the local mosque. Omar is the star attraction: *The governor's son is here from America!* The Gujar sit around trying to come up with questions for him. Finally one guy says, "How much does meat cost in America, per kilo?" That is the biggest thing anyone can think of to ask. They cannot fathom America through anything other than their own lens.

For me, America and Afghanistan are more comparable than ever before; now I have my family here. Unfortunately being together as a unit only makes the differences between the two worlds more pronounced. My father's job places us in the public eye; we can't be as teasing or affectionate as we can at home in California. And we are separated from my mother here—my brother and father and I off with the male guests in one area, while she is entertaining female relatives in another. I assumed that the presence of my mother and brother would make Afghanistan more livable. My future here seems more challenging without that promise.

On one of the few nights we all spend together, my father drags out an old movie projector. We sit before a plain white wall as he loads the reel. A man with bell bottoms and sideburns appears in the frame. It's my father—and my whole family, on vacation in Iran. My brother, perhaps seven years old, sports a stylish haircut; my sister wears a little skirt. They stand in front of a building, a monument, and walk in a park. It was just a year or two before everything happened, and their lives seem brilliantly normal. "Damn, that's a pretty happy family," Yossef says. For all of us, it's strange to see what could have been.

In another scene, at picnic area outside Kabul called Paghman, Omar and my father play soccer. By the time I was born, my father was so much older; I've never even pictured playing soccer with him. There is also footage of Rauf Mama walking around Kunar. In the years since, he's been through the most out of everyone but has changed the least of all.

There is a hushed quiet; nobody makes too many comments as the lost world flickers back to life on the screen. There is the *rat-tat-tat* of the film spinning, the cranky machine overheating.

These things are not in my memory of my family. They took place before any of the things that have come to define Afghanistan had happened; they took place before I had happened. The weirdest thing about the movies is that I'm not in any of them. That's the first thing I notice: that I don't exist. By the time I joined the family, they were refugees in Pakistan. I came along after their lives had already changed.

I fly back to California by myself and take a taxi home from the airport. My house is empty. All of a sudden I'm back in my room on my bed. *Boom, boom.* It all happened so quickly.

People often want to know what I miss about America when I'm in Afghanistan. Those who expect some big grand statement are probably disappointed to hear that it's things like paved roads and fast food. The truth is, I'm never away long enough to miss the things that matter on a deeper level, like individual freedoms.

Anyway, this spring I'm thinking more about the inverse: Here in America what I miss about Afghanistan is my family. Sofia and my nephew, Ali, also feel their absence. Before he left, Omar trained Sofia to run his mortgage brokerage offices, and now she is taking care of both Ali and the business. They live in a new neighborhood; the whole place is pin-drop quiet, amplifying every little creak, and I spend a lot of nights on their couch so that Sofia won't be nervous.

Ali is three now, old enough to know his father and his grandmother have gone to a place called Kunar. One day when I leave early for school, he toddles into the family room and sees the empty couch. "Where Hyder?" he asks Sofia. "Hyder go to Kunar?"

"No," says Sofia. "Hyder went to school." ("School?" Ali says skeptically, regarding that as a place for little kids.)

Though Sofia spent part of her childhood in the same apartment complex in which my family lived, she and Omar didn't meet until the early 1990s in India. Sofia's family arrived in Delhi as refugees several years before we joined my father; he and her mother were old acquaintances from Kabul Radio.

Sofia seems half-ready to return to Afghanistan; she wants to work in an orphanage in Kabul. But my father is wary of Omar dropping everything to settle there. In his eyes, the situation is still too unstable for my brother to give up the business for which he's worked so hard. It's different for my father, who has little interest in resuming his interrupted life in America.

All spring Omar and my father call with news from Kunar. According to intelligence reports, there have been credible sightings in the province of both Gulbiddin Hekmatyar and Osama bin Laden.

I'm skeptical about bin Laden. I can't imagine a single place in Kunar in which you could hide a six-foot-six Arab in your home. A common misconception is that Afghanistan is a country of largely uninhabited terrain. But even many remote areas are far from depopulated. Villagers are deeply familiar with one another's doings, and to disappear into one of these places would be an extraordinary feat. Many of these areas are characterized by tribal conflict; surely no one could resist dealing a blow to a death enemy harboring a fugitive, especially one with a $25 million price on his head.

Rumors that bin Laden is in Kunar have been circulating for a while. Last fall *Newsweek* ran a story that began, "Some believe life on the run has made it impossible for Osama bin Laden to control and lead Al Qaeda. In Afghanistan's Kunar province, people tell a different story." The article was riddled with overstatement and absurd speculation. "Bin Laden could hardly ask for a better hiding place," it avowed. *Yes, he could,* I said to myself, practically rolling my eyes as I read. But only one person in the article agreed with me—my father. " 'He may come to Kunar,' Akbar says, 'but he can't stay for long.' " Added the writer, "His opinion is not widely held."

Among the others interviewed for the story were a nearly toothless old man and a sheepherder "who takes evident pride in his pointed mustache, despite his tattered clothes and mended sandals." It was the Kunar equivalent of a "pulse on the street" feature, the kind of thing where the TV reporter stands in a mall, kids mouthing *Hey, Mom,* in the background.

Kunar is receiving a surprising amount of media attention these days, most of it focused on the American troops stationed in the province. *U.S. News & World Report* publishes a photo of marines exercising there; *60 Minutes II* broadcasts a segment about a new base up in the Pech Valley. And one week *Time* magazine's cover features a soldier climbing up a mountain. A valley and a river are visible behind. I can't believe it—here is Asadabad. I peer at the image, following the water's path. There at the top of the page is the house that holds my brother and my parents, a little white speck on the cover of *Time* magazine, just beneath the letter I.

Part Three

Two Rooms Full of Hope

Summer 2004

Teet meh niah bohla ghurzang rah bandai mukrah
Ze pah de oftadagay kay loy garang yem

Do not look down upon me, do not attack me.
I in all my depths am a huge abyss.

—Said Shamsuddin Majrooh

25

THE CIA GUY HAD BEEN TRYING to reach me for a while. I had some idea of what he wanted, but though I should have, I never called him back. The week the Abu Ghraib prisoner abuse scandal broke—in early May 2004—I finally picked up the phone and dialed his number. His name was Fred, and he wanted to talk to me about the death of Abdul Wali. When could I fly out to Washington and meet with him?

Fred told me that the U.S. government had been investigating Abdul Wali's death for nearly a year. I'd caught glimpses into their inquiry along the way. Within weeks of the incident, two Americans arrived in Kunar, and I gave them my account. Months later, in October, I awoke in California in the middle of the night to a ringing phone. Khalilzad needed to speak to my father about Abdul Wali's death. Had he observed anything wrong there? My father told Khalilzad, as he then believed, that everything had seemed fine.

It was the way I felt, too—until the prisoner abuse revelations. Had Abdul Wali received a severe beating, the marks of which we were simply unable to see? The death of an Afghan prisoner named Dilawar at Bagram in December 2002 was among those being investigated as homicides. According to Dilawar's death certificate, which was signed by a U.S. military pathologist, he died of "blunt force injuries to lower extremities complicating coronary artery disease." In Abdul Wali's fearful, adrenalized state, had some questionable behavior by the Americans triggered a pre-existing condition?

Rauf Mama's nephew Shohab had once spoken to me about his detention at Bagram. There was the strange, inedible food he identified as "mud" that I determined to be peanut butter; the "crazy Pashtuns from Kandahar," who, Shohab said, had been beaten. I told him he must have been mistaken. Now, of all the images from Abu Ghraib, the one of the mirthful girl standing behind a pyramid of naked men bothered me the most. When Shohab said, "You know what? The girls were kind of cruel too because they liked to humiliate the prisoners. The girls you have over in America are weird, Hyder," I just shook my head, like *you're crazy, man.*

In late spring Fred and I arrange the details of my trip to Washington. It's like playing a micromanaged spy game. "I have made a hotel reservation for you at the Courtyard Hotel," Fred writes in an e-mail. "It is being held with my government credit card number and I will go there tomorrow and present my credit card to them to hold in your folio . . . Please pay any other charges (like movies and food) in cash so the bill is just for room and tax!" I shoot my replies off to an address @ucia.gov.

The rest of my inbox—and my life—is more mundane. As is now usual at this time of year, I'm taking finals and scrambling to get ready for my summer trip. One day I agree to help my aunt move, but I don't realize how much stuff she has, and I wind up at a storage facility with couches, a treadmill, a queen-size bed, a dining table, and a pile of boxes. It's like a brain-teaser: I have to start thinking in cubic feet to figure out how I'm going to stuff it all inside. The project aggravates my back, which has been bothering me lately. I awaken in the night and am literally unable to move. My aunt teases me about having back problems at such a young age; my doctor prescribes Vicodin. I just hope the pain will go away before I find myself slamming over the bone-jarring roads in Afghanistan.

Omar returns from Kunar not long before I'm scheduled to head out. He'll take care of some things in California and rejoin me later in the summer. In early June I say goodbye to him and Sofia and Ali and take a flight from Oakland to Dulles. I'll spend one night in D.C., have the Abdul Wali meeting, then continue straight on to Kabul.

* * *

When I land in Washington, I'm in for a treat. I make plans to meet up with—amazingly—Rauf Mama. It's his first trip ever to the United States. He and fourteen other Afghan mullahs have been selected for a tour sponsored by the U.S. State Department's International Visitor Program. The mullahs will see cities as varied as New York and Salt Lake. (Alas, not Las Vegas.) Their first stop is D.C.

I drive over to see Rauf Mama at his hotel around eleven at night with my uncle Walid Majrooh. We stop on the street to get directions, the bass from a nearby car thumping in the background.

"Welcome to our barren country," Walid Majrooh says when Rauf Mama opens the door to his room at the Hilton. Rauf Mama laughs uproariously at the greeting, which is how a visitor might welcome someone to Afghanistan. Inside the TV is on, tuned to some kind of family movie. Suddenly the scene switches to show Chippendale dancers. "What are you looking at?" Walid Majrooh teases.

Rauf Mama's room is tidy, just a suitcase next to the bed. It's too late to go out, so the three of us just sit around talking. The fifteen mullahs began their trip a few nights ago at a hotel in Islamabad; by the time they got to the airport the next morning, only five were left. The more hard-core mullahs were scared of the political implications of visiting the United States. *Al Qaeda's going to come and be like, "What's with the tours in America,"* they speculated.

Sometime after midnight I mention that I'm hungry. "I actually have something here," Rauf Mama offers. "I bought two at this place and I ate one and I couldn't really eat the other one."

"Well, what is it?" I ask.

Rauf Mama opens the little refrigerator. "It's this," he says, handing it to me.

It's a McChicken sandwich from McDonald's, still inside its paper wrapper. "Why can't you eat this?" I say.

"Oh, it smells funny," he says. "It's weird." I almost have to laugh. I've shared some of the gnarliest meats in the world with Rauf Mama, and here he is, unable to stomach a McChicken sandwich.

At one point Rauf Mama and I stand before the window and look down into the street. A garbage truck approaches a Dumpster, lifts it, empties its contents, and returns it to the ground. "Nobody even got out of the car," Rauf Mama says at the end of the sequence. "Wow."

I wish we could go around the city together so that I could see his reactions to everything; I wish I could see Americans react to him. "Washington, D.C., is so green," he remarks. "So different from Afghanistan."

"Did it meet your expectations?" I ask.

"It passed my expectations," he says. "I didn't think it would be this developed."

Earlier in the day Rauf Mama visited the Lincoln Memorial, where a tour guide mentioned lines from some famous presidential speeches. "There's one president who said, 'The only thing we have to fear is fear itself,' " he tells me. "I really agree with that."

He also attended what must have been a D-Day commemoration. "There were all these old people. I guess some battles had happened, and today was the anniversary. I wanted to tell them, 'I'm kind of a veteran myself. I fought a little war, too,' " he jokes. The ceremony both touched and depressed him: "This happened sixty years ago, but the people are still so respected. In Afghanistan so many people made so many sacrifices, and all the bad people benefited from it." Afghanistan's recent struggle had rewarded "thieves and bandits," while decades later America was still honoring the contribution its white-haired citizens once made.

The next morning I take my place in a less noble chapter in U.S. military history. At eleven A.M. ("Please check out of the hotel that morning and taxi to Mr. Sullivan's office *with your baggage* . . . Following our meeting, I will reimburse you in cash for all your expenses. You are free to travel to Dulles AP"), I meet Fred outside a Department of Justice (DOJ) office building. I'm surprised to see that the deep-voiced operative from the phone calls looks like a mild-mannered schoolteacher. "You must be Hyder," he says. Inside, I open up my bags for security. "Why do you have your luggage here?" the guard asks.

"I'm in transit to Afghanistan," I tell him.

The guard takes my answer in stride—better even than that. "I'm from Pakistan," he says.

"Oh, really. What part?" I ask.

"Peshawar," he replies.

"Oh, wow," I say. "You don't happen to be Pashtun, do you?"

"Yeah, yeah!" he says.

I can't believe it—the sentry at the DOJ is a Pashtun from Peshawar. "Good luck in Afghanistan," he tells me, and Fred and I continue along to a conference room. "You can have the seat of honor," Fred tells me, and I settle in at the head of the table. It's dusty, as if it hasn't been cleaned for a while. Behind it a white board is covered in acronyms; the only one I recognize is FBI.

Fred introduces a female colleague, and a DOJ attorney named Mr. Sullivan, who earlier in his career prosecuted Manuel Noriega. They tell me to start from the beginning—from the first time I ever heard Abdul Wali's name—and to proceed as if they were unfamiliar with my radio story and with the notes I sent them in preparation for the meeting. As I speak, they break in for questions, especially when I get to something about Dave. "Okay now, Dave's part is important," they say. "We really need to find out what Dave said. Can you tell us in more detail?" As I describe the way Dave harassed Abdul Wali, Fred interrupts me so much that Mr. Sullivan teases him, "Geez, Dave!"

It's one series of questions and answers designed to illuminate another; an interrogation about an interrogation.

When I get to the part about viewing the body in the windowless hut, someone asks if we were aided in our examination by a flashlight; I say no. The light from the open door had fallen only on Abdul Wali's head.

Fred mentions Dave's urgent phone call about claiming the body the next day. "Didn't it strike you as weird?" he wonders. "Why was Dave so interested in you getting the body out of there?"

"It didn't strike me as weird at the time," I say. I'd assumed the deadline was connected to the time of Abdul Wali's death the day before. "But as I'm explaining it to you now, it's starting to seem a little weird."

They have some facts about Abdul Wali to share with me: He'd had fifteen children. He'd taken a second wife; his first had not borne him a son. And his father recently told a U.S. investigator that Abdul Wali had suffered from no medical problems whatsoever. I think of an Afghan saying—*If there's room for a thumb, an Afghan will try to fit his whole head in there*—and ascribe the father's revision to a desire to, perhaps, use what little leverage he has.

At one point Fred turns to Mr. Sullivan and asks if it would be all right to bring out some pictures. "You won't be disturbed by this?" I'm asked. The pictures are pulled out of a folder. These are not dehumanizing Abu Ghraib–style shots; they have the documentary air of evidence. In at least one photo Abdul Wali is wearing pants (as he was when we viewed him), which are rolled up near his knees. Another shows his bruised back, which we did not see. I examine photos of his discolored hand; his banged-up shins; and his cuts, one like a thick dash above his eyebrow. But the only picture that bothers me is the one on the top of the pile, of him standing against the wall, staring straight into the camera, before anything had happened.

As I leave, the subject of the undone autopsy comes up. Fred and Mr. Sullivan are respectful but honest: a post-mortem examination would have made their job a lot easier.

I know that the Americans recently approached my father and reopened the question of performing an autopsy on Abdul Wali. My father doubted that the family would agree to the procedure. Still, he got in contact with Abdul Wali's father, and in early May he welcomed him to the governor's compound. No, the father said immediately, he would not permit an autopsy. To do so would break Islamic law.

Abdul Wali had been given a permanent burial, which means that he had been laid to rest and prayed for and given over to Allah. Removing his body from the ground would be tantamount to taking him away from God.

My father said to Abdul Wali's father that he knew this must be very difficult for him. He had lost his son, a twenty-eight-year-old, presumably a family breadwinner. Perhaps something further could be done to provide for the family financially. The Americans are very interested in investigating this.

"Forget it," Abdul Wali's father said. "I don't care. Nothing can bring him back now. Even if the man that killed him is punished, he can't be brought back." Sitting across from my father in the same room where his son had trembled nearly a year earlier, Abdul Wali's father said simply, "Let us be."

26

THE DRIVE TO JALALABAD IS LIKE a family car trip: a cooler full of juice pouches on ice, my parents chatting with each other, my mother asking near Pul-i-Charki if I need a snack. It's a day after my arrival in Kabul, and we're on our way to Kunar. I lean back, put on my headphones, and tune into rapper Kanye West's album *The College Dropout*.

I flew into Kabul through an overcast sky. The haze gave the city an eerie quality; it was as if I were descending into an underworld in which I'd be called upon to fight the evil powers. Taxiing along the runway, I observed that much of last summer's debris had been removed; a man in a helmet and a flak jacket, presumably a mine-clearer, stood at the edge of a field once covered with plane parts.

Mines still dot the route to Jalalabad. Alongside the road round rocks stacked atop each other indicate their presence. Trucks go by, stirring up dust clouds. Since my last trip this road has gotten worse instead of better. I hope this isn't a harbinger of the summer to come.

In Jalalabad we exchange my father's jeep for a taxi; the security situation is not good, and the jeep basically amounts to a marked car. Now my father stands in the center of the marketplace, trying to figure out what's going on. My mother scolds him: "You shouldn't be getting out." She's probably right; my father shouldn't even be rolling down the window. His beardless face makes him instantly recognizable.

Outside the city our own security staff awaits, and when we reach them in the taxi, we rearrange ourselves in a twelve-car convoy. My mother and I join my father in the most discreet—and thereby most uncomfortable—car of the bunch, a Corolla hatchback. As we shudder over the road, I shudder in pain. (If you've injured your back, you should probably reschedule your trip to Afghanistan.)

It takes us eleven hours to travel the 150 miles to Asadabad. At the governor's compound, I collapse into bed. I ask for a glass of water, but once it's placed beside me, I find I cannot summon the energy to reach for it. I fall asleep, wake up at two in the morning and manage to take a sip, then fall back to sleep again.

Several days after my arrival my father wakes me with some news. David A. Passaro, a thirty-eight-year-old CIA contractor from North Carolina, has been arrested in connection with Abdul Wali's death. Passaro—the first civilian to be charged in the investigation of prisoner abuse in Iraq and Afghanistan—is accused of beating Abdul Wali with his hands, feet, and a large flashlight. He is, of course, the man I'd known as Dave.

"In all honesty," says my father, "it would have been better if the man had not been caught. This is good for the Americans but bad for Afghanistan. Nobody is going to voluntarily turn themselves in anymore." He flatly states: "The trust has been broken."

The official revelation renews our anger. If the allegations are true, it is abominable that Abdul Wali died in this manner. And it is infuriating to imagine that an elaborate ruse was designed to make us believe otherwise: that somewhere along the line one or more Americans endeavored to conceal the truth from us, that they thought they could.

Voice-mail messages from reporters pile up. The story is everywhere: on CNN, MSNBC, the front pages of the *New York Times* and the *Washington Post*. Now that Abdul Wali is part of a matrix of wrongdoing, he matters to the rest of the world. Or I should say, his story matters: Abdul Wali seems incidental, a supporting actor in these events. The focus is elsewhere:

on Passaro and his history of aggressive behavior, on the legal issues raised by his civilian status, on where his crime fits into the bigger picture.

Dave, a former Army Ranger, is accused of assault, not murder—a charge that, in the absence of an autopsy, could not be brought. He was indicted by a federal grand jury and will eventually be tried in federal court. Newspapers sketch a temperamental personality, a man who allegedly hit his wife and shot at his neighbor's dog. "He's got a Napoleon complex," a North Carolina neighbor tells the *New York Times*. "He's short, fiery, and always popping off. He's one of those military guys who's always got to be showing he's in charge." Dave was just five foot four, and I recall now how he had always positioned himself on the uphill slant of Toopchi, making himself a little taller.

But the prisoner abuse scandal is primarily an American obsession. In the days following Dave's arrest, not a single person sits down to discuss the situation with my father—unless you count Yossef, who, upon hearing the news, comes upstairs and says, "Hey, they announced the Abdul Wali thing." (It's not that nobody cares; it's just a hardening that accompanies the fact that thousands of Afghans died in prisons during the Communist and Soviet eras.) I wind up working on a piece for the *New York Times Magazine* about my experience in the interrogation room, and I have mixed feelings about the assignment. Of all the stories I could pick to tell about Afghanistan right now, I'm not sure if this one would even make the top ten.

As horrible as Abdul Wali's story is—and as deeply as it's affected me—a single prisoner's death is hardly the worst of what's going on here this summer. Presidential elections, for instance, are scheduled for the fall, but the registration effort is faltering. The UN's election workers have already pulled out of the province once and have threatened to do so again if affected by even a single act of violence. In Kunar, where landmines are not hard to come by, the dictate gives a single individual the power to disrupt the upcoming vote. Elsewhere in the country three governors have been forced to flee their posts in recent months. My father now sleeps with a Kalashnikov beside his bed so that he can shoot from the window if the compound comes under attack.

At the end of my first week in Kunar, Karzai stands beside President

Bush in the Rose Garden. The mood is lighthearted; the two men make jokes and their assessment of Afghanistan's progress is correspondingly cheery. (Five million children in school; 3.8 million adults registered to vote.) I find myself thinking of a GEICO commercial that played this spring on TV. As I remember it, an Enron-type CEO is indicted and will serve a lengthy jail term; that, he's told, is the bad news. But then someone tells him, "The good news is that I just saved you a ton of money on car insurance!" In Afghanistan the good news seems secondary when lined up against the bad. Events tell a different story than numbers. Chaos is rising, and exhaustion is setting in.

Two days after Karzai's appearance in the Rose Garden, I get out of the shower and can't find my deodorant. "Where's my deodorant?" I ask my mom. "You didn't bring it up here," she tells me. In the near distance I hear gunfire. "What's that?" my mom asks. "Probably the Americans," I guess. To me it sounds like target practice. But just as I'm sitting down to eat breakfast, the shots get louder, their frequency increases— *dahdahdahdahdahdahdahdahdah*—and I run outside to see what's going on. Shells have landed inside the garden. My father's aide Yossef comes out and tells me, "Your dad wants to talk to you right now." I hurry to reach him, and when I do he says, "I didn't call you. Oh, your mom did." I go upstairs, and she says she knew I'd respond more quickly to a summons from my father. She wants me to come back inside. "Don't do that again," I tell her.

The firefight rages in the marketplace, and soon my father sends me and Yossef down to the American base to ask for help. The presence of U.S. troops might quiet things down.

Yossef is in his late thirties. He began working for my father in the 1980s in Peshawar. During the Taliban times he worked for the same NGO as Sartor; there he set up a kind of credit system comparable, he says, to my brother's mortgage brokerage business. "We did the same thing here," Yossef told Omar this past spring. "We did it with cows. We'd take the interest rate from how much milk they produced. Our credit check was the tribal shura. They would come, do *zamanat,* say, 'This is a good guy; he'll pay for his cows.'"

Today when Yossef and I arrive at the base, the major there tells me that they can't interfere in a local disturbance; and besides, all of their special forces "are in the mountains right now."

"It's crazy in A-Bad," I overhear one marine say to another. "Good thing we're not there."

A couple of hours later, the firefight dies down. We never get a clear picture of what caused it; eventually we come to believe that the firefight was a bid to create an appearance of instability, which is different from actual instability itself. People simulate disorder to achieve their own ends—in this case, to chase away my father. We learn that in the midst of the chaos, a local military official called the Defense Ministry in Kabul and told them that the compound was under attack and that my father was trying to flee.

Such false reports increasingly dog him. Not long ago, for instance, a former local government official with ties to the Taliban gathered a jirga for a visit to Karzai. This "jirga" was hardly a formal tribal delegation; the official and his coconspirators probably rounded up a bunch of taxi drivers, paid them ten bucks, and told them, *We're going to say Fazel Akbar this and Fazel Akbar that, and you just nod your head.* But Karzai decided their complaints warranted an explanation. When my father arrived, he regarded the official and said, "Excuse me. Aren't you the same guy from whose house we seized the Taliban car? Whose son is a driver for the Taliban's shadow government?" The official admitted, "Yes, that's me." Another man addressed my father: "If you don't want *badi*"—bad things to happen—"don't come back to Kunar." My father walked out.

The false reports are frustrating enough; the fact that the central government takes them seriously is even worse.

One week later I find myself heading back toward Kabul. It's four in the morning, pitch dark when we leave. Near Khas Kunar one of the pickups gets a flat tire. While we wait around for it to be fixed, I get out my new digital camera, and we take some pictures. The river behind me glistens in the early light. Green islands rise to the surface, just the high tops of the land the water has swallowed up. Our figures make long shadows on the adjacent sand.

As soon as we arrive in Kabul, we learn that Kunar is casting a shadow of funhouse proportions. The problems in the province have been grotesquely exaggerated. My father tries to correct the perception, but his meetings during our stay do little to assuage his frustrations. Since his very first speech to the people of Kunar, he's been endeavoring to strengthen the province's ties to the central government. But he isn't getting anything back. While warlords and others who openly flout the rules get a free pass, people like my father are scrutinized, perhaps because they seem easier to control.

What my father does ask for is ignored. For months he has requested the removal of several Kunar security officials involved in smuggling and other illegal activities. Yet the central government has done nothing. How can you battle the big guys—wealthy, entrenched warlords like Ismail Khan and Rashid Dostum—if you can't even summon the strength to take the little people down?

Yet in some sense, it's absurd to expect the capital to effectively manage the countryside; the central government can hardly handle itself. During our stay in Kabul, an Interior Ministry official seizes some opium, and a Defense Ministry commander requests that the load be turned over to him. The Interior Ministry official refuses; the commander has him beaten and the opium taken from him by force. Presumably he plans to release it back into the black market. If you require any proof that Afghanistan is turning into what foreign policy wonks call a "narco-terror state," you need look no further than this.

"Trouble in Asadabad?" my father says. "They have trouble here."

Several months ago the International Monetary Fund estimated that the opium trade comprises between forty and sixty percent of Afghanistan's economy. The central government prefers to tout the figure that in the past year, the economy has grown by twenty-five percent. Whatever the money's provenance, its impact on Kabul's infrastructure is finally evident. (The city looks so good; how long can the disconnect between the capital and the countryside continue?) A couple of glass buildings that would look at home in Silicon Valley arise from the streets. You need a lot of confidence in Afghanistan to erect something so fragile. Across the street from the U.S. embassy, ground has been broken for a $40 million Hyatt Regency. (People say that the hotel will be open only to Americans, which probably isn't true, but that is the rumor nonetheless.) NO WALKING and NO STANDING signs flag the American presence at the Ariana Hotel, widely known to be the CIA's local headquarters. (Afghans refer to suspected CIA operatives as "Ariana Americans.") Sartor jokes about the contradictory directive: if you can't walk and you can't stand, what are you supposed to do?

We check out the residential building boom in a neighborhood called Wazir Akbar Khan. The architecture is alien, imported from Pakistan and India: big columns, bright colors. (This is bling-bling, Afghan style.) My father is constructing a modest new home here; nearby Massoud's son is building a house in the shape of the map of Afghanistan.

Kabul is no longer plastered with pictures of Massoud, but his Panjshiri colleagues continue to exert a real, if less visible, influence on the city's streets. One day we drive past a building that was once a photo finishing studio owned by relatives of Sartor's. During the Taliban times it was famous all over Afghanistan as a place you could get film developed. Sartor says you'd carry fruit as a cover for your errand when you went to pick up your prints. After the Taliban fell, the building was seized by the Panjshiris. Sartor's relatives came to see my father; an evacuation order bearing Karzai's signature was drawn up. Yet nothing has ever come of it. Journalists often call Karzai "the mayor of Kabul," referring to the central government's lack of control over the countryside; few note just how fractious the capital city itself remains.

The Taliban had basically no recognition outside Afghanistan, yet inside the country their power was undeniable. This government is in the opposite predicament: though its leader doesn't have enough authority to restore rightful ownership of a building within a few miles of his palace, red carpet rolls out for him all around the world.

And if this government derives its legitimacy from outsiders, then who is the presidential election for? The firefight near the governor's compound was about trying to create the appearance of instability. The elections are the opposite. The people behind them seem more interested in the appearance of stability than in actual stability itself.

27

W E'RE ON OUR WAY TO REGISTER to vote, and Sartor is giving me
tips on how to make it seem like I'm a native. "Don't tell them you're
from Asmar right away," he says. "You've got to make it complicated.
When they ask you where you're from, say, 'Oh, from up north.' Or, 'From
the village on the other side after that valley.' And keep cussing them out,"
he adds. "Then they're believe you're really from Asmar."

Sartor's just joking around; I'm not doing anything illegal. I'm carrying
my very own Afghan citizenship certificate, same as he is, and we're driving
past Kerala to the local registration site. (I have dual Afghan-American citizenship.) My father said that even though I wouldn't be around in the fall
to vote, I should still go ahead and sign up; it would set a good example.
My father has been promoting the elections for several months. Attendees
at a kick-off meeting got a crash course in democracy, absorbing lessons
like *Nobody gets to see your vote; don't believe anyone who says anything
else.* He asked locally prominent men to encourage women to vote by en-
suring that their own wives register. "Yeah, I agree," announced warlord
and military commander Malik Zarin. "I will bring out all four of my
wives. I'm not going to leave one of them at home." (Later my father jokes
that if all the men bring all their wives, the female turnout will exceed the
male.)

We pull up outside the registration site, Sartor still making jokes about how to talk like a "Shalozai." (Shal is the name of my father's home village; Asmar is the district in which it sits.) We enter the plain white building by going up a set of stairs that shake. Inside there are long tables, three election workers, and perhaps ten others like us who've come to register. First I get my photo taken. It's like school pictures, sitting on a chair pulled up to a little line. There's a beep and a big flash, and then I move onto the next station. A worker is asking another guy how old he is. "I think I'm thirty," he responds.

"Can you sign your name?" the worker asks.

"No, I can't," the man says. Instead he fingerprints the necessary document.

When it's my turn, I give my name, my father's name, my district, my village, and my age: *noolas*, nineteen. Then I scrawl my signature, and that's pretty much it—we're ready to go. Sartor and I walk back to the pickup, our voter registration cards in hand. I tease him about his photo—he looks like he has no neck. But these cards are no joking matter. Just two weeks ago, in Uruzgan province, the Taliban killed sixteen people found carrying these cards. We've been having our own problems here.

The registration process in this region got off to a rough start. In May three election workers were killed in neighboring Nuristan. One was a British man I met on my visit this spring. He was a nice guy, more like a vacationer than a security consultant. At the time of his death, he was scouting registration sites, a task that in Nuristan could involve hiking for several hours at a stretch.

The elections are being organized in part by UNAMA, which stands for the United Nations Assistance Mission in Afghanistan. After an explosion south of Asadabad injured several election workers, UNAMA shut down operations for a month. When they came back, they announced a new policy: they would work only along the main road. The strategy ensures a quick escape route, but it also effectively eliminates from the voting pool between sixty and eighty percent of the population. The decision to stay on the main road is an inflexible solution in a place where agility is paramount.

But logistics are only part of the difficulty. Even election supporters worry that democracy will not solve the country's more immediate problems. Afghans still need so many basics: food, water, shelter, roads, electricity. *Hungry? Thirsty? No place to rest your head? Hey, at least you're free. Welcome to liberty.* One of my favorite writers, Fareed Zakaria, cites in his book *The Future of Freedom* a study that found a democratic regime in a country with a per capita income of less than $1,500 had a "life expectancy" of just eight years. Afghanistan's per capita income is $190. No, I did not miss a zero.

But you don't need to be conversant in political theory or economic indicators to recognize the problem. Though warlord Malik Zarin may proudly supervise his four wives' voter registration, he tells my father, "This country was ruined by communism. Now democracy is going to turn it into chaos again." Malik Zarin's prediction is not academic. (This is a man who is not literate enough to take down a phone number.) Rather, it is based on decades of first-hand experience—with war, bad government, occupations, and tyranny—that has taught him to recognize a bad deal when he sees one.

On the ride home from the registration site, Sartor continues to tease me: "So where exactly is your house in Shal? I don't think I've come across you in Shal before." Back at the compound I look around for my mom so I can show her my card. I find her in the kitchen. "Did you get the card?" she asks. "Yeah, yeah," I tell her. (Later, when my father sees it, he gets annoyed that the official wrote Bar Kunar—*Upper Kunar*—instead of Asmar in the spot for district; the registration tally may serve as an unofficial census. But it's funny—all of Sartor's jokes about geographic evasiveness were right on the money.)

"What are you doing?" I ask my mother.

"Oh, I'm just cooking some *shorwa*," she says. It's soup for my father, prepared in a way that does not exacerbate his high blood pressure or his gout.

"What's that over there?" I ask.

"Potatoes," she replies.

We don't use the kitchen for cooking much—the stove is electric and therefore unreliable. Most of our food is prepared outside. Sometimes the stench of spoiling meat arises when the butcher leaves his scraps around.

The other bad odor comes from the bank next door, whose employees go to the bathroom in the bushes that separate our properties. "If you guys need a budget to create a bathroom, I'll give it to you," my dad offers.

The compound wasn't set up to receive visitors before my mother got here: ten guests would sip from the same glass of water. Hospitality is so important in Afghanistan—the central government gives my father a *distarkhan,* or hospitality budget, of about $1,000 per month—that my mother's days are full of real work. Still, she wishes she could do more. But she says that "conditions are not right right now to leave the compound much." Culturally, Kunar is worlds away from Kabul; in at least one nearby village, drivers kill their headlights at night so that the beams won't accidentally stray over women who have come out to collect the water.

This spring my sister Zulikha announced that she wanted to come to Kunar. Omar put her name in for a plane ticket, but I thought we should talk to our parents first. Zulikha is twenty-seven now; she works in a bank and drives a Jaguar. I worried that for her Kunar would feel like a prison. Ultimately, it was decided that this was not the right time for her to come: for women, just being in a public space here is intimidating.

My mother, Nadera Akbar, was born around 1947 in a place named for her father: Pacha Kelay, or King Village. This was in Laghman province, which borders Kunar. During her youth, Laghman had an outsize influence in the central government. (One illustrative joke tells of a disgruntled man who gets into a land dispute with a Laghmani and takes his case to a supreme court justice. But the justice is no help; he is a Laghmani, too. Next the disgruntled man tries Kabul's security chief—also a Laghmani; then the interior minister—Laghmani; and finally the prime minister—another Laghmani! Hearing of his troubles, a friend advises, "There's no way around this. All you can do is pray to God that you'll get your land back." The disgruntled man replies, "I'd love to. But I'm scared God will turn out to be from Laghman too.") My mother's father, Said Ahmed Pacha, was one of the most influential leaders in the eastern region, a wealthy landowner and a confidant of national political figures. In 1929, when the future king Nadir Shah (father of Zahir Shah) came through Laghman on his way to seize back

Kabul, some of his entourage hid in my grandfather's house. My mother remembers a visit to her home years later by Prime Minister Shah Mamoud Khan. As everybody in the house yelled, "He's here! He's here!" my grandfather just sat calmly, waiting for the prime minister to come to him.

For much of her childhood my mother had a private tutor because there was no girls' school in Laghman. In sixth grade she began attending a school in Kabul. (Her large family—her father had six children by my mother's mother, who was his second wife, alone—divided its time between there, Laghman, and a mountain village where they went to stay cool during the summers.) Around this time King Zahir Shah lifted a requirement that had made veils compulsory for all women over a certain age. My grandfather told my mother and one of her sisters to travel to Jalalabad and represent him at a formal unveiling ceremony. When the governor saw the two girls there, he ran to call Prime Minister Daoud Khan. "You'll never guess whose daughters are here," he said excitedly. Daoud Khan, who had been instrumental in this reform, was happy but not surprised; he had expected my grandfather to be among the first to support the unveiling.

Said Ahmed Pacha was close to my father's grandfather, Shal Pacha—so close that he gave him one of his daughters for his second wife. (And thus my father and his grandfather married half-sisters.) When Said Ahmed Pacha learned of Shal Pacha's death, he beat at his thighs, hurting himself so badly that he was unable to walk. He himself died of diabetes. But at that time, around 1960, most people in Laghman didn't know what diabetes was, or that it ran in our family. *Oh,* people speculated, *he's been cursed.*

Thereafter my mother offers a neat summation of her tumultuous life: "Basically I went to school. Started going to college. Got married. Became a teacher. Went to Moscow. Worked alongside your father in radio. Came back. Revolution. Became refugees in Peshawar. Then to America. Then to India. To America again. And then back to Afghanistan."

The days after the Soviet invasion, during which she and my father waited for the right moment to leave for Pakistan, were difficult. "We'd have these conversations at night: expect the worst," she remembers. "We would sit down and come up with the worst situation that could happen": a refugee camp, my father dying. "You have to be prepared for whatever," my mother says.

Thankfully, none of their imaginings came to fruition. Their house in Peshawar was always filled with guests. A stream of mujahedeen, diplomats, and foreign journalists trod a path between our home and my father's office next door. "No house was as bustling as your dad's," my mother recalls. At our first family meal in America, my sister Mariam, then fifteen, looked around the table and said, "Oh my God, Mom. This is the first time we've actually had a meal just among ourselves." It had been years since my family had dined alone.

"America, if I can be honest, was very difficult for me," my mother has said to me. The years she spent in Peshawar irrevocably altered her propriety, making her more conservative. But cultural unease was not the only source of her discontent: "In Pakistan, despite our difficulties, despite security threats, our sacrifices made me feel good. We were working in all of our capacity to help the jihad. And we hoped that one day the Russians would leave, and we would go back. We were all working toward that goal. By the time we came to America, we saw that slowly disappearing."

Now, having finally returned to Afghanistan, my mother seems spiritually more at peace; she relishes being among her own people in her own land. "To see people tired of war, and want peace, and want the country to get back on its feet again makes you hopeful," she says. "But it is kind of bittersweet. There is still a very dark past."

Now my father enters the kitchen. "Are you already done with work?" my mother asks.

"There's nothing really to do in the office so I told Haji Rousi to go ahead and send somebody over if they need me," my father says, referring to the deputy governor. He regards the dinner preparations. "What's that?" he asks.

"That's the *gutchey,*" she replies. My father recently purchased two pounds of this mysterious vegetable. It was expensive, so it's somehow fitting that the item's Pashto pronunciation matches the name of a luxury goods manufacturer. (Months later, shopping at a specialty food store in Lake Tahoe, my parents will run across the plant again. It's grown in the forests of Oregon, they're told, and its name in English is *morel mushroom.*)

"Oh, are you cooking it in a pan?" my father asks.

"Yeah, I'm going to make it in a pan," my mother says.

"I'm sure you're not supposed to eat it for a meal," my father says. "I think you're supposed to put it on something."

"I'm going to cook it as a meal by itself," my mother disagrees. "It doesn't taste like a side to something else."

"I don't know," my father says.

I wonder how much it would sell for in yuppie America, I say into my minidisc recorder.

"Have you got to record everything, Hyder?" my father laughs. "Look," he says to my mother. "He's talking about this." *Sounds like a very family environment,* I say into the mic. *Mom in the kitchen, Dad just got back from work. Feels kind of weird.*

The scene's ordinariness is what makes it worth capturing. Of all things, it may be the least likely to last.

28

T HEY TOOK ME TO A PLACE where the people had even longer beards
than me," Rauf Mama tells me. He's returned from America, full of
stories, including some about Amish country, where people relinquished
electricity by choice. Where else did he go? "Chee Cahgo," he tries. "I can't
pronounce those crazy names. You guys have crazy names for cities," he
says, and gets out a list. He saw D.C., Philadelphia, Vermont, Salt Lake
City, Houston, Chicago, and New York. Manhattan was impressive, the
White House less so. Likewise the food: Rauf Mama didn't care for what
he was served in restaurants. At hotels he would get permission to use the
kitchen, and then he would go to a grocery store. "You have every kind of
vegetable!" he marvels. He'd buy a huge variety, set himself up at the stove,
and make soup.

Other settings were less hospitable. At an airport one of the mullahs left
the group to spit out his chewing tobacco. Some security officials—seeing a
guy with a big beard and weird clothes hovering over a garbage can—called
for him to wait. The mullah, who didn't know English, was terrified: in his
experience, policemen had ways of making you disappear. He fled, hid, and
was eventually discovered. The group's bags were searched and their trip
delayed three hours.

Rauf Mama's favorite place of all was Philadelphia. He liked the history there, especially this quote from Ben Franklin: "Those who would sacrifice liberty for security deserve neither." As it happens, some of the people in Kunar this summer might do well to consider Franklin's remark. Liberty is being sacrificed for security by democracy's very promoters: the election workers.

One afternoon we welcome two of these men to my father's office. One is an angular British guy with a square forehead, square jaw, and square haircut. The other is a Scot with a big red beard and the burly bearing of a rugby player. The two are employees of a private security firm assisting UNAMA; their upbeat tag line is that they're "problem solvers." They ask us for business cards, and I say that we don't use them.

The problem solvers start with some news that seems too good to be true: of all the provinces, Kunar now has the second-highest percentage of its population registered to vote. The men tell us that 105,000 people are on the rolls. But our estimates of the eligible-voter population differ wildly: their figure is 170,000, while ours is more than double that. UNAMA's figures here and elsewhere will likely be used to determine representation for next year's parliamentary elections, and Pashtuns are on edge, believing that the Panjshiris in the central government are purposely undercounting them, trying to give them the short end of the stick.

We spend much of the meeting discussing the problem of Shulton. Shulton lies across a river from a village called Shigal. Shigal, which is on the main road, has a registration site; Shulton, which is off the main road, does not. Inhabitants of Shulton and Shigal are of rival tribes; so to register to vote, the people of Shulton will have to venture into enemy territory. Most will also have to cross the river on a *jahla*—a raft made of animal skin that carries five or six people at a time. One way, the crossing takes twenty minutes, meaning that maybe fifty people can register to vote each day. There are at least twenty thousand people in Shulton.

"Five persons," my father says to the election workers, emphasizing the raft's meager passenger capacity. His words are misheard as "five percent."

"Five percent is better than no percent," one of the election workers says.

"But we want to show to the world that the president was chosen by the majority of the Afghan people," my father argues. "Not five percent. If the next president is chosen by five percent, this is not a legitimate government."

My father tries to convince the election workers to set up a site in Shulton. He tells them that the people there have guaranteed their security. "No one can guarantee security," one of the men says.

"In Kunar if the elders of a tribe guarantee security, nobody can go against the tribe," my father explains. "They can go against the government, but not the tribe." He adds: "I can give you five or six police, but they can give you hundreds of men. Their security is stronger than the government's."

My father makes the point that Shulton is a tribal area only loosely affiliated with the Afghan government; any steps we can take to strengthen those ties reduce the possibility that Shulton will slide into the hands of the insurgents. If the tribesmen feel that they are a part of things, they are more likely to help with the struggle against the opposition.

But the conversation doesn't solve anything. We're frustrated, not so much with these two men—we know these aren't their own decisions—as with the situation in general. Imagine if the citizens of New York City were told, *We can't register you guys. Transportation is a hassle, and the threat of a terror attack is too great.* People would be furious, especially if the registration effort were then deemed a success, as it has been in Kunar.

One morning I set out to talk the people in Shulton about the problems with the election myself. Rauf Mama comes along. The trip takes us along a side valley that follows a dried-up stream. The road is like the one up to Kurangal—handmade. Our progress is too slow for the car's speedometer to register; the line hovers a hair past zero. The landscape is beautiful, terraced green fields and mountains. (*Terraced farming,* I say into my minidisc recorder. *Not terrorist.*)

When the road ends, we ask a guy for directions. We'll have to walk the rest of the way to Shulton. The path is steep. Outside it's hot, maybe ninety degrees, and it isn't long before my back is soaked. There's a calm feel to the area—and there's a distinct smell. In the mountains, you can usually count on good lungfuls of fresh air. But here the air is heavy and sour, like spoiled milk. I wonder if it's because of the shrubs.

It takes us forty-five minutes to hike up to the village. Rough green grasses and simple mud houses stretch the few miles toward the mountains that mark the border with Pakistan.

We're escorted to the hilltop home of a tribal elder. From the ceiling of his *hujera* hangs a decorative chandelier made of cassette tape. The tape is tied in bunches, like pompoms. On the wall someone has drawn the outline of a big flower. It's unevenly colored in, the way a little kid would do it, with white spaces in what should be solidly green leaves. We rest here while somebody goes to fetch the others. Rauf Mama tells me that people here are reluctant to come out of their houses because everyone is out to get one another.

"Why is this place famous for tribal feuds?" I whisper to him. "Is there a shortage of water or land or something?"

"There's a shortage of brains here," he says.

"What?" I say.

"There's a shortage of brains."

Our host is avidly hospitable, bestowing pillows upon Rauf Mama so he can lie more comfortably on the bed. "Oh, that's not enough," he observes. "I'll bring another."

"No, no," Rauf Mama protests.

"No, no, I'll bring another one," our host says firmly, walking away.

"You've got to give up with these people," Rauf Mama tells me. "Let them do what they want."

So we do: we eat lunch, because they wouldn't have it any other way, and we drink tea, because they wouldn't have it any other way, and finally, two hours after we arrive, we—me, Rauf Mama, our host, and three other tribal elders—begin to talk about the elections.

They start by naming some of the thirty-five villages in their area that have been effectively disenfranchised. "Slow down, slow down the names, man," Rauf Mama says, as the elder barrels through the list.

"Okay," I say. "Has anyone been here for the registration yet?"

The elders say that people have come to register them but that they were from Shigal. They recorded the registrants as residents of their own area, not of Shulton. "So we told them to get out of here," an elder says. When the people of Shulton complained, they were told that "somebody from the

mohseesa"—a catch-all term for NGOs, the UN, and other organizations—
"was going to come and help us register. But somebody from over there"—
the speaker points at Shigal—"told them that there is no security here or
whatever, so because of that, it has been delayed."

"What results do you think you will get from this election?" I ask.

"Peace for Afghanistan," says one of the elders.

"You think peace will come after the elections?" I say skeptically.

"Yes, of course, peace will come after the elections. Of course."

"Why?" I ask.

"Because the people's choice will be elected."

"Well, you haven't been registered yet, so your choice won't be in it," I
point out, and everyone laughs.

I ask which candidate they like. "Personally for my own vote, I like
Karzai, because he's Pashtun," says one of the elders. "And his work was
good, too," he adds.

"Okay now, what does Karzai have that, for example, Mr. Assefi doesn't
have?" I ask, referring to Humayoun Assefi, who is among the twenty-
three presidential candidates. Assefi, a brother-in-law of King Zahir Shah's,
works well with foreigners, and represents a viable alternative to Karzai.
The villagers return a blank look.

"Do you know Assefi?" I say.

"No."

"Do you know Siraat?" I ask, naming another candidate.

"We don't really know any of these other people," one of the elders tells
me. Here they have neither electricity nor radios.

"Do you know Qanooni?" I try, thinking they'll at least recognize this
candidate, a prominent figure in the current cabinet.

"They should know Qanooni," Rauf Mama puts in.

But they don't. "Qanooni," I say. "The Northern Alliance, the Panjshiri,
briefly the interior minister?"

"No, no, no, no, no!" they respond vociferously.

"Why? Because he is Tajik?" I ask.

They hedge—"Yeah, well, no, not really. Yeah, that too, but not just because of that"—and then one of the elders tells me with finality, "Karzai is
the choice. We aren't going to vote for anyone else. Karzai is our king."

"How do you know that Mr. Assefi might not be the better leader?" I ask.

"Karzai is a Pashtun!" our host exclaims. "Who knows what this other person is?"

"Actually he's Pashtun, too," I say. "In fact, he is related to Zahir Shah."

"Really?" another checks.

"Zahir Shah has thousands of relatives," another elder says. "We can't keep track of all of them." Again everyone laughs.

The people of Shulton do not seem to be seeking an alternative to Karzai. They just want to be acknowledged, to cast a vote for what they see as the country's current course toward peace. But to their minds, this course has little to do with democracy. Its roots are in war weariness—in Afghanistan's own past. "Nobody is ready for *khoon-rezey*"—bloodshed—"anymore," an elder says. "We need to give *khoon-rezey* a break. And everything will be fixed by itself."

"To destroy their own country again, nobody is ready for that," agrees Rauf Mama. "Nobody wants to fight anymore." (It is decided that any current troubles are the doing of people who "get trained in Pakistan" and "come over here to explode bombs, or plant mines.")

Afghans are tired of war: I think that's one of the most important things to understand about this country. Twenty-three years of war: that's the figure you use if you start at the 1978 coup and continue through the fall of the Taliban in late 2001. (Others begin their count at the 1973 ouster of Zahir Shah.) But I've noticed that people are starting to extend the war's length into the present. They don't know whether to stop at twenty-three or keep going. *Is what's going on now war? You can't really call it peace.* So time goes by, and the tally increases: as of this summer, twenty-five years of war.

I ask the elders if they will still believe in the elections, even if they are unable to vote. One hesitates, then replies: "Yeah, we'll still believe in the elections. But we are going to want proof from the governor, proof that we were tribals"—by this he means a sovereign tribe—"and that we have remained tribals." He continues: "They should at least keep a tribal relationship, like the way they used to, *kah na?*" *You know?*

The relationship to which he refers was characterized by government payments to ensure the tribes' allegiance (as well as to get them to foment trouble in Pakistan).

"If we are not counted and not registered," another affirms, "then we would want tribal autonomy. We would not recognize this government officially, only on a casual basis. We would go the way that Zahir Shah and my grandfather did."

"Yeah, there is a tribal office in Jalalabad, right?" one checks. "They would deal with us."

It's the point my father tried to make to the election workers. Allegiance here is to the tribe, not to the nation; but the election is the kind of thing that might give the people of Shulton a stake in Afghanistan, pull them in. But if Afghanistan doesn't care about their votes, why should they care about Afghanistan?

"If we are ready to participate in the government, and we want to vote in this government, and we are not given the chance to, then that is the government's fault, not ours, right?" our host says.

I agree.

"If we are left out of this process, left out of the stakes—remember these words—we want tribal papers," another concludes. Suddenly they're bargaining with me as if I'm an official representative of the government.

I tell the elders that since they're being recorded, they should mention the things their village lacks, like electricity and roads, "because in America, it's considered unusual to not have those type of things."

"*Sayeeba*," one of the elders says to me with mock patience, dragging out the word for sir, "we don't have water for us. We can't even feed our crops, which we had prepared." For several years now Afghanistan has been suffering from a major drought; news of this devastating environmental crisis has taken a backseat to that of the war on terror. "It takes us four hours to reach the nearest water," the elder continues. "We are dying from thirst, there is no road, we don't have electricity. Every little job is a huge burden on us."

"What else can we say?" another shrugs. "No need to sit here and talk about our unhappiness. We are in need of everything."

"This road that you drove up, we built that ourselves with our shovels as much as we could," one of the elders wants to make sure I know.

"That was pretty impressive," I say, genuinely meaning it.

"Yeah, now we are forced to stop because we don't have any more resources to keep the road going."

"What's more important for you," I ask, "a road or the elections?"

"They are both important," our host begins. "The road and the elections go hand and hand." Development and democracy: they both matter. But it's clear to him which should come first. "If there is no road, how can we have proper elections?" he asks. "We can't even have a car come up here to register us." The elders look at me as if I have a shortage of brains.

29

THE ONLY CROPS I RECOGNIZE IN Afghanistan are rice fields and corn fields. Rice fields I know from Vietnam movies, and the corn from *Field of Dreams*. Driving south to the American base in Kunar, I picture Kevin Costner among the stalks, searching for a voice in the sky.

This summer the U.S. military seems similarly adrift. I'm still hoping there's a grand scheme I'm just not getting; that the policy experts in the Pentagon and State Department are working from a master plan that's just too complicated for me to understand. But as the years pass, I'm losing faith. The Americans' quick defeat of the Taliban is often touted as a measure of their success here. But the Russians had every major Afghan city controlled within a week, and they got bogged down for the next ten years. Same too with the British: an early victory preceded a mighty struggle. The long haul is what matters here: "Unlike other wars," wrote one historian, "Afghan wars become serious only when they are over."

Here in Kunar the Americans are retreating, barricading themselves in. This is entrenchment, not engagement. From the road you can no longer see the base at all. The primary interaction most people in Kunar have with the Americans is watching their helicopters, and this summer there are more than ever. At night they wake me up. I'll hear them approaching—the distinctive *chtch-chtch-chtch*—and soon they'll be directly above me, low overhead, shaking my room a little as they go by. We never know what the helicopters are doing. One time I ask an American what's going on, and he tells me it's a "clusterfuck." I have no idea what this means: whether they're bombarding a village, or searching for an insurgent, or resupplying a base up north with Gatorade.

This morning we're on our way to the Asadabad base for a meeting. Approaching the entrance, we pass a photo of Osama bin Laden ringed by dollar bills. This is just one of a number of the Americans' wanted-men posters. On another, faces of terrorists shoot up from a map of Afghanistan like rockets. (Those with information can e-mail cjtf18orewards@hotmail.com.) Then there's something that reminds me of a hall pass, except instead of indicating that you have permission to go to the bathroom, this card announces, ATTENTION COALITION SOLDIER. THIS INDIVIDUAL HAS INFORMATION REGARDING TERRORISTS. REPORT TO COMMANDER IMMEDIATELY.

"Are you coming in with the car?" an Afghan guard asks. We're at a checkpoint outside the base, having just passed the sign that warns, STOP. DO NOT ENTER OR YOU *WILL* BE SHOT.

"Yes," my dad affirms.

"Hold on, I've got to talk to my superior," the guard says.

"Okay, hurry it up," my dad replies. "Our appointment's at eleven."

If my father's response seems irritable, it's only because he finds it offensive that the Americans do not trust him enough to allow him straight through. It's one of the small things that doesn't help their cause here. On a recent day, after waiting outside for ten minutes, my father finally received permission to enter, but first he would be frisked. "I'm not going to come in then," my father said. A man with whom my father works closely named Colonel Thomas intervened, instructing the American guard on duty to search my father only "briefly."

"If the whole place blows up, I don't care," the guard responded petulantly. My father was furious. When the Americans come to the governor's compound, both they and their M-16s are immediately welcomed into his own office. We offer them tea and Coke and fresh juice—which a guy will run to the market to get—and someone will bring the biscuits my mother special-orders from Pakistan. Beyond the personal affront, my father was troubled by the display of arrogance. If the Americans respond to the governor of the province this way, how are they treating the others?

Our car idles as we wait for the guard to return. "Don't they have radios?" I wonder aloud.

Five minutes pass. I kill some time practicing my Pashto literacy skills, reading from a nearby sign: *You can use the other gate from six to seven. After seven o'clock, don't enter the base.* As I'm deciphering it, the guard returns. "You can come in, but they can't come in," he announces. Only my father and the driver can enter; his guards will have to wait outside and be searched.

"Did you tell them the governor is here?" my father asks.

"Yes," the guard says.

"Are you sure?" my father confirms, and when the guard replies yes, my father says, "We're going to go. Tell them we came, and we left."

We start away from the base. My father is so annoyed that he's silent. Then he decides that I should get out of the car and double-check that they know that we came and we're leaving.

We stop at a different entrance, this one staffed by Americans. They send me to see Colonel Thomas, and we return together out front. Colonel Thomas announces that he'll be escorting my father, and that "he will not be searched." As we walk toward the base, Colonel Thomas apologizes. A couple times my father has visited the base's clinic to get his blood pressure checked, and Colonel Thomas asks if he would like to do so today. My father would, and the two men discuss their numbers. My father's is 172 over 110, which is really bad—especially considering the surge-effect of encounters like the one today.

The triggers add up. After nearly three years of exposure to Afghan cultural mores, the U.S. soldiers still walk along the Kunar River in shorts in view of women. (Their thoughtlessness begets rumors—for instance, that their night-vision goggles allow them to see through women's clothes.) They are sometimes careless; shortly before I arrived, they killed two civilians while unleashing fire at a band of wild dogs. A soldier at a base staffed by special forces in northern Kunar fails to recognize my father's name when he receives a letter from him; that base seems like the domain of high school kids whose parents are permanently away for the weekend. And even now, after Abdul Wali's death, problems with the handling of detainees remain. Two of my father's own guards allege that they were beaten at Toopchi during an interrogation; they return with bruises and we have no reason to doubt their story. Misinformation still sometimes results in mistaken detention. One time Yossef himself is held at the base overnight. Secrecy is another problematic issue. "I, as governor, have no idea why certain people have been captured," my father says. "When families and tribes come to me wanting to know why their people have been held for six months, I can't tell them anything. The lack of details creates serious animosity."

One man, who is known as "Marble" Jahan Dad because of his business extracting marble from rocks, was detained by the Americans last fall and hasn't been seen since. In the months Marble Jahan Dad has been held, my father has made repeated requests for information about his detention; he has even spoken to Lieutenant General David Barno, the new head of the U.S. operation in Afghanistan. "At least give me a reason why he is still there, at least tell me you have proof, so I can face his family," my father laments. He has done *zamanat* for the Americans, but they are not reciprocating.

There are exceptions, of course. This summer there is a friendly, level-headed State Department representative at the base named Mr. Hunter. He walks around in khakis, a blue button-down shirt, and a bulletproof vest, and he packs a pistol—a getup as close to civilian as the Americans come in Kunar. He gathers information about the situation in the province; my father briefs him on such things as the intratribal feuds of the Safi. (One time, at a going-away lunch for a U.S. official, my father noticed that representatives of the State Department, the Pentagon, and the CIA were not mingling. "Do you want to sit in the same room?" my father checked, half-jokingly, with Mr. Hunter. "We're all Americans," he replied. "But we're kind of like Safi ourselves.")

But it is Mr. Hunter's colleague Colonel Thomas who does the most to ameliorate the tension that characterizes some of our other dealings with the Americans. Colonel Thomas is a reserve who, in his civilian life, works as an assistant attorney general for the State of Washington. Here in Kunar he leads the PRT, and this spring he and my brother collaborated on reconstruction projects.

At first Omar and Colonel Thomas thought big: they would reconstruct the Jalalabad-to-Asadabad road. Local Afghans were invited to apply for security positions. (A regular American job application was translated straight into Pashto, resulting in a request for information that was wildly irrelevant: names of high school, college, previous employers; three references with phone numbers; street address.) Omar tried to coach the locals for the interview portion. "Don't be too aggressive," he suggested. "Act peaceful and calm." Still the applicants were thrown some curveballs. "What would you do if you saw somebody trying to lay a mine on the road?" an American asked one applicant. "Um, walk over to him," the man replied. "Okay," the American said. "When you walk over to him, what are you going to say?"

"I'll say hello," the applicant guessed. Nobody seemed to know how to talk to a troublemaker, much less to a potential employer.

But the project, at least on the scale envisioned, fell through. The road would cost at least $20 million; the PRT could dole out only $25,000 at a time. So Omar and Colonel Thomas—and Yossef, who plays a major role in our NGO—set their sights elsewhere. This summer I monitor the progress of the projects. Several schools are being rebuilt, including one for orphans in which previously sweltering classrooms have been equipped with fans. Then there are new plumbing systems, including one being constructed in the village of Dam Kelay which will replace a three-hour walk down a cliff to the water supply. It feels good to visit these sites, to see the immediate impact of our efforts.

"My mission here is to help accelerate the reconstruction of this province—everything from roads to schools to bridges to clinics," Colonel Thomas says, explaining how the PRT's role differs from that of other U.S. forces here. "The other mission here, of course, is the war-on-terror mission of killing or capturing anti-Coalition militia forces. The two missions are different."

But sometimes the distinction is not drawn clearly enough. PRTs all over Afghanistan are rumored to trade aid for intelligence: *If you saw bin Laden come through here last week, we might be able to build that road you're talking about.* The line between militarism and humanitarianism has been blurred, affecting traditional relief workers, who are now seen as legitimate targets. (One of the world's most respected aid groups, Doctors Without Borders, pulls out of Afghanistan in July after five employees are killed along a road in Badghis province.)

Colonel Thomas will return to the United States in the coming months and he hasn't accomplished as much as he'd have liked. "I've been a little disappointed in the rate of progress," he says. The security situation in the province makes it difficult for him to woo aid groups; U.S. military bureaucracy slows other things down. He's assessed Kunar's needs, but "now it's just a question of will. Are we willing—we being the American military and the international community, organizations like the United Nations and the Red Cross and all the different aid agencies—are we willing to come in here and dedicate ourselves to some of these large-scale reconstruction projects? I hope we are." The clock is ticking: "I think there's a window of opportunity—a definite, finite period of time we have to succeed here in Afghanistan," he says bluntly.

Colonel Thomas worries that people like my father "can't be here forever"; that to continue to delay progress is to risk pushing him, and our family, out. "I will always think of the Akbars as Americans," he confesses almost apologetically. "I know they are Afghans, but they've made my job easy. . . . It's a unique province because of the resources that are here and because of the governor it has and his understanding of the way the West works."

Colonel Thomas makes an important point. My father is a moderate who believes in democracy for Afghanistan, and from an American perspective, he is almost certainly the most culturally accessible governor in the entire country. Yet despite this a chasm of understanding remains between him and the U.S. forces, a fact that belies the enormous difficulties the Americans face in establishing partnerships here.

"If we can't succeed here in this province," Colonel Thomas says, "I don't know where we can succeed in Afghanistan."

In spite of everything, there is still a lot of goodwill toward the Americans here. It's not like it is in Iraq: in Afghanistan the U.S. troops have legitimacy. The Americans did not invade this country: they helped overthrow an occupying force. Since then they've decreased the detrimental influence of neighboring countries. And perhaps most important, their continued presence prevents a return to chaos. But even this substantial benefit cannot placate Afghans forever.

From Afghanistan, it seems as though attention is lavished on Iraq at our expense. The numbers are stark: international donors have pledged more than $30 billion to rebuild Iraq and only $13 billion for Afghanistan. (The earlier figure of $4.5 billion was supplemented in spring 2004 at a reconstruction conference in Berlin.) Both countries are home to approximately 26 million people; Afghanistan is larger, poorer, more destroyed, and almost entirely bereft of infrastructure. And really, that's all the country wants the money for, is to rebuild; after so many years of entanglements with outside powers, the last thing Afghans want to do is rely on foreign aid.

Some posit that the United States is content with the current situation. The Americans don't necessarily want Afghanistan to develop quickly; they're happy with the status quo. This is not an exercise in nation-building—this is about maintaining a military base that offers the United States easy access to Iran, Pakistan, and China. (Or, to put it another way, a critical perch between one Muslim country with a nuclear bomb and another Muslim country about to get one.) So as the Americans see it, Afghanistan has exactly the right amount of chaos—sufficient to justify their continued presence here.

Of course, the fact that there is as yet no fully functioning Afghan army is justification enough.

One day we're driving home, and two donkeys run straight toward us in the road. We see them burst out of the entrance of the local Afghan military base. This mud-brick building, flanked by statues of missiles, houses the Ninth Division of the Afghan Military Force (AMF). Exactly what goes on inside there is a mystery; this regiment is shockingly lazy and inept. Staring at the donkeys in the road, Yossef jokes, "The transformation is finished—the military has morphed into complete jackasses."

Afghanistan's military leaves a lot to be desired. The Afghan National

Army—the ANA, which will eventually replace the AMF—is still in the works. Only fifteen thousand of the required seventy thousand troops have been trained. So all across Afghanistan private militias remain in place, headed up by local warlords.

The commander of Kunar's Ninth Division is Malik Zarin, the man who assured my father that all four of his wives would register to vote. Malik Zarin has an uncomfortably close relationship with Pakistan. He is an elder of the Mashwanai tribe and bears resentment toward Rauf Mama and other elders of the Salarzai. The feud erupted years ago, and when my father came to Kunar, he sat down with the two tribes to negotiate a truce. Officially the feud was forgiven. But though my father is on good terms with Malik Zarin, Rauf Mama doesn't trust him. And with good reason: this summer, Malik Zarin is spreading rumors designed to damage him. (Even Karzai has been taken in by the rumors, which are outlandish. They include coded messages sent to Kabul by former governor Jahan Dad like, *On Wednesday night Mullah Rauf is going to kill everyone in the governor's compound.*)

Malik Zarin runs the Ninth Division as he sees fit. Take, for instance, the disarmament effort. Known as the DDR (Disarmament, Demobilization, and Reintegration), this program offers incentives to turn in weapons. When Malik Zarin heard news of people being disarmed in other provinces, he realized that Kunar was falling behind the rest of the pack. So he designed a scheme to catch up. In Pakistan he purchased a couple hundred Kalashnikovs—for $20,000, more than fifty times the average Afghan's yearly salary—then presented the guns to the proper authorities.

Malik Zarin's age does not match his appearance. My first summer in Afghanistan I sat in while he and my father met with some CENTCOM officials. "How old is he?" the CENTCOM guys wanted to know. "He thinks he's around seventy," I told them. They were sure there was a mistake; Malik Zarin doesn't look a day over forty. But my father confirmed the estimate. "When I was a teenager, he was a grown man," he said. When the CENTCOM officials asked for a rundown of the people causing trouble in Kunar, Malik Zarin mentioned a name that caused my father to pause. "Wait, you're talking about your cousin," my father said. "And isn't that your enemy, too?" My father explained to the Americans that Malik Zarin was trying to fold a personal enemy into the list of wanted men.

But it would take a couple dozen smart bombs to wipe out all of the enemies on Malik Zarin's list. He has so many outstanding *patneys*—formal declarations of revenge on another family or tribe—that most of the time he's not even in Kunar. His whole life is one long duck and cover.

"If you want to fix Kunar, you have to bump heads with Malik Zarin," I've advised my father. He disagrees. With or without my father's intervention, the ANA will make warlords like Malik Zarin irrelevant. Tribal factions like his will not be incorporated wholesale into the new army—leaving Malik Zarin with little to gain from the establishment of strong institutions in Afghanistan.

Malik Zarin's militia is not the only security force in Kunar taking advantage of the army's absence. The Ninth Division, the border brigade, the police, and the intelligence service: These rival gangs have all staked out the same turf, Kunar's main road. They're supposed to secure its safety, but the only thing they secure is their own wealth, by collecting "tolls." There is no such easy money along the border or in the mountains.

"People fire rockets from the mountains. The army should go there," my father says. Likewise the border brigade: "I say, 'Why are you here? Go to the border. This is your job. What are you doing on the road?' Nobody's listening. When the national army is here, I'll be able to tell them, 'Do this,' and they'll do it."

Some Americans involved in recruiting ANA soldiers stress to my father that they're striving for ethnic balance, and if there is any worthy excuse for the army's slow progress, this is it. But there's another security issue on which I often wonder if any progress is being made at all. One day Rauf Mama says, "The way I can tell this has been an absolute failure is that every time I turn on the TV, I see Karzai and his American bodyguards around him. After three years there is nobody to protect our president." That there are too few Afghans to secure an entire country is one thing; that there are too few to secure one man is another. The reminder stings: *This is how little things have changed.*

Then one day there's a big change. Yossef approaches me and says, "Don't tell anybody, but Malik Zarin might be dead." Malik Zarin was shot several times upon emerging from a hotel in Kabul; the news makes Al Jazeera and the AP. But he survives and soon after the incident he gives an interview on one of the local-language radio services. He says something like, "Yeah, yeah, what can I do? Al Qaeda and the Taliban are my enemies. I've always fought against them. Now they're coming after me again." For a guy who can't even write down a phone number, Malik Zarin is pretty slick. Al Qaeda and the Taliban had nothing to do with the assassination attempt; the men arrested for the crime tell the police that they'd been paid to settle a private feud. But Malik Zarin is probably betting that the Americans, whom he's been manipulating from the get-go, won't pay close attention to what really happened. Because his personal rivalries happened to place him on the anti-Taliban side after 9/11, he was able to paint himself as a champion of peace and democracy, and simultaneously portray his enemies as terrorist sympathizers. Now he's skillfully folded his own feud into the war on terror. He deploys the right buzzwords: Taliban, Al Qaeda. He's a trickster; his success is predicated on chaos. The conditions in Afghanistan allow him to flourish.

Malik Zarin seems indestructible. He's been shot at several times, and has always come away unscathed—like a cat with nine lives. We have a similar saying in Pashto: *de peesho sa rari,* or "he has a cat's breath." It's not an exact equivalent. The American version might indicate someone charmed—someone who narrowly escapes danger—but the Pashto version is invariably used as an insult. And there's another difference. In Afghanistan, cats have only seven lives—perhaps an adjustment meant to reflect the shorter-than-average Afghan lifespan, forty-four and a half years old.

Malik Zarin gets out of the hospital, and his life resumes. In my room at the governor's compound, I think of death feuds and schemers; and of Abdul Haq, of Said Bahauddin Majrooh, and of all the extraordinary Afghans who breathed not as cats, but as men.

30

WE'RE PLANNING A MISSION. A military force of my father's own composition will travel to Kunar's rural reaches, keeping watch for insurgents and timber smugglers, and generally letting people know that there's a government presence here. Lacking support from both the central government and the U.S. military, my father is taking things into his own hands.

There will be 150 men on the mission, and funding from the Interior Ministry will cover their AKs and RPGs. This much we know. Everything else remains to be determined. There is no armory from which my father can requisition even the most essential supplies. The troops need transportation, for example, but nobody wants to rent out a pickup to a government security force that might get ambushed. We debate what to do about food: do we sacrifice a whole truck to pots, pans, and sacks of rice? Instead we decide to give the men money and hope that they will be able to find and compensate gracious hosts along the way. A shoemaker in Asadabad will provide footwear; we asked the Americans for boots, which they cannot supply on such short notice. (Nor can they help us with backpacks and water canteens.) But when Colonel Thomas learns I'm going on the mission, he says he'll try to get a pair of boots for me. Then I tell him my size, thirteen, and he shakes his head, saying he'll have trouble finding a spare pair that big.

It's just as well; it's exactly the kind of special treatment my father said that I must avoid when he gave me permission to go along with the troops. "You can't go and be the governor's son," he warned. "Don't be a burden on them. Don't let people carry your stuff. Don't let them give you extra blankets. You've got to do everything the way they do it."

The mission will be my father's second significant effort this summer to reform Kunar. In June he hosted a shura of religious and tribal elders that had been nearly a year in the making. Three hundred men from all over the province came to the governor's compound and assembled in chairs that poked down into the garden's grass. My father stood before them and said, "How long are we going to wait and see what the Americans will do? See what the central government will do? If we are united and act united, one people can do anything. We can create security ourselves." It was inspiring to imagine Afghans taking charge of their own destiny; as my father often said, it was the only permanent solution.

But while we made plans, the mukhalafeen took action. They were getting bolder: one early morning, for example, they attacked a U.S. base in northern Kunar, launching twenty rockets and unleashing machine-gun fire. Elsewhere in the province, they made direct assaults on local district offices. Fed up with playing defense, my father created the *ketai-muntazayra*: forces-in-waiting. (Despite the name's implication, the forces-in-waiting are a ready-action unit.) In consultation with Kunar's various security organs, he cobbled together a hodgepodge of untrained and undisciplined young men. (The improvisational assembly reminded everyone of the resistance; it was sobering that we were back to that.)

One of those untrained young men will, of course, be me. Among other things, I'm excited to learn how to fire an RPG. I know already that you have to hold it at a certain angle, that fire can shoot out and burn you badly, and that the weapon's force can both take down helicopters and blow your pakol off of your own head.

Though the mission is dangerous, it is an acceptable risk. "Acceptable risk": the phrase has come up a lot this summer. I determine that the experience I'll gain on the trip outweighs the possibility of harm. My father agrees. If I want a future in Afghanistan, I can't just sit around the governor's compound all day.

* * *

I'm all set to go when my departure is delayed: Rauf Mama, who's also going on the mission, gets held up at a jirga in Shigal. The forces leave without us, and I wait at the compound for him to return. Together he and I will travel north to meet the troops, carrying blankets along. It's only their first night out, and already they've found their supplies to be insufficient; they call and report that they're on the side of a mountain near the border, freezing cold, huddled together and wrapped in plastic bags.

But only hours later something much worse happens: the troops are attacked.

I hear the news the next morning. The story goes like this: some people approached the camp at night. The troops yelled for the people to stop—*Dresht!*—and, when they didn't, began to fire. One intruder died; two others were injured. Now our men fear a retaliatory strike is imminent. Their reports are alarming and contradictory and trickle in throughout the day:

Salarzai tribesmen are coming across the border and gearing up for the attack.

Pakistani forces have crossed and are aiding the opposition.

The Taliban are entering the area while Pakistan looks the other way.

Al Qaeda has arrived with heavy weaponry.

A cry for jihad has gone out in mosques all across Bajaur.

It's impossible to determine what's really going on. All we know for sure is that our troops have been surrounded, that the threat is escalating, and that they need help. For much of the day Yossef and I shuttle back and forth between the compound and the American base. We're hoping that the Americans can provide air support—at least a flyover to deter the attackers. Sitting with Mr. Hunter and Colonel Thomas, we try to pinpoint the forces' location on a detailed topographic map that lacks the one place-name we need: Letai Kandao. (*Letai* is a kind of mushy oatmeal; *kandao* is a mountain pass.) Every couple of minutes Yossef checks in with the troops by phone; the situation remains unchanged. Then suddenly he's yelling, "Hyder, *saboor kawa!*" *Hold on!* The stand-off has broken: our forces are being shot at from up above. We all lean back over the map, as if our heightened sense of urgency will somehow summon Letai Kandao.

Bagram relays the message that they're inclined to arrange a flyover. The

Americans seem freaked out by the possibility that Pakistan might be involved. "If we bomb the place and it turns out people from Pakistan were inside Afghanistan—" Mr. Hunter starts. "Hyder, I think you know what that means."

Back at the compound we sit in the courtyard. Under a starry sky, my father talks on the satellite phone. Karzai agrees that showing support for government troops in this remote area is vital. Khalilzad leaves a message that the Americans have sent a B1 bomber to survey the area. And from the forces, we hear that four of our men have been killed, and that their bodies are on the way back to Asadabad.

We get ready to leave for the hospital. Yossef and I slide into the pickup, and security guards start piling into the bed. "Whoa, whoa," Yossef says. "I think it would be good to have a couple people at the compound."

On the drive over our two-way radios squawk. "So where are they?" someone asks, referring to the cars transporting the bodies.

"They have just reached the Marawarai bridge," comes the reply.

"Can you bring somebody over here for the night name?" a man calls out, referring to the code word that checkpoints require at this hour.

As we approach the hospital, Yossef says to the guards, "Make sure your eyes are on the car the whole time. There are intelligence guys all around. I don't trust them."

"They're *beysur*," one of the guards replies: *out of tune*.

A crowd is gathered outside the small one-story building. Aside from a couple of pairs of headlights and the weak glow from an outdoor fixture, the area is dark. Four empty coffins sit just outside the door. I recall how just yesterday I was thinking, *I've never been to the hospital; I should visit the hospital here.* Then the pickups come around the corner with the bodies.

We all move inside to a plain, dim room. There is commotion, everyone yelling at once. The bodies come in one by one, laid out on stretchers. The first man's head is smashed. I can't tell where he was injured. "Where was he shot?" I ask. He was shot in the eye. His skin is tinged yellow.

"Get out of the way! Get out of the way!" somebody yells. The second body arrives. Blood is still dripping from a wound in his head. His arm is bent completely backward, as if popped out then replaced the wrong way.

"Over here, over here!" somebody cries. "Put him down right here," a doctor says. The third body is set down, and I see where bullets pierced his skin.

Around me people try to make identifications: "Who's this *alak*?" someone asks, using Pashto's closest word to teenager.

"This is Sher Wali," another replies. "And he's from the Ninth Division."

"I think this guy's from the border patrol," someone says.

"Yeah, I think his name's Amanullah."

"You guys know whose son this is?"

Someone comes over and begins to root around in the pockets of their uniforms for ID cards.

Then there's a wave of something: *Oh my God*, I realize. *The stench.* It's the first time I've smelled death, and I can't compare it to anything. (Haji Qadir's body had been cleaned and kept cool; Abdul Wali had been dead only a short while.) The scent is strong and musky. The discussion shifts accordingly. In this hundred-degree heat, the odor will only worsen. So despite the hour, the decision is made to immediately inform the families of the deaths.

Suddenly a voice is shooing back the crowd. "Hold on, hold on, he's my brother," someone says. Then he's standing next to me, at his brother's feet. He takes in the whole of him, all the way up to the mud matted in his hair. "Yeah, I'm his brother," he says evenly. "Yeah, where do we go now?" He is just a young guy himself.

When we get back to the compound, Yossef throws up. I go to my room. I lie on my bed and say the names of the four to myself: *Najmuddin, son of Said Jalali, was killed today. Sher Wali, son of Mirwais Jan, was killed today. Nazamin—can't figure out who his father is. Amanullah—can't figure out who his father is either—passed away today.*

My own near-miss has been subsumed all day by the frantic efforts to aid the troops, but now I allow myself to think, *I could have been one, too.* These were kids, my age. At the hospital I'd had a fleeting image of my own body laid out upon one of the stretchers: of villagers hovering at the fringes, trying to figure out my face.

Hyder Akbar, son of Said Fazel Akbar.

I close my eyes and try to go to sleep.

* * *

It's only over the next few days that we begin to understand what happened. And it turns out that the lenses through which Westerners view Afghanistan—the night-vision goggles through which the war on terror is fought—will not work here. The Taliban were not involved, nor was Pakistan, nor was Al Qaeda. This was a tribal fight.

The man our troops killed that first night was a timber smuggler—not a hostile insurgent hell-bent on attack. More important, he was the teenage son of a prominent Salarzai *malik,* or landowner. Making matters worse, our troops had set up their camp in a hotly disputed territory. To sum it up: they had blithely entered a sensitive area, then overreacted to an unlikely threat.

The Salarzai were not then aware that these were my father's men. All they knew was that one of their tribesmen had been killed, and that they needed to respond to the attack. So they formed a *lashkar,* or tribal army, composed largely of tribesmen from the Pakistani side of the border. The *lashkar* killed the four men whose bodies I saw and took thirteen more troops back with them to Pakistan as hostages.

Though the Taliban were not involved, they immediately take credit for attacking our forces; their reputation is now wholly dependent on acts of insurgency. They aren't the only ones trying to get a piece of the pie. The ISI—Pakistan's intelligence service—requests that the Salarzai turn the thirteen hostages over to them. The Salarzai refuse. *Okay,* says the ISI. *We won't take the hostages—only their pictures.* The Salarzai refuse again. Perhaps the ISI wants to hand the hostages over to the Taliban; perhaps it wants to use the photo of uniformed soldiers as "proof" that Afghan forces are crossing the border. Whatever the case, it seems to boil down to an attempt by the ISI to undermine the Afghan government.

But it fails. As soon as the Salarzai realize that their hostages belong to my father, amicable talks begin. Though they live in an area clearly demarcated as Pakistan, their loyalty to the guy across the Durand Line surpasses anything they feel toward the government of their own side.

Over the next couple days my father negotiates with the Salarzai as a sovereign power. We plan a trip up to the Dangam Valley—the site of the attack—so that my father can talk to the people there face-to-face. A handful of Americans will come along, too.

The day before we leave, I head down to the base with several servings of my mom's *joshi* kabob: fried meat mixed with potatoes and vegetables and eggs. During one of my recent visits, Colonel Thomas had lamented, "You get to go back to your delicious homemade food from your mother, and we get to go up and heat up our MRE"—*meals ready to eat.* So now here I am, standing at the checkpoint with my Tupperware containers, as if I'm welcoming a new neighbor rather than trying to get a security clearance to enter a military base.

I deliver the food and Yossef and I sit down for a talk with Mr. Hunter. Then there's a *boom!* unlike any I've ever heard in my life. "What's that?" I ask.

"Hold on," Mr. Hunter says, "I'll be right back," leaping over a chair as he exits.

"That was not from them," Yossef says. "This is someone attacking the base."

"Get out! Get out right now!" Mr. Hunter yells.

Yossef and I run outside and crouch below a little roof. There's a whistle and then another *boom!,* this one maybe twenty meters to our right. "Hyder, let's run out of here," Yossef urges.

"Calm down," I tell him. "We'll look like we're really weak to the Americans." Yossef is the only person I've been around in Afghanistan whom I actually have to calm down; usually I'm the one whose nerves are being managed. "I've never been this close to death," he quakes. A shift in the wind might have meant the end of us. *If a missile is going to hit on top of you, then it's fate,* I say to myself. *It's your time to go.*

Though nobody is hurt, the attack is significant. It's the first time in my father's two-plus years here that a missile has actually landed inside Toopchi. Back at the compound, less than an hour later, the call to prayer echoes as a B52 hums above us in the sky. The B52s always look like they're barely moving—they're like slow shooting stars. I'm not so naïve as to think that the Americans are going to devote as many resources to protecting us as to protecting themselves; and I'm sure they have a pre-planned response for such direct attacks. But it's hard not to compare the speed with which this bomber was scrambled to the hemming and hawing and delays that accompany our requests. The B52 continues its flight, high, high up above us, seemingly part of another world none of us down here will ever be able to reach.

3 1

Y EAH, THAT WAS PRETTY CLOSE LAST night," I agree with the Americans the next morning. We're standing around outside, waiting to leave for Dangam, talking about yesterday's missile attack. Though it's only nine A.M., we're already baking. This whole summer has been hot; I sometimes awaken drenched in sweat, as if I've just gotten out of the shower. Today I rose early in preparation for this trip. For breakfast, I had eggs and turkey sausage my mother recently purchased in Pakistan. As I finished eating, I noticed that the mood was unusually relaxed; nobody was making an effort to get going. My father was outside, meeting with some visitors, and now I interrupted to tell him that we were going to be late. He'd thought the Americans were picking us up here.

You should have told me about this before.

I mentioned it several times last night.

Yeah, but you never made it clear—

But Dada—

Then I stop myself, conscious of the guests around me.

We meet the Americans outside a building known as the *barq-fabricah*: the electricity factory, or power plant. (Actually, power*less* plant: bringing this place back to functionality is an unfunded $6.7 million project.) There are a couple Humvees full of U.S. troops—including Colonel Thomas and

Mr. Hunter—but the majority of the men who will be accompanying us today are ANA soldiers who've come up from Jalalabad for this trip. Their presence is a real sign of progress. The preparations for our journey take forever. Finally they're complete, a formation is agreed upon, and the twenty cars in our convoy are off—for a moment. The lead driver has forgotten to fill his tank with gas. The huge line of us wait alongside the pump, then sputter away to Dangam.

You could throw a football from one side of the Dangam Valley to the other and run out of room. We edge into the corridor through dusty sunlight. I see that despite the drought, this place is really green; trees carpet the massive mountains that rise on either side.

At the district office there's more green: wild marijuana plants, which the Americans helpfully identify. Nearby, tribal elders wait along a dirt road to greet my father. He holds out his hands to each man in the long line, and then we walk up to the local mosque for our meeting. The sun is out, and a breeze ruffles our shirts.

The mosque is a low white building. A couple hundred tribal elders assemble on rugs laid out in the dirt courtyard. Some of the rugs have a tropical motif, palm trees and round suns. My father sits on the mosque's long front terrace, facing the group. He's in the center of a line of people that includes Mr. Hunter, who's wearing a bulletproof vest; and Rauf Mama, who's next to my father, dressed the same way he is, in a light-colored kameez partoog. Both wear round wristwatches. Occasionally Rauf Mama adjusts his pakol, revealing his balding head. My father's sleeves are rolled midway up his forearms, and his feet are covered in gray socks.

He opens the meeting by saying that he is here to talk about peace, and to clear up any misunderstandings. He addresses the problem of outside interference: "There are people who see benefits in destroying the alliances and relationships in this area," he says. "But now it is our Islamic duty, our duty to this nation, not to let small incidents like these be fanned by people who have other agendas. I consider Pakistan our friend, and I have this request of them: That instead of trying to fan the *leman*"—literally, to fan the bottom part of a kameez partoog, but used the same way as *to fan the flames*—"in situations like this, if they could help us."

My father curves his hands, the tips of his fingers touching as he talks. "I consider you all my brothers," he says. "I'm from this area. I refer to some of you as *mamas,* some of you as *kakas.* . . . The Salarzai tribe is very close to me. I've spent a lot of time here in this very valley. I moved up and down this valley several times during the jihad. And on the other side, in Bajaur, I've spent even more nights there, and I know all the elders. In situations like this, let's keep our brotherhood intact." He continues, "I don't want the people here hurt. Even if I was not the governor of this province, as somebody from this area, as one of your brothers, I would consider this my duty. That is why I came to Kunar, to try to help the people here and to try to protect the people here. That is why I came to Dangam today."

Above us, leaves flutter a little in the breeze, and my father explains the reason for the presence of the U.S. and ANA troops: "The people that are here with me wanted to come and see this place," he says. "Please don't take this as I've brought soldiers and convoys with me to intimidate and scare people. We're not here to perform operations. We're not here to patrol. I truly believe if I come here empty-handed, if I bring nothing with me, that you will be my *lashkar*"—tribal army. "I don't need other *lashkars.*" It is as my father told the election workers: the support of the tribe is everything in Afghanistan.

As I've done since my father began speaking, I whisper a translation into Colonel Thomas's ear. Later he tells me, "I thought how different this is, the way people resolve conflicts here in Afghanistan. . . . It was moving to me to see your father, without protection, without weapons, without body armor that we all carry, sit in front of a group of two hundred folks that could be hostile. They could have done anything they wanted at that point to your father. But he walked right into the middle of them, sat down, and began to tell them, 'This is the way we need to resolve this conflict, and this is why I'm here, and we can go forward peacefully.' "

We finish the meeting with a prayer, then head for lunch. Our host is a jovial man with a two-packs-a-day rasp. The food is set up on a perch overlooking the spine of the sunlit valley. People crowd along narrow carpets on which silver bowls and platters of rice are spread. Mr. Hunter and Colonel Thomas try to fold their legs, their huge boots getting in the way. With our fingers, we eat meat—lots of it.

The villagers would like to construct a plumbing system, and after the meal Colonel Thomas is shown to a mountain spring. "It was one of the most beautiful things I've ever seen," he says to me later. "The cleanest, purest water I've ever had." There, he reports, one of the villagers tells him, "This is where Governor Akbar stayed during his time over here commanding units that were fighting the Soviet occupation. This was his sanctuary, where he had fresh water, and the ability to refit and replenish himself." Something about the scene really gets to Colonel Thomas: "And here's your father back here again, trying to move this place forward," he tries to explain to me. "I wrote to my mother about it. She said, 'Oh, I've sent it to everyone in town.'"

After lunch we visit the proposed site of the Asmar bridge, which will provide a critical connection between the northern and southern parts of this district. But the locals are worried; this site, chosen by the Americans, is disaster-prone. Floods might wash a bridge away; falling rocks might snap its pillars.

Engineer Will, who has a shaved head, assures the villagers that this spot is fine. He's planned it all out; it's going to work. He's unyielding, yet the villagers press their case: to construct here would be wasteful. The bridge will not last one spring.

As I translate, I have one foot here and the other in the pages of one of my favorite books: *Caravans,* a James Michener novel set in 1946 Afghanistan. It's as if I'm channeling the character of Nur Muhammad, repeating the words he speaks to American diplomat Mark Miller in chapter 6:

These bridges are far more important to us than they are to you. They're our first contact with the western world. If they succeed, we who want to modernize this nation will succeed. If they fail, dreadful consequences may follow. Now please, Professor-Architect, listen when I tell you that sometimes in the spring what you call our trivial desert streams roar out of the mountains two miles wide. They move boulders as big as houses. They destroy everything not perched on a hill. And the next day they're little streams again.

Eventually Colonel Thomas takes over from Engineer Will, and when we leave, Rauf Mama asks me about the "red-faced small guy who seemed to be the leader." I tell him that was Colonel Thomas. "I really liked how he talked at the bridge," Rauf Mama says. "He seemed to be genuinely concerned, and he talked to the people on an equal level. He also seemed really comfortable—not paranoid, looking over his shoulder as if we were all going to shoot him at once. This is a guy I could be friends with."

I too had marveled at Colonel Thomas's effective style. Though he had not managed to give the people what they wanted (perhaps the PRT's budget could not be stretched to cover the villagers' more complicated proposal), he had succeeded in befriending them.

Sometime later I decide to give Colonel Thomas a copy of *Caravans* as a gift. When I present it to him, he tells me he's already read it. "Have you seen the part about the bridges?" he asks me immediately. "Yeah, yeah, yeah," I say. There's something special about this shared reference. Later Colonel Thomas shows the section to Engineer Will.

Soon we leave the bridge site, pile back into the convoy, and head down to Asmar, where we and the rest of the group will split: we'll stay the night and they'll proceed back to Asadabad. Rauf Mama keeps turning around in his seat, checking to make sure that the Americans' Humvees are still in line behind us. That the U.S. forces are bringing up the rear worries him; this should be our position, so that we can look out for them. Finally I explain, "They want to be in back."

"Oh, you mean they're providing the security for us?" Rauf Mama realizes. The arrangement baffles him. Because the U.S. troops are unfamiliar with this area, attackers would force them to flee; Rauf Mama, who knows this land, would be able to engage. I realize I'm seeing two very different perspectives. To the Americans, security is armor and weapons. To Rauf Mama, security is knowledge—of mountain passes and alternate routes.

And so like this we continue along the open road, each side thinking they're keeping the other safe.

* * *

In the morning we wake in the home of a wealthy tribal elder with whom we've stayed for the night. When everyone is up, we decide to walk down to the village of Shangar. My sandal strap rips the skin off my toe, and eventually I decide just to go barefoot. The relief is so great that I don't even mind the pebbles pressing into my soles.

Shangar is Sartor's home village, and I get on the satellite phone and let him know we're here. I reach him in Kabul, where he's been supervising the construction of my father's new house. Sartor tells me that he really wants to come back to Kunar, and would I ask my father if he could? My father says yes, and then it's time to go. We're off to Shal, his own home village, a place to which I've never been.

This is probably the first time in Afghanistan in which I consciously do not want to turn on my minidisc recorder. Even before we get to Shal, I've decided to keep this moment to myself.

On our way my father and Rauf Mama tell stories about their childhood. They point out the mountains they used to climb. They show me the place on the road where they'd stand to block the kids from Shangar from coming into their town. They did not have to worry about traffic disrupting their play; a car came up this road only once every two weeks, ferrying supplies to a northern checkpoint. Villagers would assemble, as if for a parade, to watch its passage. My father's family eventually bought the first car in Asmar. They kept it on the other side of the river, in a place that, thanks to them, became known as Garage Village. After they parked, they would stand on the banks and fire a gun into the sky to signal their arrival. Little *jahlas*—those animal-skin rafts—would be sent to fetch them. They'd pile on, float across the river, and climb forty-five minutes back to their house. This was my father's boyhood; this was all happening in the 1950s. It's strange to think how different my life would have turned out if I'd been born here. A particular chain of events propelled me not only out of Shal but several generations into the future.

Now we approach the village's soaring peaks. (In the winter, my father claims, Shal had only four hours of sunlight: at eleven A.M. the sun would finally heave itself up over the eastern mountains, and at three P.M. it would duck back down behind the peaks to the west.) Along a dirt road, we greet another long line of well-wishers; and then we go to see my father's old house. As we head over, I think I know what to expect—something mud-brick. What I don't realize is that his childhood home will be almost completely flattened. I am seeing a site rather than a structure. The feel is archaeological; the walls that remain offer only a sense of the outlines of rooms. There are many people here, and we walk through the dirt and overgrown grasses. We raise our hands and pray before the grave of my grandfather—my real grandfather, my father's father, who died when he was even younger than me.

Afterward, the villagers welcome us into a tent and serve us tea. Soon I tell my father that I'm going to walk around and take some pictures, and he says, "Don't take too long. We are going to have to get going," as if we are just anywhere—as if this is a normal trip.

Yossef and Rauf Mama and I return to the house, and someone snaps a picture of me before a section of wall I'm told was my father's room. I sit down, and Rauf Mama tells me the story of the day during the Soviet war when my father's house was bombed. He actually saw the explosion from a mountain perch. The hit was so direct that it almost seemed like the house was a high-value target. But of course it wasn't—it was just our family home.

"We better hurry," Yossef says. "I think your dad is leaving." I take a final look around the place where my grandfather walked, where my father and Rauf Mama crawled. Then I grab my camera and run to the pickup. My father is already sitting inside.

Our last stop is Asmar, the main village in this district of the same name. There we visit a girls' school, where a group of students—all of them perhaps ten years old, their heads wrapped in thin white chadors—perform a song specially prepared for my father. The girls stand on a rug in a patch of grass, and we regard them from a row of plastic chairs. My father holds a bunch of red flowers. In the distance there's a river, terraced green fields. The girls sway back and forth, as if in time to the light wind. They sing:

Our esteemed guest, our brother, congratulations on your return.
You have come back to your country.

But they don't say country: they say *watan,* which is more expansive. Afghanistan is my father's *watan*; so is Kunar; so is Asmar; so is Shal.

It is a good thing that you have come to the destroyed village
    Asmar.
The hopeful eyes are widened.
Everybody is looking at you with hopeful eyes.
A bridge, will you please plan a bridge here on this ravine?
Will you please build a bridge right away?

Congratulations on your return.
You have come back to your *watan*.

You are the governor of all of Kunar.
Of the poor people, you are on top of their hearts.
You are the leader of the Pashtuns.
You are the integrity of all the people.
Please bring us peace and brotherhood.
Please bring it to us in your ways.

Congratulations on your return.
You have come back to your *watan*.

The children have come out, the children of heroes.
Some have fathers next to them, but mostly they are the countless
    orphans.
Tell the tormentors to go home, to get on their way.

Congratulations on your return.
You have come back to your *watan*.

And then, our visits finished, we're on our way back to Asadabad. I slip on my headphones, and I'm succumbing to a U2 CD when Rauf Mama taps my shoulder.

"You see that place right there, across the river, next to that field?" he says.

"Yeah, I do," I tell him.

"That is where Nizamuddin's dead body was taken out of the river by the people," Rauf Mama says, "and beaten again with rocks and sticks and stones." Rauf Mama is referring to the governor who was one of the masterminds of the Kerala massacre.

"Wow," I say. "I see."

"That's it," he tells me. "You can put your headphones back on now." And so I do, as if he's just pointed out any old roadside attraction.

We're on the Asmar Road in the Kunar Valley. Sartor has mentioned a commercial—it sounds like something from a tourism board—that plays on TV in Kabul. It shows the Bamiyan Buddhas, a mosque in Mazar-i-Sharif that is believed to hold the tomb of the son-in-law of the Prophet Muhammad, and an overhead view of this road right here.

Colonel Thomas once told me that this area reminded him of an old movie called *Lost Horizon*. He said you might see it on the Turner Classic channel. The plot goes like this: In the 1930s some Westerners are in a plane crash in a remote valley in Tibet. It turns out this is Shangri-La: a special place of extraordinary purity where everyone lives for hundreds of years. At first all of the travelers just want to get the hell out of there, except for one, who continues to dream of the place once he's gone. Colonel Thomas said this valley, the Kunar Valley, reminded him of the one in the movie: the one to which the dreaming man spends his life trying to return. And at the end of the movie, he actually gets there. You see him returning: you see him being welcomed back.

Congratulations on your return.
You have come back to your *watan*.

32

MY BROTHER AND I ARE AT OSAMA bin Laden's house. The roof is gone and the wind blows through the bombed-out rooms. Below us is dirt, and above, a big blank blue sky. Bin Laden doesn't live here anymore, of course. This compound, which supposedly once housed twenty-six families, sits between Jalalabad and Tora Bora and was destroyed after September 11th. The imprint of the American forces is now more visible than bin Laden's. Graffiti is scrawled across the remaining walls:

Quinn + Rose
OSAMA→SUCKS
hDS A5R -2004 OGF.
CINCINNA (a subsequent bombing may explain the missing *TI*)

We're here with our cousin and one of his friends. When we arrived, they told us that this place is mined. But I don't think that Omar heard them, because he walked straight inside. I had to follow; I didn't want them to think Omar was braver than me. Now our companions regard us from a distance. There's a cursed, haunted-house feel, and they don't want to come too near. (They also don't want the Americans, whom they believe still monitor this place, tracking them down, asking what they were doing here.)

I imagine that this hot desert area must have reminded bin Laden of his home in Saudi Arabia. My brother carries a tall plastic bottle of Nestlébrand water around as we make our tour. The place is huge, and I ask Omar to use his expertise as a Bay Area mortgage broker to assess the space.

"This right here is about ten thousand square feet," he says, calculating a partial section. "So twenty thousand, thirty thousand, forty thousand, eighty thousand, a hundred—at least—" He looks around.

"Yeah, yeah, there's more beyond that wall," I tell him.

"At least four or five hundred thousand square feet," he decides.

"Four or five hundred thousand," I say. "Wow."

"How many square feet is equal to an acre?" Omar wonders.

"I don't know," I laugh.

We regard the property with a critical eye.

"It's all house," I say. "It's not like, four hundred thousand square feet, and like a ten-thousand-square-foot—"

"There's no lot," Omar interrupts. "It's all living area."

Omar got to Afghanistan just a few days ago. His arrival coincides with my departure: I'm leaving from Kabul this week. I'll start school almost immediately after I return. (It's strange: I'm forgetting what summers are like in America. An entire season has been subtracted from my life there.) My mother's going back to California, too, mainly to be with me, about which I feel a little guilty. Here in Afghanistan Omar will resume work on the reconstruction projects he began last spring. But now we're off for one last adventure: we're on our way to Tora Bora.

After the feverish campaign of 2001, Americans largely forgot about Tora Bora (the cave complex from which the U.S. troops attempted to flush out remaining members of Al Qaeda). If they remembered it at all, it was as a relic of a particular era, one characterized by Ashleigh Banfield's eyewear. But Tora Bora did not shut down once the cameras went home. It turned into a sort of shrine for the Arabs who died fighting there. Their passing has been mythologized: it is said that when people tried to loot their dead bodies, they could not remove the watches from their wrists, nor the money from their pockets. It seemed that God was protecting them. Now people bring deaf and blind kids to Tora Bora, as though they might be healed by its spiritual force field.

When a cousin of mine from that region came to Kunar for a visit, I told him of Tora Bora's status in America as the sensational climax of the war. He started laughing. "Oh my God," he said, remembering the fighting. "The Americans couldn't go beyond a certain line. They made the Afghans do all the work." I wanted to see what had become of this place that had figured so prominently in the popular imagination, and I told my cousin that later in the summer I would come for a visit.

A few weeks later my cousin's older brother Naray Lala showed up and tried to change my mind. "The security is not good there," he said. "A lot of *daaz o dooz*." *Daaz o dooz*: a Pashtun phrase for "action." (*Daaz* and *dooz* are not real words; just sounds that represent commotion.) To me Tora Bora sounded no more dangerous than Kunar: tribal disputes, rocket attacks, some mines on the road. So I made my case to my father, he gave his permission, and Naray Lala, shaking his head, reluctantly agreed to take me with him when Omar showed up.

We awoke at four in the morning to prepare. The goal was to do the trip in a day: make the drive, plus complete the hike, before dark. While I got my things together, Omar did pushups and crunches.

The air was still thick with crickets' chirps when we went to say good-bye to our parents. We whispered; a morning program played softly on the radio. "Kiss the Koran Sharif," my mother said, and I touched my lips to the book, as is traditional before a trip.

"Hyder, are you taking a bodyguard with you?" my father asked.

"No," I told him.

"Make sure you take a rifle with you," he said. "And make sure you have a registration card with it."

I went to ask Naray Lala if he thought we should bring a gun. "Yeah, yeah, that wouldn't be too bad of an idea," he said. "It would be better than the option of having to beg for your life."

I went back to my father in his bedroom. "Here, you can take this one," he said, handing me a Kalashnikov. "Sartor has the card. I think we have an extra clip."

I carried the gun into the courtyard. "It's a good thing you have the Kalashnikov," said Rauf Mama's son Salaam. Morning prayers had finished, and people were already up. "You want to take a pistol, too?"

"No," Naray Lala said. "What would you do with a pistol if you have a Kalashnikov? A pistol is good if you want to do something small, but it can never do a *toura*"—an amazing feat.

We finished gathering our supplies—a holder for the Kalashnikov, the extra clip of thirty bullets—and then a taxi came for us and we crammed inside. Omar wanted to listen to some kind of Arab techno music he'd picked up in Dubai. He craned around from the front seat and regarded me, Sartor, and Naray Lala in the back. "I'm telling you," he said, "this is supposed to be really good. The man kept raving about it." But the tape was horrible: a mixture of classic Middle Eastern music and club beats topped off with an occasional, extremely embarrassing, seductive female moan. It sounded like something Saudi sheikhs would listen to in their Ferraris. The beats were as repetitive as the scenery: *mountain, mountain, mountain, boom, boom, boom.* Naray Lala closed his eyes and Sartor just shook his head. Finally Omar relinquished control of the tape deck, and we put in our choice: a rare Ahmed Zahir cassette for which I'd searched in every single music store in Kabul. It was a *khanagee,* a live performance recorded in a private home; in this case, that of one of my cousins. I thought maybe my father had attended: in the background, you can hear people calling out to Rayees-Saib, or Mr. Director, which was what my father was known as back in his Kabul Radio days.

The taxi driver raced over the roads at an insane speed, and we got two flat tires. We used our spare the first time; the second all we could do was wait at the side of the road and hope for assistance. Finally there rose a cloud of dust, and a car swerved and stopped. Inside was a bank official from Asadabad. "What are you guys doing here, just standing along the road like that?" he said. While his driver hurried to fetch a spare, the bank official addressed me and Omar: "You really shouldn't be standing on the side of the road like this, the both of you. Somebody might just pop you off, you know?" We nodded politely. It had already been suggested that Omar and I ride in separate cars, lest one of us die, and our father be left without a surviving son. As soon as we had the tire, the bank official sped off, as if evading snipers perched all around us in the mountains.

* * *

314

We were already exhausted by the time we reached Jalalabad. We got out of the taxi, our faces painted with dust. "Are you sure you want to go?" Naray Lala, who was still reluctant, checked. (*Naray* means "slender," and *lala* is an endearment for an older brother or for another family member who is not quite an uncle. His real name is Ekraam, which I've never heard anyone use.) We were still game, so we began a seemingly fruitless search for a friend of Naray Lala's who would serve as our guide. Omar was getting irritated. "We should just go ahead and go to Tora Bora," he said to me impatiently, as if we could just rent a car for a leisurely drive to the cave complex. "You know, Omar Lala, you can't just freakin' *go* to Tora Bora," I said, my own irritation getting the better of me. "We need someone from the area to come with us." Finally we found our guide—an NGO worker with thick glasses that shrank his eyes—and we were on our way, making a quick detour to bin Laden's house.

Now we leave that bombed-out compound and get back in the car. The desert landscape through which we travel is bereft of pretty much everything: I observe no signs of government control—no police, no security guards, no soldiers. (I do see a wedding party: cheering, music, kids dancing on moving trucks.) We pass fields burned up by the drought. The scorched earth is just one indicator of this area's lack of progress. During my stay I'm told that maybe ten percent of the people here are happy with the Americans, while eighty percent were behind the Arabs. This is not indicative of a nationwide sentiment: the Jalalabad area was the first place to which bin Laden came, and he had a lot of connections here. (Afghans in Naray Lala's own village, Khugyiano, are said to have sheltered bin Laden after 9/11.) The Arabs were concerned with international issues and with their own goals. They didn't interfere in the lives of the local people—except to pay them off and fund their projects. So this was not an ideological alliance. The people here liked the Arabs because they did things like build wells. But there is little to show for the U.S. presence in the way of infrastructure. And, I'm told, "The Americans can't even have a car come too close. They shoot the people." (A taxi driver is said to have recently been killed by a U.S. soldier in such an incident.) I can tell that even though some of those with whom I speak don't want to admit it, the Arabs still hold for them some pull. It makes me worry about the prospects for the Americans here.

"You can see it from here," says Naray Lala. "It's that black hill right there before that mountain." Here, finally, is Tora Bora: a black, charcoal-colored mound set before a larger range. We attempt to drive up an access road, but when this proves impossible we get out of the car and start to walk.

It's a hundred degrees, maybe 120, but the heat doesn't bother me as much as my illness. Of course I'm sick; I haven't eaten more than a bite of a single meal in three days. Everything I swallow, I throw back up, including liquids. I wonder if I might have dysentery. "How are you even alive?" Naray Lala wonders now. But I try to put my discomfort out of my head; we're here, the day is dwindling, and we need to move really fast.

The hike is steep and exhausting and we have no water. We didn't really take into account the drought. Naray Lala points out the shrine for the Arabs—their graves are marked with flags—but it hardly seems to matter. The sun bores down, and I have a pounding headache. I think I'm doing pretty bad until I take a look at Sartor. He's been on edge ever since we started, directing his wrath first at Osama bin Laden—*Why did that Arab jackass pick this wretched place to come to? What was he thinking?*—and then at the land itself—*Afghanistan will never be stable until we get rid of these damn mountains! How are you going to tame this country when we have these in which to run and hide?* Now, as we approach a tank, Sartor remarks, through a hallucinatory fog, "Look, it's a house." We start to worry, perhaps too late, about heatstroke.

Finally we get to the top. We see some caves but don't even attempt to check them out. Omar and I literally collapse on our backs. We bend our knees, as if about to do situps, though there is no way I could muster the strength. I speak into my recorder: *Tora Bora beat me good.* But there's no time for a real rest: the sun is setting. A bright band of light stretches atop the peaks across from us; most of their long bulk is already dark.

We return down the steep slope as fast as we can. We've heard three large explosions and spied two reconnaissance planes. Meanwhile Naray Lala has white stuff coming out of his mouth, and my brother tells me I don't look so good either: the color has drained from my face. Then, a ways away, I see a trail of water. "Oh my God, yes!" I cry. I shuffle toward it down a vertical wall; finally I let myself go and begin to run. Sartor reaches out to grab me, but I'm already too far away. Before me I take in the spring. It releases its bounty: one drop. Ten seconds. Another drop. Ten seconds. Drop. And so on. I can't believe it.

Then Omar appears. He points and says, "I just drank some of that puddle of mud."

"How did you drink that mud?" I say skeptically.

"I got on my hands and knees and pressed my lips to it and sucked the water out," Omar claims.

"No, you did not," I say. "You're trying to trick me. You're trying to get me to do that so that you can take a picture." Luckily dehydration has not shut down my powers of logic: "If you did that, your knees would be dirty," I reason. "Lift up your kameez partoog and show me if your knees are dirty."

As soon as I see the spots on Omar's pants, I get down on the ground and literally begin to eat the mud. It's the only way I can get any water out of it. I'm consuming so much that the others tell me to stop; I'm going to make myself sick.

So I stand back up and we continue along the bottom of a canyon. "Are you okay?" Naray Lala asks. "Can you walk a little faster? It's not too good to be in this area." We speed up. Naray Lala starts to jog. "Are you okay?" he checks again. And then he just starts sprinting. "We need to get out of here!" he cries.

Finally we reach the access road. We still have some distance to go to get to our taxi, and when we see a truck, we yell to the driver to slow down. Everyone runs to hitch themselves up on the rear, but I'm tangled up in my recording equipment, and by the time I unfurl myself, the truck is fifty yards in front of me, accelerating to twenty, thirty miles an hour, everyone is on it, and I'm all by myself.

But the mud puddle has rejuvenated me so much that it doesn't really hit me that I should be scared. I amble along for about twenty minutes, and then I run into Naray Lala, who lost his grip on the truck and turned back to find me. Almost as soon as we meet, a pack of wild dogs rears up. Alone I wouldn't have known what to do, but Naray Lala just picks up a rock and the dogs back off.

At eight o'clock we reach Omar and Sartor and our taxi. Some kids offer us water; we drink so much, they go back to their house four times to fetch more. We get in the taxi, which balks when we reach an uphill stretch. So we drag our sore legs up the road while the driver goes ahead, the car more agile without us. It's so dark that when he gets too far ahead, we can't see in front of us.

Then we're back in the car, bouncing along, when we realize, *Hey— aren't we in the middle of the river?* We're driving inside the dry, rocky bed of the river—its quality is no worse than the road—and now the driver sticks the taxi in reverse and we try to figure out where we lost our way. The moon illuminates the desert floor, and I gaze out at what seems to be one of the most remote areas in the whole world.

Two days later in Kabul, Omar and I go shopping on Chicken Street and then to a restaurant for lunch. At our table we flip through a copy of an English-language magazine called *Afghan Scene*. There is an article by author Ahmed Rashid and an ad for a photo exhibition; there's even a fashion spread. As we sit there, marveling at how much Afghanistan has changed, the phone rings.

"No, no," Omar says. "What happened?"

Immediately I feel queasy. We're staying at a guesthouse—a little hotel— with our parents here in Kabul. There's not much in the way of security, and now I wonder, *Has something happened to my dad?*

But when Omar hangs up, there's relief: our father's okay. The trouble isn't here in Kabul, it's up in Kunar. Last night eight rockets were launched at the governor's compound from three different locations. The coordinated effort is alarming—and just as representative of the new Afghanistan as any fashion spread.

"How do you want me to start?" Sartor says.

It's my last morning in Kabul—my flight leaves in four hours—and I'm doing an interview with Sartor as my final recording.

"For instance, you were born in Shangar," I say.

"Okay," he says. And then like everyone he jokes: "Don't ask about dates. I can describe to you what has happened, but don't ask about dates.

"I was born in the Kunar province, Asmar district, Shangar village," he begins. He lived there until fifth grade, when the Soviets invaded; then he moved to a refugee camp in Pakistan, where he worked for a shopkeeper who paid him one and a half rupees a day.

"What could you get with one and a half rupees?" I ask.

"It was kind of cheap back then," Sartor says. "Three rupees for a kilo of rice, five rupees for a kilo of oil." At some point Rauf Mama showed up and told Sartor he was taking him to Peshawar for three months. (Rauf Mama and Sartor belong to the same tribe.) "I came to Pacha Saib's house," Sartor says, referring to my father. And he stayed not just three months but almost twenty years.

Of course there have been interruptions, a date Sartor knows among them: "In your calendar, it was in the year eighty-nine, I think," he says. "The twelfth month of the eighty-ninth year and the twenty-fourth day." This was Sartor's wedding day. A week later Rauf Mama announced his plans for an attack on a Communist post. "I went with him," Sartor says. "We were going to attack the village at night and nobody was willing to stay behind to take care of the food. One white beard volunteered to stay, and Rauf Mama turned to me and said, 'Sartor, you're going to stay, too.' So I stayed. At night the fighting got really intense. There were missiles landing around us. We had a lot of injured mujahedeen. They were bringing them back on donkeys. And when I saw those wounded mujahedeen, I remembered an old saying. They say that anybody who marries between the two Eids"—two important Muslim holidays—"the small one and the big one, will die very soon. Both my brother and I had gotten married between the two Eids. I said to myself, *You're going to die tonight.* But I made it out alive."

"What was the most difficult era for you?" I ask.

"The Taliban time was the most difficult for me," he answers. "There was nothing to do in Shangar, no work. You'd just be home all day."

"What if you needed money to get something?" I say. "What did you do?"

"We didn't have a choice," he says. "We couldn't get any money."

"Okay," I say. "What would be the best time you've spent in life?"

"The best time, I would say, is this current time right now," Sartor replies. "Karzai's government."

"Why?" I ask.

"Well, because the salaries are a lot better than they used to be," he asserts. "Employment is getting better. People are starting to have jobs again." (To give an idea of just how little it takes for things in Afghanistan to start looking rosy: unemployment here has been estimated as high as seventy-eight percent.)

"Do you think Afghanistan could slip into chaos again?" I ask.

"No," he says. "The international forces are here from all over the world to help us. If the foreigners run away, then it's back to the old game. But if the foreigners stay here, I think things will get better. People know now, nothing can come from the chaos we went through. We had chaos for twenty-five years. Those people that got rich off of that are plenty rich now. I don't think they want to fight anymore. I think they just want to invest their money."

Sartor offers an explanation for the problems that remain in Afghanistan: "When the Taliban fled, anybody who grabbed anything stayed in that place. So we have a lot of that left over." It's actually a nice sketch of the first post-Taliban government: the Karzai administration came in, surveyed the country, took note of which warlords had already seized what, and issued edicts proclaiming them the official authorities of their domains.

Sartor believes the elections will bring positive change. Like the tribal elders in Shulton, his confidence in this outcome is unshakable—even when I remind him of the stasis that followed the first loya jirga. That too was supposed to be a marker, the point at which things would finally get serious; what happened? "At that time, everybody was new," he points out. "The foreigners had just come. The new government had just come. Everybody was scared, playing conservative. Everyone was counting their moves, thinking ahead."

When Sartor is not with us at the governor's compound in Asadabad, he returns to his family in Shangar. He and his wife have seven children, six daughters and one son. Right now they do not have their own home, so they are renting a place from friends. "We only have two rooms," Sartor says. "In one room we have all of our animals—the cow and the chickens all in one room. And the rest of us all in one other room."

"How many people are in this house now?" I ask.

"Well, we're nine, plus five more. We are fourteen people in this house," he says.

Soon Sartor gets impatient. "I've got to go downstairs and get the car out of the main road," he announces. "Shopkeepers are going to come and open up their shops."

He leaves, and I look out the window at a collapsed wall of bricks. I think of Sartor as cynical, wisecracking; I am surprised by his bright view of the future. *The best time, I would say, is this current time right now.* His optimism gives me pause, at the end of my pessimistic summer.

Sartor returns from the street and stands in the doorway. He has introduced me to so much in Afghanistan; now, as I leave, he has reinstilled in me some measure—at least two rooms full—of hope.

Epilogue

*San Francisco
International Airport,
August 2004*

O KAY, SO BE TOTALLY HONEST WITH me," the airport official says. "How do you feel about U.S. foreign policy?"

I'm standing at SFO with my four suitcases, answering a barrage of questions from this woman and others, including someone from the Department of Homeland Security. We've just finished the marathon journey from Kabul. My mother passed through without incident, but I'm stuck here, being searched. It started with my carry-on: the first photograph they looked at showed me kneeling high above the Panjshir Valley on a cloudless day, wearing sandals and a kameez partoog, laughing a little, and holding an AK. "You're going to be here for a while," someone told me, putting that picture to the side. The officials continued shuffling through, making a little pile and pointing the original shot out to one another: *Check this one out.*

"Are you trained in the use of weapons?" they say. "Explosives? Have you ever been a member of the U.S. military?"

They press for details about individual pictures. "Who's this guy?" they say.

"Um, Hamid Karzai," I reply.

"Who's that?" they demand.

"The president of Afghanistan," I say. It's a casual photo of my father and Karzai.

"How does your father know him?" they ask.

"They've been friends a long time," I say.

"Since when?"

"The resistance," I tell them.

"The resistance against?" They wait expectantly for me to fill in the blank, seemingly thinking I'm going to say *Against freedom and democracy* or *Against the U.S. and its allies and the infidel troops currently occupying Afghanistan.*

"Against the Russians," I say.

They move on. "Who's this guy?"

I do what I can to prove that I'm not a terrorist. I show them a copy of my *New York Times Magazine* article about Abdul Wali, but the color photo identifying me as the author has no effect. They continue to rifle through my belongings. They hassle me about having not one but two copies of historian Louis Dupree's *Afghanistan*—a book that is rare and expensive in the U.S. but relatively easy to come by in Kabul. They pull out George Soros's *The Bubble of American Supremacy: Correcting the Misuse of American Power.* "This is interesting," they say. "Is this supposed to be a terrorist handbook?" They flip though, examining the notes I've made in the margins.

My heart stops when they pull out a piece of propaganda from the Taliban. *Anybody who cooperates with the Americans will be killed:* that's the basic message of the leaflet. It hits me that I might get stuck here for two days. But they clearly can't decipher the Arabic script; they ask neither about the leaflet nor about a missive from Gulbiddin Hekmatyar. They're skipping over all of the most damning documents, things I've kept for their historical worth, but that in another young man's possession might indicate suspicious sympathies, or contain within them a personal message from Osama bin Laden.

Then they scoop up a pile of items and say, "We have to go verify all this."

"How long is this going to take?" I ask. "I had a very long trip, starting from Kabul."

"A half-hour."

"A half-hour?" I grumble.

"Excuse me, sir, we could hold you a lot longer than a half-hour if we wanted to," one of them announces.

They return after fifteen or twenty minutes with my stuff and say that I can go. Heaving my luggage behind me, I walk down the concourse toward home.

For the first weeks I'm back, I feel almost like a one-man threat-advisory system. I want to warn people that things in Afghanistan are getting out of control. *Look at Afghanistan's history,* I want to say. *This is a place that has often come out of nowhere to shape world events. Its stability is important for international security.*

Each day my mother waits to hear from my father. When the phone rings, it's like he's giving attendance. There are three or four days in September when we don't hear from him at all—*Fazel Akbar, Absent*—and she really starts to worry. I see on my cell phone I had a missed call at three-thirty in the morning and wonder if it was him.

In the end it's nothing; we hear from him and everything is fine. But fine is relative. My father has had a tough life ever since he was born. He's nearing sixty, and it's time for things to start getting good.

In October the elections surprise me—they go better than even the most optimistic predictions. The day proceeds almost without violent incident. What disruption there is fails to deter voters: when a rocket explodes near a line of women outside a polling site in Kunar, nobody flees. "We shouldn't run away because then the men will get scared," one woman is said to have advised. (A rocket also lands inside the garden of my father's compound; thankfully, it malfunctions and does not blow up.) Eight million voters come to the polls, some of whom, as my father points out, had probably never before touched a pen to a piece of paper. In at least two provinces—and at least two districts in Kunar—the female turnout surpasses the male. At one point during the day Rauf Mama sees an old lady struggling down a mountain, using a branch as a cane. "Here, let me help you," he offers. "Where are you going?"

"I am going to vote today for Karzai," she tells him proudly.

Karzai wins easily, with 55 percent of the vote, which is sharply divided along regional and ethnic lines: 95 percent for Qanooni, for example, in Panjshir, and 95 percent for Karzai in Kunar. For almost the past three years Afghanistan has been struggling to build national institutions out of a coalition of regional governments. Now there is hope that Karzai will realize he has a mandate to set up something truly united.

The peaceful elections are a positive sign. Afghans have stepped up to the plate and shown they're ready to work with the Americans and the international community. Now the gesture must be returned. There is still a chance in Afghanistan; there's still time to get things right.

Unfortunately, in the weeks that follow, the Afghan elections do not inspire renewed commitment; instead they are used to promote personal agendas. In a presidential debate with John Kerry, Bush employs the election as a symbol of American success rather than of Afghan strength: "As a result of securing ourselves and ridding the Taliban out of Afghanistan, the Afghan people had elections this weekend. And the first voter was a nineteen-year-old woman. Think about that. Freedom is on the march." (At times the blind ambition to spread "freedom" across the world troubles me. It makes it hard for people like my father to promote democracy without seeming as though they are serving American interests.)

As America's own elections near, the country is polarized. I recommend a book of Fareed Zakaria's to a girl in my comparative politics class, and the first thing she asks is, "Is he liberal or conservative?" I don't know what to say; I don't read Zakaria for his party affiliation. The Afghan elections recall some lines from his book *The Future of Freedom*: "In an age of images and symbols, elections are easy to capture on film. But how do you televise the rule of law? Yet there is life after elections, especially for the people who live there."

I see that life like this. Yes, the people of Afghanistan backed Karzai. But they've been weakened to the point that their backing doesn't amount to much. They are tired, desperately poor, and have few opportunities—and they are thus at the mercy of warlords, terrorists, opium, the country's carnivorous neighbors, you name it. They need long-term help, not the shaky presence of the aid community. Omar tells me that as the election approached, aid workers arranged for tickets out of Kabul, for fear of getting killed in some kind of bombing or other attack. After the election was deemed a success, everyone came back.

I find myself returning to Rauf Mama's measure of Afghanistan's progress: Karzai still has American bodyguards. You can have ten elections, but if the country can't keep its own president secure, then we haven't accomplished anything.

The guards are far from a benign presence. The French ambassador tells my father that one shoved a gun into his ribs when he came to see Karzai. In early fall one slapped the minister of transportation. And Omar returns to California with his own story. One day before he left, he was making a video of the presidential palace. When my father and Karzai emerged from a meeting, Karzai ordered, "Stop videotaping!" Omar snapped the camera shut. "I'm sorry," he apologized. When they sat down for lunch, Karzai softened. "Come on, Little Pacha," he said to Omar. "You can take the picture now." Omar picked up his camera and positioned himself. "What are you doing?" an American bodyguard asked my brother. "I'm going to take a picture," Omar said. "No," the bodyguard replied. "That's not allowed."

My father got up from his seat. "Excuse me, the president of Afghanistan said he wants him to take the picture. Why are you interfering?"

The only good news about the bodyguards is that maybe Karzai is tired of them, too. I read in *Time* magazine that one day Karzai sneaked out of the palace, evading his American wardens. In the market he bought himself a pomegranate. A guy in a shop recognized him: "Karzai!" he exclaimed. He grabbed him and hugged him. Others approached with the same joviality. Among those with whom Karzai spoke was an old man whose son had long been imprisoned. He took the man to the palace with him to see what he could do to get his son back.

In early winter the prisoner story with the most personal resonance for us remains unresolved. Dave Passaro has yet to stand trial for the assault of Abdul Wali. In late November, my father returns to California for a visit, and one morning soon afterward we drive down to the Marriott in Walnut Creek to meet with Fred and Mr. Sullivan.

In the lobby the two men introduce us to James Candelmo, an assistant

U.S. attorney. We take the elevator to the second floor and enter a conference room named for a California city: San Diego, maybe, or Santa Cruz. The men begin by asking my father how it was that Abdul Wali came to us in the first place. He explains about tribal feuds. "Like Sicilians," Mr. Sullivan jokes.

"Oh come on, don't bring Sicilians into this," Mr. Candelmo says.

They want to know why somebody would have gone after Abdul Wali. "Was he an important person?" they wonder. "Did his family have a lot of land?" No, says my father. Then what was the feud about? "Somebody mentioned it was over a woman," my father says.

"Oh God," both Mr. Candelmo and Mr. Sullivan laugh. "Isn't it always?"

They confirm that Abdul Wali had come to clear his name, not to admit to any wrongdoing. The defense may argue that Abdul Wali showed up at the base in guilty surrender. *Abdul Wali was a terrorist, a bad guy; if he died, it's okay.* But my father explains that if Abdul Wali had been guilty, he'd have had no incentive to turn himself in. If he'd had anything to hide, his Salarzai tribesmen on the Pakistani side of the border would have given him shelter; the Americans would have been unable to capture him there.

The thorniest issue is the heart attack. In the days following the indictment, Dave's lawyer had seized upon comments my father had made immediately after Abdul Wali's death. The Associated Press reported that the attorney had "a transcript of an Islamic radio broadcast from June 27, 2003, in which an Afghan official said an examination showed Wali suffered a fatal heart attack." The transcript was an English-language version of an Iranian radio broadcast available in news databases: "The former spokesman of Afghan President Hamid Karzai and new governor of Kunar province, Said Fazel Akbar, told reporters on Thursday 26 June that the post-mortem carried out by doctors and the history of his heart disease indicated that a heart attack had been the cause of death." (My father may have mentioned that he had been told that Abdul Wali's body had been checked by medics.) Of course, Dave's lawyer neglected to mention what followed: "Iranian radio on 24 June quoted 'reliable Afghan sources' as saying that the man had died as a result of torture by U.S. forces during interrogation."

When, a year later, the AP called my father for comment, I'd picked up the phone. "Spokesman Hyder Akbar, who is also the governor's son, said that his father's initial assessment was 'just speculation,'" the reporter wrote of our exchange.

Now, over and over, Fred and the others ask my father how he came to believe Abdul Wali died of a heart attack. Who first suggested it: the Americans or us? Neither my father nor I can say. "Did it seem like they tried to put thoughts in your head?" they ask. Again my father can't remember; he explains that we didn't then have "suspicious minds." He tells them: "The thought of something like this happening from the Americans, I couldn't have even suspected it. I thought it was a tragic event. I did not even think about the possibility that he had been beaten." My father points out that he didn't even feel the need to see the body.

"How come you didn't want to see the body? Weren't you concerned?" they wonder.

"No," my father says. "I had no suspicion. And seeing a dead body is not something I look forward to. It's something I don't want to do unless I absolutely have to."

My mind catches on his admission and, for a moment, drifts away from the proceedings. I remember my father leaning over Haji Qadir's body, touching his skin; back then I'd marveled at his remove. *He's completely numb,* I'd concluded. It changes things to know that the prospect of that task may have filled him beforehand with dread; that I was not the only one whose mind was unsettled as we drove to the hospital along that dark road, that he was feeling at least some version of what I was, there beside me in the backseat.

The men return to something Dave said during the interrogation: *Is there anything you want to give to your family?* They ask me, "Did that seem strange to you?"

I remember translating the question and Abdul Wali's stuttered response. "I just assumed it was part of the protocol," I reply.

"No, no, it's not part of any protocol," the officials tell me. One speculates that Dave was trying to "scare the bejesus" out of Abdul Wali. My father confirms that the question would have elicited terror. From those words Abdul Wali would have surmised that he was going to be taken and shot: "That would have brought him down to zero. He would have had no feeling left."

My father is shown the photographs of Abdul Wali's body. Today the officials are curious about his clothing. The defense may argue that Abdul Wali's teal-colored kameez partoog identifies him as a rich man; they may characterize his attire as "very upscale dress." The concept is absurd. "There are no dress-up clothes in Kunar," we tell them. "There are no variations. There are no separate clothes for casual and for work. These are very normal clothes."

"Even the vest?" they check.

"Even the vest," we tell them.

After we see the pictures, things start winding down. The meeting has lasted four and a half hours. Dave's trial is scheduled for sometime in 2005; both my father and I may be called to testify. The government has witnesses. According to a news report, they include one who says that Abdul Wali pleaded just to be shot rather than face further abuse; two who say they saw Dave beat Abdul Wali with a steel flashlight.

That same summer the Americans gave one of their flashlights to Sartor, who really liked it. Sometimes I'd borrow it from him. The flashlight was a long tube, like something a movie detective would use to see into a room's dark corners. I'd lie on my bed on the balcony and aim it high above me, shining it into the vast Afghan night.

My father is home for almost six more weeks after our meeting. It's a regular vacation, like all of them. He gets his doctors' appointments taken care of. I memorize information about dicots and monocots for my final exams, and I start looking over transfer applications; I'm gearing up to switch to a four-year college. We celebrate my twentieth birthday at a restaurant; for his fourth birthday, my nephew Ali gets a SpongeBob SquarePants moonwalk brought to his backyard. My little cousin Hares comes to visit from Atlanta, and we get snowed in at Tahoe.

As always, we keep an eye on the news. (Of course, there is little of it from Afghanistan; by now only three major U.S. news organizations have full-time reporters there, all of them in Kabul.) America's drumbeat toward

Iran continues; journalists and pundits discuss the possibility that the Bush administration will confront the regime about its nuclear development program. An article by Seymour Hersh in the *New Yorker* lends support to the theory that the U.S. has an ulterior motive in retaining Afghanistan as a military base. "Previously, an American invasion force would have had to enter Iran by sea," Hersh writes. ". . . [N]ow troops could move in on the ground, from Afghanistan or Iraq." He says that American commando units have already gone into Iran from western Afghanistan.

Not long after Hersh's article appears, Senator John McCain travels to Kabul and announces that "permanent bases" in Afghanistan are desirable "not only because of our appreciation of Afghanistan, but because we believe there will be vital national security interests in this region for a long time." I'm shocked that the plan is this overt. Apparently so is the Bush administration. A Pentagon spokesman immediately refutes McCain's contention: "It's premature to even consider something like that." McCain's own office issues a statement that the senator "did not mean to imply" that the ongoing mission in Afghanistan "would necessarily require permanent U.S. military bases."

Of course, Afghans might not mind some long-term U.S. presence if such a scenario took into account their interests as well as American ones. The very same week McCain makes his remarks, the United Nations issues a report on Afghanistan that places the country near the bottom of its Human Development Index. The country ranks 173 out of 178; the five countries doing worse than Afghanistan are all in sub-Saharan Africa. Life expectancy remains a dismal 44.5 years. Afghanistan's education system is "one of the worst in the world." Opium production has increased to the extent that Afghanistan is now "the world's largest producer." (Elsewhere it's reported that last year, Afghanistan was responsible for nearly ninety percent of the world's supply.) The report points out that the U.S. spends $1 billion each month on the war on terror, while "much less than that is being spent on curbing the poverty that could breed extremism"; in addition, "Given that Afghanistan's human insecurities have been the result of conflicts compounded by foreign interference, the world now has a particular obligation to help resolve them."

But this report hardly makes the news at all. It doesn't square with the storyline that Afghanistan is a success.

Soon after my father returns to Afghanistan, he calls and says that the inevitable has happened: I myself am the target of a false report. Apparently I am a gemstone smuggler—my father and me both. The report has made it all the way to the presidential palace.

A few days later my father calls again with more sobering news. Rauf Mama's brother Ghousoudin Mama is dead. He and his son were gunned down together outside their mosque in Bajaur.

Ghousoudin Mama was the one the grandchildren called Kabul Baba. He was deeply peaceful; he hated guns. "Stay away from that stuff," he would tell me. "Try not to get involved."

Because Ghousoudin Mama had stayed out of the fray, he had no fear. He focused his concern on others. "Hyder, you need to talk to your dad and Rauf Mama," he'd tell me. "They're really loose about security. Your dad is too brave for his own good. The hopes and the future of Kunar rest upon him. Please, please tell him to be careful."

Eyewitnesses saw someone in a green car shoot Ghousoudin Mama on a rainy, foggy night; at first we know only this. Then the police get involved and the car turns up at someone's house. The people there are arrested. Various theories are floated: that Malik Zarin may be involved, that Ghousoudin Mama may have been killed for his involvement in a commission charged with preventing timber smuggling. (Much of which is done by border and military units that sneak the wood from Kunar over into Pakistan.) But nobody can say for sure what happened.

Rauf Mama can barely say anything at all. When I talk to him on the phone, he is so quiet that I can barely hear him speak. My mother is also distraught. Ghousoudin Mama spent a lot of time at the compound this summer—he was Kunar's director of environmental affairs—and he and my mother had gotten to know each other. His passing is a grim reminder that at any time such a fate could befall my father. So many days go by without incident, and then something happens. It catches you off guard.

* * *

Epilogue

Only a couple of hours before we first learned the news of Ghousoudin Mama's death, my father and I had spoken. In that conversation he mentioned that he was as frustrated as ever with the situation in the capital. People in the countryside were putting their lives on the line for Afghanistan and were still not receiving enough support.

Several times in the past year my father has spoken to Interior Minister Jalali and others about resigning from the governorship; he has made his displeasure clear. His promises to the people of Kunar are beginning to seem empty; without support, he is hamstrung. Always before, my father has been urged to stick it out. But this winter, the depth of his frustration is finally understood. In February 2005 it is announced: Kunar will have a new governor. My father prepares to leave the compound and return to Kabul. He doesn't know what he will do next, and it may take a while to figure it out. It's disheartening that my father's commitment to Kunar was unmatched; though he tried, in the end he could not do it alone. Now he will work through a different channel; he has no wish to extricate himself from Afghanistan entirely. He probably couldn't, even if he tried.

At one point I consider going back to Afghanistan during the winter. I imagine seeing the country covered in snow. On the plane I'd listen to the new U2 album, *How to Dismantle an Atomic Bomb*. I'd take off into the California sky, the same voice in my ears that had accompanied my first trip to Afghanistan now nearly three years ago.

It's hard to say how I've changed since then; mostly because it's hard even to remember what things were like before. Everything before September 11th now seems like a completely different life. I think about the past less than the future. So far I've been an active observer of Afghanistan; to me, this isn't enough. I want to tip the balance, become an active participant in moving the country forward.

There's something we call *sher swayee* in Afghanistan: *riding the lion*. The story behind the phrase goes like this. The lion is sleeping. A daring person sits atop the silent creature. Then the lion wakes up, and the person is caught unawares. Now he is riding the fierce animal, and he doesn't know how to get off.

A lot of people compare trying to rule Afghanistan to riding the lion. While Afghanistan is sleeping, it's easy to sneak in; it's trying to get out that's the problem. My father, Karzai, the Americans—they are all riding the lion.

And then there's me. Even in my room in California, I feel like I am astride that same golden beast, my hands tangled in its long mane.

Acknowledgments

A number of books about Afghanistan provided background for the writing of this one. Among them: *The Fragmentation of Afghanistan*, by Barnett R. Rubin (the quote in chapter 14 is from Rubin's book); *Soldiers of God*, by Robert D. Kaplan; *Afghanistan*, by Louis Dupree; *Taliban*, by Ahmed Rashid; *Ghost Wars*, by Steve Coll; *The Baburnama: Memoirs of Babur, Prince and Emperor* (in which the quote in chapter 11 appears); *Crosslines Essential Field Guide to Afghanistan*, edited by Edward Girardet and Jonathan Walter (Girardet's 1985 book, *Afghanistan: The Soviet War*, includes a description of the Kerala massacre); *Afghanistan and the Soviet Union*, by Henry S. Bradsher; *The Soviet Occupation of Afghanistan*, by John Fullerton; and *The Pathans*, by Olaf Caroe (Caroe is the source of the quote in chapter 29). Both *The Future of Freedom*, by Fareed Zakaria, and *Colossus*, by Niall Ferguson, have informed my thinking about America's role in the world.

A lot of people have helped me along the way on this project, but there is one person who made all of it possible from the beginning: Susan Burton. When Susan and I first spoke, it was December of 2001 and she was doing a story about Abdul Haq for the *New York Times Magazine*. We chatted on the phone and when I brought up my plans to go to Afghanistan, she told me that she was also a radio producer—maybe I would be interested in taking a tape recorder with me on my trip. I am glad to have taken her up on that offer. Working with her has been one of the most rewarding experiences of my life; together we have made two documentaries for *This American Life* and coauthored this book. I am incredibly grateful to have her as a partner, a mentor, and a friend.

This American Life recognizes that a personal story can illuminate a larger political one; I don't know of another place that would have taken a seventeen-year-old like me so seriously. Ira Glass was as invested as we were in making our documentaries perfect, and remained a generous advocate of our work long after the final mixes were finished. Julie Snyder and Wendy Dorr listened for hours and offered invaluable suggestions.

This book found the perfect home at Bloomsbury. We would like to thank everyone there, and especially our editor, Gillian Blake, who recognized the potential of our proposal and saw the book through with enthusiasm and intelligence. Jud Laghi at ICM worked hard on our behalf. Amy O'Leary provided much-needed transcriptions. And at the *New York Times Magazine*, Paul Tough and Alex Star published some of our earliest work on the book.

All of this took place as I was trying to be a normal college student in America. I'm grateful to Professor Mikolavich, my English professor, who gave me advice and encouragement, and helped me grow as a writer and thinker; to Professor Walters, my math professor, for her patience and understanding; and to Professor Young, my economics professor, who always had his office door open for me. I'd also like to thank Rahman Arabshahi, Tariq Azim, Yossef Azim, Haris Ibrahimi, Omar Poya, Matin Sayed, Soliman Sultani, and Frank Vesely. And Susan and I were lucky to have as our first reader her husband, Michael Agger, who quickly became as familiar with these stories as the two of us, but always offered a fresh perspective. Then there's Nick Agger, who, though he may not have known it, was there for every single sentence.

I would like to thank my family: my father, Said Fazel Akbar, for being my guide to Afghanistan, for teaching me everything that I would not be able to learn in books, and for giving me the opportunity to spend my summers shadowing him; my mother, Nadera Akbar, who has been the pillar of this family, for all her love and patience and support that made it possible

Acknowledgments

for me to take on Afghanistan; my brother and sister-in-law, Omar and Sofia Akbar, for being my first audience, sitting patiently and listening to me give foreign disquisitions, even if they had only stopped by for some tea; and my sister Zulikha Akbar, who does not have the patience to sit through my talks, but has always been there in time of need.

Hospitality is a very important part of Afghanistan's culture and I am thankful to all the people who made me feel at home there. To Rauf Mama, whose confidence in me led to memorable adventures into Nuristan and across mountain passes and borders; to my uncle Minister Abdullah Ali, who always gave me a place to stay in Kabul; to my other uncle Walid Majrooh, who would always make sure I did the "Pashtun thing"; and to Sartor, whose jokes and stories made driving on the country's bone-jarring roads go by quicker. I would also like to thank Salaam, Shohab, and Yossef—among many others—for initiating me into the country.

A Note on the Authors

Said Hyder Akbar is currently a college student. He is also the codirector and founder of his own nongovernmental organization, Wadan Afghanistan, which has rebuilt schools and constructed pipe systems in rural Kunar province. He is now twenty.

Susan Burton is a contributing editor of *This American Life* and a former editor at *Harper's*. Her writing has appeared in the *New York Times Magazine*.